Strategic Alignment Process and Decision Support Systems:
Theory and Case Studies

Tamio Shimizu
University of São Paulo, Brazil

Marly Monteiro de Carvalho
University of São Paulo, Brazil

Fernando Jose Barbin Laurindo
University of São Paulo, Brazil

IRM Press

**Publisher of innovative scholarly and professional
information technology titles in the cyberage**

Hershey • London • Melbourne • Singapore

Acquisitions Editor: Michelle Potter
Development Editor: Kristin Roth
Senior Managing Editor: Amanda Appicello
Managing Editor: Jennifer Neidig
Copy Editor: Nicole Dean
Typesetter: Cindy Consonery
Cover Design: Lisa Tosheff
Printed at: Integrated Book Technology

Published in the United States of America by
      IRM Press (an imprint of Idea Group Inc.)
      701 E. Chocolate Avenue, Suite 200
      Hershey PA 17033-1240
      Tel: 717-533-8845
      Fax: 717-533-8661
      E-mail: cust@idea-group.com
      Web site: http://www.irm-press.com

and in the United Kingdom by
      IRM Press (an imprint of Idea Group Inc.)
      3 Henrietta Street
      Covent Garden
      London WC2E 8LU
      Tel: 44 20 7240 0856
      Fax: 44 20 7379 0609
      Web site: http://www.eurospanonline.com

Library of Congress Cataloging-in-Publication Data

Shimizu, Tamio, 1938-
   Strategic alignment process and decision support systems : theory and case studies / Tamio Shimizu, Marly Monteiro de Carvalho and Fernando Jose Barbin Laurindo.
      p. cm.
   Summary: "This book deals with strategic organizational decision-making providing techniques for improving the intelligence of actions by organizational decision-makers"--Provided by publisher.
   Includes bibliographical references and index.
   ISBN 1-59140-976-4 (hardcover) -- ISBN 1-59140-977-2 (softcover) -- ISBN 1-59140-978-0 (ebook)
   1. Strategic planning. 2. Decision making. 3. Management information systems. I. Carvalho, Marly Monteiro de, 1965- II. Laurindo, Fernando José Barbin. III. Title.
   HD30.28.S4323 2006
   658.4'012--dc22
                                        2005023878
British Cataloguing in Publication Data
A Cataloguing in Publication record for this book is available from the British Library.

Dedication

The authors dedicate this book to:

To our parents, Fuminobu, Sotoe, Maria do Carmo, Lenny, and Sylvio (all in memoriam) and Mauro for their example and dedication.

To the wives and husband, Sumie, Margarida, and João Alexandre, and daughter and sons, Alice Maria, Luiz Fernando, Lucas and Diogo, sources of inspiration, who fulfill our lives with motivation and joy.

Strategic Alignment Process and Decision Support Systems:
Theory and Case Studies

Table of Contents

Chapter III.
An Overview Of Value Chains, Supply Chains And Strategic Alliances Issues

Chapter IV.
Aligning Strategy With Organizational Structures And Project Deployment

Chapter V.
Alignment Of Organizational Strategy With Information Technology Strategy

Chapter IX.
The Structuring Of The Strategic-Decision-Making Process 213

Chapter X.
The Nature Of Strategic-Decision-Making Models 241

Preface

Developing strategies in organizations requires the use of wide and deep participation of organizational intelligence. Research on strategic organizational decision-making seeks techniques for improving the intelligence of actions by organizational decision-makers. The strategic-decision-making process falls into the category of non-structured and is a complex problem mainly due to the difficulties caused by the ignorance, conflict, and ambiguity to define the objectives. The scope of the objectives, the range of period of duration, and the non-repetitive nature of strategic problems are sources of difficulties to reach some kind of reasonable and reliable decision results.

Problems of strategic decision making can be structured and analyzed through methodologies and instruments provided by Operations Research and Management Science, augmented by knowledge of organizational theory, sociology, psychology, etc.

Simon (1997) stresses that the solution to any decision problems in the business, scientific, or artistic areas can be visualized in four stages: the perception of the need for a decision or an opportunity; the formulation of action alternatives; evaluation of the alternatives in terms of their respective contributions and the choice of one or more activities to be carried out.

Organizations often find themselves faced with serious decision-making problems. An individual can analyze the problem and choose the better alternative in an entirely informal manner. In an organization, the problems are much broader and more complex, involving risk and uncertainty. They require the opinion and participation of many people at different levels of hierarchy. The decision-making-process in a business or organization should be structured and resolved in a formal, detailed, consistent, and transparent manner.

In addition to making the BEST DECISION at the time, the company might also like to know the other possible decision alternatives. The company could be content with a GOOD DECISION within its possibilities or, the SECOND BEST DECISION might be more appropriate. A procedure known as SENSITIVITY ANALYSIS, which analyzes the possibilities of a decision around a chosen solution, is usually used. In general, the company or the decider would like to ask the following type of question (known as WHAT-IF? question):

"WHAT WOULD HAPPEN to the chosen decision, IF the panorama or conditions were different?"

Usually *decision-making models* fall into one of the following categories:

a) **Normative Models** – discuss and present the mathematical or algorithmic aspects of the decision-making process, taking into consideration the formal aspects (theoretical or "ideal") about *"what should be done"* in a decision-making situation. Because they usually consider quantitative values, decision-making problems at the operational and tactical levels are mostly analyzed. The books of Keeney and Raiffa (1976), Luce and Raiffa (1957), Gregory (1990) and Bunn (1984) are worthy of note in this category.

b) **Descriptive Models** – show discussions and cases involving practical aspects of *"what is usually done"* in decision making without distinguishing among the operational, tactical or strategic decision levels. The books of Clemen and Reilly (2001), and Goodwin and Wright (1996), are examples of this category of books.

c) **Prescriptive Models** – seek to answer the question *"what can be done most realistically"* to improve the decision-making process, including analysis and resolution of problems with multiple criteria, conflicting objectives, and fuzzy variables. Books of Saaty (1980), Poulton (1994), Kickert (1978), and Negoita (1985) belong to this category. The books in categories a) and b) also make a prescriptive analysis of the decision-making process in their final chapters.

d) **Decision Support Systems** (DSS) and Business Intelligence (BI) using Data Mining techniques – present a general analysis of the models, structure of data and mathematical algorithms utilized to form a guide to orient the use of Decision Support Systems and Data Mining techniques. The books of Mallach (2001), Turban and Aronson (1998), and Witten and Frank (2000) are examples in this category.

In this book, strategic-decision-making process is, at the starting chapters, based on normative and descriptive models. Then the decision process is expanded to the prescriptive and other related technologies, such as DSS, BI and GDSS (Group Decision Support System) to encompass the nonstructured and complex nature of strategic-decision problems.

The structuring process of a strategic-decision-making model starts using the of bounded rationality principle stated by Simon, based on the world of the administrative man who works with a drastically simplified model of reality, and adopts a "satisfactory standard" of the world formed by a limited number of choice alternatives that satisfactorily meet the problem, and is content to find satisfactory or adequate solutions.

First, problems can be classified into three categories: *structured, semi-structured* and *nonstructured problems*, according to Turban and Aronson (1998).

In addition, a decision about any one of the three kinds of problems (structured, semi-structured and nonstructured) can be differentiated by the *level of decision:*

- **strategic** (usually, a decision for two to five years);
- **stactical** (decision for a few months up to two years);
- **operational** (a few days or a few months); and
- **dispatching** (an "in loco" decision just for some hours).

The choice of a model depends on the purpose of the decision, time, cost limitations, and on the *complexity* of the problem. A problem can be considered to be complex when:

a) the number of variables and/or objectives increases (these are the *multi-dimensional problems with multiple objectives*);

b) when the occurrence of the values of the variables and/or objectives is subject to *risks or uncertainty*; and

c) when some variables or objectives are defined in an *imprecise or ambiguous way (they are fuzzy)*.

It is then possible to classify decision-making problems according to their *degree of uncertainty* (from absolute certainty to total lack of knowledge of the problem) and the level of *conflict of objectives*. According to this classification, we may have four basic models of decision problems: *rational model, descriptive model, political model,* and *ambiguous model*.

The Rational Model

This type of model, based on the principle of bounded rationality, defines structured decision making in situations with various possible decision alternatives. Often they are simplified representations of real problems and provide us the first trial of the decision-making process.

The Descriptive Model

In this type of model, a decision is made according to a descriptive process similar to the procedure adopted in practice. The decision-making process is aided by having the person or organization assign values to risk and uncertainty in an attempt to minimize the effect of uncertainty in the choice of alternatives. The resulting decision depends on the administrative behavior or structure adopted by the organization.

The Political Model

In this case, while the decision can be based on a rational model or a descriptive model, the increase in size and complexity of the problem does not allow an individual or small group of persons to choose the best alternative, since it could depend on a more extended analysis of the problem or, on negotiation or consensus among the parties involved.

Ambiguous Model

Depending on the nature of the problem and type of persons involved, problems whose descriptions are difficult or incomplete can occur. The problem may be described in an insufficient or imprecise way. On the other hand, the problem can be well-formulated, but the decision-making process can be difficult or fuzzy. As a result, decisions alternatives may be "ambiguous," as frequently happens with qualitative judgment or judgments involving the merits of people or organizations.

The basic types of decision models (rational, descriptive, political, and ambiguous models) rely on quantitative values (money, time, or probabilities) that are most suitable for structured and semi-structured decision problems. These basic models can be used as starting models to guide the structuring process of strategic-decision-problems.

First, a systematic procedure for structuring the strategic-decision-making process is presented, using decision matrix and decision trees. Some problems that must be considered in this structuring process are presented in the form of *hidden traps* and *paradoxes*.

To expand the characteristics of the four types of basic models to encompass the difficulties and complexities found in strategic decision problems, the following factors are considered:

Multiple Criteria or Goals and Multiple Scenarios

An efficient algorithm for this kind of problem has not yet been presented, unless using some kind of heuristic techniques. It should be noted that the mathematical programming problem does not consider the event of uncertainty or risk, which, in this case, would involve the resolution of stochastic or probabilistic mathematical programming.

Thus, the decision-making process is one of the methodologies indicated to resolve these problems, since it does not depend on complex mathematics involving scenario restrictions and multiple goals functions.

It is often interesting, or even necessary, to represent and analyze a decision problem from the standpoint of its optimum or optimized solution. In an optimization scenario, criteria or goals may be considered as objectives to be optimized or as part of restricting conditions. In the formulation of Nonlinear Mathematical Programming models, every goal or criterion except one can be described as a restriction, in order to maintain the mathematical formulation of the optimization problem with a single objective. However, if someone needs to proceed in finding an optimized solution, the linear versions of the problems are usually adopted, enabling the use of the Simplex method of Linear Programming. The two methods for multiple linear criteria optimization problems used in the book are:

- "Global criterion" method (Kinoshita, 1996) and
- "De Novo" Programming (Tabucanon, 1988).

However, today's management systems have become complex and are seldom evaluated in terms of quantitative linear components. Multi-criteria problems arise in the design, modeling, and planning of many complex systems in the areas of industrial production, urban transportation, energy production and distribution, health care, etc. These problems can be formulated and optimized using the quantitative approach of linear or nonlinear mathematical programming, but real-life decision problems involve many conflicting goals expressed by quantitative and/or qualitative criteria.

The AHP Method

AHP is a method for choosing the best decision alternative considering multiple criteria and goals expressed by qualitative or quantitative values. This method created by Saaty (1980) has been used for the decision problem to establish: priority definition, cost and profits assessment, resource deployment, benchmarking, market survey, strategic decisions, conflict negotiation and resolution, social or political decisions, and forecasts.

Complex problems and non-structured (known also as ill-defined) problems are often considered as similar problems, but it is possible to find complexity (in the sense of NP or Non-Polynomial complexity defined in Mathematics) in well-defined problems (small number of variables and functions), as in the case of optimization of nonlinear problems.

Complex strategic-decision-problems often require the use of multistage decision trees. For each event located at one of the tree node, an estimation of the probability values corresponding to the level of uncertainty of occurrence of this event is calculated. The estimations of these probability values based on historical data or subjective assessment of experts are unlikely to be efficient because of the large number of nodes and branches of the decision tree involved. The chain of conditional probability values formed along a branch of the decision tree may cause difficulty to conduct the decision based on a single value of the Expected Monetary Value.

Simulation or Monte Carlo process generates a large number of random results for the problem, forming a statistically acceptable sample of the population of events of the real problem. Simulation provides the determination of the probability distribution of intermediate or final event of the decision process, making it possible to compare different strategies using the stochastic dominance technique.

Decision-making process involving competition among companies can be better understood and explained through the use of appropriate business games. Business game is an efficient tool to create a virtual environment for strategic competitions and can be used mainly for training purpose.

In Chapter XII, two approaches to make decision based on organizational knowledge or organizational intelligence are presented. The first approach is of exploiting nature and serves to found refined solutions around an existing one, using expert systems or the "if– then?" alternative of a Decision Support System (DSS). The second approach uses the benefits of the data mining techniques found in Business Intelligence (BI) or Knowledge Data Discovery (KDD) environment, exploring different databases to discover new facts, new relationships or previously unknown trends.

While a DSS is a mean to refine the existing information and data searching for refined or optimized results, a BI or KDD is a technology used to explore the data files searching for new knowledge (new information or new relationships hidden inside the database).

Individuals may differ in their subjective value of probabilities, their utilities of outcomes or in their perceptions of the subsequent actions available. Strategic-decision problems involve not only one person's opinion, but involve a group of individuals belonging to different classes and levels of interests inside and outside the organization. No longer is the problem concerned with the selection of the preferred alternative of one person. The analysis must be extended for a group of decision-makers behavior, each one exhibiting a certain preference structure, perceiving different consequences, and corresponding to a diverse set of interest and responsibility.

Behavioral perspectives of competitive decision-making are neither as well articulated nor as complete as those of economic view. In contrast to the rational approach of the economic perspective, the behavioral perspectives acknowledge that players may adopt different kinds of rationality.

Summarizing the results of decision based on the models and examples shown, one can say that the selection of the best or top best alternatives of decision is a difficult task. We must think about certain personal considerations and organizational biases a decision analysis should overcome, and the concept of "good" rather than "best" decisions must be considered.

The choice of an adequate decision-making methodology will be one of personal or organizational preference, and we can not decide a priori which particular methodology is appropriate. Rather, we may analyze a problem according to different points of view to see what the outcomes are for different ways of analysis, and in this way determine which course of action is most justifiable.

A brief description of each chapter follows.

Chapter I

Chapter I introduces the historic origins of the strategy concept, which was born in warfare. The evolution of strategic thinking is discussed through the presentation of different schools, according to Mintzberg, Ahlstrand, and Lampel (1998), highlighting the complementarities rather than the differences among them. The main characteristics of strategy are analyzed, considering the aspects of design and implementation of a business strategy. It is also stressed the importance of understanding the environment and the internal aspects of the organizations, in order to formulate a strategy to occupy a unique and sustainable position in the competitive market. The case studies discuss these ideas.

Chapter II

Chapter II presents the main aspects to develop a good competitive strategy. This chapter focuses on the mapping of competitive environment, showing the main aspects of the model for industry analysis. The need of constantly monitoring is also highlighted and strategic groups and pressure maps are presented as useful tools that allow the understanding of main players' movements and help companies to capitalize quickly on opportunities or neutralize threats. Five cases are presented in order to illustrate these concepts.

Chapter III

Chapter III intends to present a more in-depth discussion of the supply chain, introducing issues such as location, networks of cooperation, and the study of governance, both of local and global scope. The concept of value chains, both in product-based and in service-based industries, are presented. A case illustrates the main concepts of this chapter.

Chapter IV

Chapter IV discusses the main concepts related to project management as a tool of strategic change and also to achieve competitive advantage. The alignment between strategy and project management structure is also addressed. Finally, the competences and capacities needed to achieve maturity in project management are presented through the most widely spread maturity models. Two cases discuss the value of project management to a company and the maturity diagnosis process in an Information Technology company and in a multinational belonging to a telecommunication sector.

Chapter V

The increasing importance of Information Technology (IT) for facilitating decisions, enabling, and creating new strategies is the main issue of Chapter V. The concepts of IT Effectiveness, Critical Success Factors, IT Strategic Impacts, and Strategic Alignment between IT and Business are discussed. The focus is the importance of the appropriate use and management of IT for increasing companies' competitiveness. The analysis of IT role in the organizations is done through the presentation of case studies.

Chapter VI

Chapter VI presents the issues related to the strategic alignment of the organization to effectively implement the outlined strategy. The main strategic-performance-measure systems available on literature are discussed, as the key tools to monitor and measure the results obtained from the actual strategy. A case illustrates the BSC implementation in a financial institution.

Chapter VII

The turbulent environment that demands for agile strategic-decision making is the background for the discussion in Chapter VII. The existence of a "New Economy" is analyzed, considering different points of view, stressing the importance of strategic thinking following the changes in the economy and society. The main strategic alternatives and impacts brought by the Internet are presented, emphasizing e-business and e-commerce models, and the creation of new models for doing business. Actual situations of today's fast-changing market are studied in different cases.

Chapter VIII

Starting with the model of the administrative man suggested by Herbert Simon, this chapter presents different ways to classify a decision-making process in order to see the characteristics of decision models mostly used for strategic decisions. We know that for the decision-making process to be viable, we need to adopt concepts based on bounded rationality such as "near resolution of problems" or "minimizing uncertainties."

Decision problems can be classified into structured, semi-structured and non-structured problems. Structured decision problems have low levels of complexity while non-structured problems present medium to high levels of complexity. To start with the structuring process and the analysis of strategic decision problems, we can use these two criteria. Then it is possible to say that strategic-decision problems are semi-structured or non-structured with medium to high levels of complexity.

Chapter IX

In this chapter, steps to structure a decision model through a systematic way, based on the PDCA (Plan, Do, Check, and Action) principle, are presented. Decision matrix and decision tree are tools used to organize a starting model of a strategic-decision problem. Decision matrix is used to represent a one-stage decision problem while decision tree is used to represent a sequence of decision-making stages.

Examples of problems to select the best alternative under no risk and under uncertainty or risk situation are presented. For each case, decision problems with single or multiple criteria or goals, using utility values, are presented. A decision model updated using feedback from an additional information is also presented.

Difficulties to be considered in the structuring process of decision models are illustrated in the form of paradoxes and hidden traps that reflect the different aspects of human behavior under uncertainty, risk, and complexity, to determine a consistent list of decision alternatives.

Chapter X

In this chapter, complexity in decision problems due to uncertainty or risk factor, multiple-scenario definition and multiple-criteria decision, are presented. Subjective assessment of probability values, scenario definition, and multiple criteria decision with or without optimized solution, are problems that do not have definitive answers, requiring several steps of decision- making-process to reach favorable and consensual results.

As a solution to the difficulties found in the ambiguous model of decision, often presented in real case problems involving uncertainty and multiple criteria,

a) Lower Probability or Belief Function and

b) Upper Probability or Plausibility Function from fuzzy possibility theory (Shafer (1978), Terano and others (1984) are used.

Chapter XI

In this chapter we show how simulation method can be used to evaluate complex decision problems involving uncertainty. Simulation is the most appropriate tool for visualizing, testing, and evaluating the parameters and the dynamic behavior of a probabilistic process. Simulation uses algorithms that generate a population of probabilistic events which makes possible the estimation of the values of parameters of the problem. The results of a simulation can be proven to be valid approximations of the values of the real phenomenon which it simulates.

Chapter XII

This chapter presents an attempt to see how new software technologies such as the Decision Support Systems (DSS) and Knowledge Data Discovery (KDD) have been developed as an effort to obtain new knowledge to support decisions in the organization.

Chapter XIII

Three decision-making models are analyzed in this chapter: the first model is based on the economic win/lose perspective of game theory; the second is based on the behavioral view illustrated by the garbage can model; and finally, the third model is based on a perspective of negotiation and co-evolution. An attempt to understand the characteristics and feasibility of the use of group decision methods (NGT, Delphi and GDSS) is made.

In any of these three perspectives, group decisions may lead to the need for a decision using a voting system. Despite the problems found in voting systems, and the objection raised by Arrow's Impossibility Theorem, election is an important process for selecting strategic preferences.

Audience of This Book

The book will provide instructive material (models, exercises, and cases) for classroom teaching to undergraduate, graduate, or extension course students.

Texts and cases presented in each chapter can be used, in an independent way, as reading or discussion material by professionals, analysts, and executives.

Acknowledgments

The authors are indebted to many persons and organizations that, in a direct or indirect way, contributed to make the edition of this book possible. The authors wish to thank:

- The head board of the Production Engineering Department and the Polytechnic School of University of S. Paulo, whose support made possible the edition of this book.

- Colleagues and friends of Production Engineering Department, Polytechnic School, University of S. Paulo, who promote a dynamic knowledge environment.

- The FCAV – Fundação Carlos Alberto Vanzolini who provided the financial support.

- The anonymous reviewers who pointed out errors and made valuable suggestions for the improvement of the draft.

- The editors and editorial staff at Idea Group Inc. who gave us kind support and advice.

- FAPESP – Fundação de Amparo à Pesquisa do Estado de S. Paulo (State of S. Paulo Research Foundation) for sponsoring our research projects.

- CAPES – Coordenação de Apoio ao Pessoal do Ensino Superior (Federal Agency to Support University Education), for sponsoring our research projects.

- CNPq – Conselho Nacional de Pesquisas (Federal Council of Research and Development) for sponsoring our research projects.

- Professors, instructors, and students from many universities and colleges, who made valuable comments on the early version of the draft.

- Our families, who gave entire support and understanding for the needs to write and publish this book. A special acknowledgement to Margarida, wife and friend, for the support that allows the necessary concentration in the work, providing dedication, patience, and love. To João Alexandre, fellow always together, who has given the necessary support to the work and to the children. To Mauro, beloved father, always unconditionally dedicated to his grandsons. To Sumie, friend and enthusiastic of my career.

Thank you very much.

Chapter I

Concepts And History Of Strategy In Organizations

The Rise of Strategic Thinking

The concept of strategy was born in military campaigns whose results, whether good or bad, were largely the product of the minds of strategists. From ancient times, much has been said about great military commanders and their strategies.

The word strategic comes from the Greek *stratego*, which literally means general. In the classic division of war into operational, tactical, and strategic aspects, strategy is linked to planning, to the broader environment and the longest time frame. Even though its meaning has changed over time, since the Napoleonic wars it has encompassed military, political and economic dimensions.

The first writings that contain thoughts about what today we would call strategic thinking go back to antiquity, authored by Greeks and Romans. Even in the Bible, there are passages where one can perceive the strategies used to win conflicts. Perhaps the oldest text that deals systematically with this matter is "The art of war," written by Sun Tzu (1983) of China in the fourth century, B.C. This book appeared in the West in the 18th century and became well disseminated by the end of the 20th century. At the time the text was written,

China was the scene of constant warring among feudal lords. Sun Tzu traveled throughout the country disseminating his teachings, as a kind of consultant (Hurst, 2001). *The Art of War* deals with principles of a general nature, which aid a sovereign in winning wars. For Sun Tzu, the art of war is governed by five factors:

- **Moral Law:** the degree to which the people are dedicated to and trust their government;
- **The Sky:** the climatic conditions;
- **The Earth:** the conditions of the land, of distances;
- **The Chief:** represents the virtues of wisdom, sincerity, benevolence, courage, and righteousness;
- **The Method and discipline:** the correct deployment of the army, supplies and cost controls.

The book strongly emphasizes the need for generals to know themselves and their adversaries well, which is summed up in the phrase: "If you know your enemy, you do not need to fear the result of a hundred battles." Another aspect that he stresses is the importance of avoiding direct confrontation, where force meets force. On the contrary, the adversary should be convinced to not to want to fight: "The greatest merit consists in breaking the enemy's resistance without fighting." Sun Tzu's writings had a lot of influence on the thinking of business people and there are several extensions of his ideas which focus on different aspects of business in the literature. His influence was particularly important for authors seeking guidelines and declarations of principle devoted to business strategy. Among the most noteworthy are the authors who originated a school of strategic thought called the "school of positioning" which flourished in the 1980s, and in which Michael Porter is usually included. This and other schools of strategic thinking will be examined later in this chapter.

Niccolo Machiavelli's most famous work, *The Prince* (Maquiavel, 1976), was a kind of manual of politic science, written in the 16th century. This was during the Italian Renaissance, a time of extreme turbulence, when kingdoms were warring among themselves and many struggled to govern them. Machiavelli's thinking, often expressed in the "Machiavellian" phrase "the ends justify the means", had broad repercussions in political and military thought over the years and in 20th century business ideas as well. Notions about how to form alliances and to deal with enemies appear throughout his work: "The prince should become the chief and protector of his less powerful neighbors, work to weaken the stronger and avoid the entry of a prince stronger than he at all costs". Machiavelli exalted governors who were alert and ready to fight decisively: "Princes lose their states when they dedicate themselves more to voluptuousness than to arms." Audacity is another virtue he extols in his work: "I am of the opinion that it is better to be daring than prudent".

Machiavelli influenced not just politics but business literature as well, especially in recommendations for executive actions. This vision is found among thinkers included in the "school of entrepreneurship," which highlights the role of the (CEO – *Chief Executive Officer*) in formulating strategy.

The concept of strategy focused on military matters arose in the 18th century amidst the valorization of thought which oriented the ideas of Illuminism.

Influenced by the success of scientific principles in explaining physical phenomena, theoreticians examined military successes with the same criteria, trying to distill the principles of strategy.

These theoreticians were influenced by Frederick the Great of Prussia who was successful with small, well-trained armies. Scholars of the time perceived mathematical and geometric principles in these victories.

However, at the end of the 18th century, Napoleon's armies crushed the armies mounted along Prussian lines, disorienting theoreticians who struggled to explain what had happened in order to create new principles.

In this context, two theoreticians who studied Napoleon's successes arose: the Prussian general Karl von Clausewitz (1780-1831), still famous today both in military and business circles, and the French-Swiss general Antoine-Henri de Jomini (1779-1869), who although very influential in his day, has now been nearly forgotten.

Of those who wrote interpretively and contemporaneously of Napoleon's successes, Von Clausewitz's works had the greatest impact on concepts of military strategy. His main contributions were in understanding the relationship between theory and practice and his vision of war as a dynamic process. For him, strategic theory should have a descriptive rather than prescriptive nature, i.e. there is no "recipe" for strategic success; rather it is possible to learn from observing outside experiences. The study of strategy, with a descriptive focus, aids in training the judgment and intuition of the commanders, but it cannot be used as a basis for action, since command is seen as something essentially creative. Decisions have to be made quickly in situations which are essentially unique and thus it would be hard to prescribe actions beforehand. On the other hand, the commander who learns from former experiences can use them in a rational or even intuitive manner to make better and faster decisions.

Clausewitz's book, *On War*, has been used by military academies since its publications and as business literature since the 1980s.

Curiously, de Jomini was more influential in his time than Von Clausewitz. Today, however, few remember his ideas. For Jomini, there were scientific principles of military strategy that not only should be prescribed, but should be followed. Since there were many commanders who were avid to discover the secrets of Napoleon's military successes, the idea that they could be transformed into a collection of recipes, which could be used repeatedly, was extremely attractive. His was, therefore, a prescriptive approach. De Jomini considered that the principles of war were always valid, independently of the situation or the technology employed. His ideas remained in vogue in military circles until the beginning of the 20th century.

However, with the advent of World War I, the reality of its bloody combat overthrew his "immutable principles." In his writings, de Jomini defended the effectiveness of massive frontal attacks and argued that this was valid independently of the technology employed. These ideas of direct attacks had their basis in the era of muskets and became a lot more expensive with the advent of repeating rifles. But with machine guns, widely disseminated in the first world war, direct attacks became prohibitive (to illustrate, there were more than a million casualties just between the Battles of Somme and Verdun). Therefore technology deeply affected the supposed validity of his principles.

Ideas of military strategy were transposed to the business world during the second half of the 20th century, and the use of the same concepts and terms was common.

The use of analogy, especially taking cases from military strategy, is very frequent in the study of business. Nevertheless, there should be a certain caution since this is a resource to facilitate comprehension that should not be taken literally. As was said regarding Von Clausewitz, analogies should be used as a source of inspiration.

The lines of thinking of the previously cited authors, von Clausewitz and de Jomini, influenced the rise of currents of strategic thinking devoted to the world of business. They can be grouped generically in two ways: descriptive and prescriptive. Alternating between these two basic ideas, Mintzberg, Ahlstrand and Lampel (1998) identified 10 different currents of strategic business thinking detailed in the following.

Investigating the Concept of Strategy

What is understood by strategy has not remained the same over time, but has run a long course to arrive at the present. What factors should be considered in developing a strategy? How to analyze these factors? How to develop a strategy? Should strategy be planned or generated as facts develop? How to view strategy? Is there a recipe for successful strategies? These questions, and others that come up, will be discussed in this chapter and in this book.

Strategy as a subject for business arose in the 1950s and flourished in the 60s, 70s and 80s. There was a period of apogee, and with the birth of the so-called "New Economy", it came to be strongly questioned. Then with the developments in the wake of the bankruptcy of the Internet companies it came back into view. From all we have seen up to now, the importance of having a better understanding of strategy is clear.

The concept of strategy, in business as well as the military realm where it originated, has several approaches and remains in constant evolution. There are different ways to understand strategic thinking. Thus, definitions of strategy will be different. Instead of trying to define strategy, various factors within the concept of strategy and various views on the subject will be presented.

The Evolution of Strategic Thinking

We have already seen how the concept of strategy had a military origin and two of the thinkers who had a major influence on strategic theory: von Clausewitz, who adopted the descriptive approach and de Jomini whose writings are of a prescriptive nature.

According to Hurst (2001) there is a continuum of strategic thinking that ranges from description to prescription, the two basic ideas presented earlier. In this context, Mintzberg & Lampel (1999) listed 10 different "schools" in one of the most well-known taxonomies about strategic thinking. For them, they signify different processes for determining strategy—all parts of the same process.

Among the schools of thought that formulate analytic and prescriptive strategy (the "ought to" schools, which aim to instruct), Mintzberg, Ahlstrand, and Lampel locate the following Design, Planning, and Positioning.

- **Design (Strategy as a process of conception).** This school views the process of forming strategy essentially as a fit between strengths and weaknesses and threats and opportunities from the external environment. This was the dominant thinking in the 60s, and beginning of the 70s. Among the representative authors of this school are Philip Selznick, Alfred Chandler, and Ken Andrews.

- **Planning (Strategy as a formal process).** Developed concomitantly with the school of Design, the school of Planning came into being with Igor Ansoff in 1965, and had its apogee in the 70s. Russell L. Ackoff is another representative author of this school. Although it lost some importance at the beginning of the 80s, it remains an important school.

- **Positioning (Strategy as an analytical process).** The school of Positioning predominated in the 1980s, thanks mainly to the work of Michael Porter. This is descended directly from the ideas about military strategy of various authors, among them Sun Tzu. It is based on the idea that strategy can be reduced to some generic positions, which can be identified by analyzing the situation of the industry (industry here used in the sense of a sector of activities). In this view, the strategist is, above all, an analyst.

Among the *schools of thought about formulating strategy of a descriptive nature* (the *"is"* schools) which seek to inspire the imagination rather than to instruct, Mintzberg, Ahlstrand, and Lampel (1998) list the following: Entrepreneurship, Cognition, Learning, Power, Culture, Environment, and Configuration.

- **Entrepreneurship (Strategy as a visionary process).** Like the Design school the school of Entrepreneurship focuses the process on the CEO — *Chief Executive Officer.* However, in a very different manner, it bases the process of creative intuition in a visionary leader and in the capacity to control and implement his/her ideas.

- **Cognitive (Strategy as a mental process).** This school appeared in the 80s and is still developing today. It is based on the ability to understand people's mental processes and how reality is perceived. More recently, the focus has been on a more subjective, interpretive, or constructivist approach to creating strategy.

- **Learning (Strategy as an emerging process).** Developing in parallel with other schools, and in a certain sense taking on a position of challenging the dominant school at every turn, it has an incremental view of implementing strategy. Strategy is seen as an emerging process, strategists can be present everywhere in the company, and the formulation and implementation of strategy are not separate.

- **Power (Strategy as a negotiating process).** In this school, not among the largest, strategy is based on power. In a micro approach, power is viewed as being internally disputed in the companies in a natural political process involving negotiation, persuasion, and bargaining. In a macro approach, it views the company as an entity that uses its power over others to form partnerships, joint ventures, or other interrelationships to negotiate collective strategies in its own interest.

- **Cultural (Strategy as a social process).** This school, equally small, considers strategy as a social process based in culture that has to do with common interests and integration. Most of the school's writings have to do with the influence of culture as inhibitors of more important strategic changes.

- **Environmental (Strategy as a reactive process).** This school seeks to understand the degree of freedom a company has to move within its environment, as well as to understand the demands it makes on the organizations. Included here are Contingency Theory (which studies the expected responses of companies under certain environmental conditions) and Institutional Theory (which studies the institutional pressures organizations face).

- **Configuration (Strategy as a process of transformation).** This is the school of strategic thinking in a more inclusive and integrative practice. There are two aspects to this school which are mutually complementary: one is more academic, the other is professional, with nuances of consulting. The first, more descriptive aspect, understands the company as a configuration for each situation, integrating the different views of each school, all capable of being used, according to each case. The second, which is more prescriptive, views changes as dramatic transformations from one state to another.

Table 1.1 shows a summary of the characteristics of the 10 schools of thought on formulating strategy.

Table 1.1. Characteristics of the schools of thought on the formulation of strategy (adapted from Mintzberg & Lampel, 1999)

Schools of Thought	View of the Process of Formulating Strategy	Examples of Authors	Intended Message	Message Delivered
Prescriptive				
Design	Conceptual Process	Selznick; Newman; Andrews	Fit	Think
Planning	Formal Process	Ansoff; Ackoff	Formalize	Program
Positioning	Analytical Process	Porter; Schendel; Hatten	Analyze	Calculate
Descriptive				
Entrepreneurial	Visionary Process	Schumpeter; Cole	Envision / Project	Centralize
Cognitive	Mental Process	Simon; March	Cope or Create	Be concerned
Learning	Emergent Process	Lindblom; Cyert & March; Weick; Quinn; Prahalad & Hamel	Learn	Play
Power	Negotiating Process	Allison (micro); Pfeffer & Salancik; Astley (macro)	Promote	Treasure
Cultural	Social Process	Rhenman & Normann	Coalesce	Perpetuate
Environmental	Reactive Process	Hannan & Freeman; Pugh et al.	React	Capitulate
Configuration	Transformative Process	Chandler; Mintzberg; Miller; Miles; Snow	Integrate, transform	Accumulate

With the view that various schools can live together at different stages of the process of formulating strategy, Mintzberg and Lampel (1999) point out how each of the schools can contribute to a vision of the process as summarized in Table 1.2.

To complement the classification they proposed, Mintzberg & Lampel (1999) point to new approaches to the formation of strategies that combine aspects from the 10 schools as shown in Table 1.3. This table reinforces the idea that

Table 1.2. Characteristics of the schools of thought on the formulation of strategy (adapted from Mintzberg & Lampel, 1999)

School of Thought	Contribution of Each School in the Process of Formulating Strategy
Design	Look to the near future to find a strategic perspective.
Planning	Look to the immediate future to program the execution of a defined strategy.
Positioning	Look to the past within a defined timeframe and the analysis will contribute to formulating strategy.
Entrepreneurial	Look to the distant future in search of a unique vision.
Cognitive	The thinking of the strategy formulator which is at the heart of the process.
Learning	Look to detail in search of the root cause of events.
Power	Look for the points hidden within the organization.
Cultural	Look to the process within the subjective perspective of beliefs.
Environmental	Look to the process as a whole within the perspective of environment.
Configuration	Look at the process more broadly, examining all aspects.

Table 1.3. Combinations of the schools of thought on formulating strategy (adapted from Mintzberg & Lampel, 1999)

Approach	Schools of Thought
Dynamic capacities	Design, Learning
Theory based on resources	Cultural, Learning
Analysis of Scenario and Analysis of Stakeholders	Planning, Learning or Power
Constructivist	Cognitive, Cultural
Chaos and evolutionary theory	Learning Environmental
Institutional theory	Environmental, Power or Cognitive
Intrapreneurship (Venturing)	Environmental, Entrepreneurship
Revolutionary Change	Configuration, Entrepreneurship
Negotiated Strategy	Power, Positioning
Maneuver Strategy (or Movement)	Positioning, Power

schools of strategic thought can be complementary since they can contribute in a specific way to these new approaches, showing that ideas about strategy continue to evolve, without, however, disregarding earlier thinking.

In addition to these schools and approaches there are other currents of strategic thinking that are gaining visibility, according to Hurst (2001) and focus on implementation rather than formulation (although the separation between these two stages is more of a didactic nature than what really happens):

- The Balanced Scorecard (Kaplan & Norton, 1992, 1996, 2000), which focuses on iterative processes, discipline, and a search for means for companies to develop performance indicators that encompass aspects in addition to the financial.

- Administration by self-control (Drucker, 1974), which considers that the final goal of administration is to produce a self-governing community; this requires productive work, feedback for self-control, and continuous learning.

- Creative destruction (Foster & Kaplan, 2001), which shows that long-lasting companies have a lower than average market performance, which negates the hypothesis that companies survive as long as they perform better than their competitors. In this view, the greatest gains are obtained by companies that are industry entrants. Thus, companies need to undergo a process of creative destruction in order to cease being mere followers of average market performance.

- Rupture or disruptive models (Christensen & Overdorf, 2000) show the inability of companies to reinvent themselves. According to these authors, small new entrants in an industry dethrone the old leaders with disruptive business models, based on new technologies, which in turn lead to resources, processes, and values that allow them to be exploited adequately. The rupture is based much more on these factors than on new technologies which are not often radically innovative.

Thus, strategic thinking continues to evolve.

Strategy and Competition: The Deliberative and Revolutionary Nature of Strategy

The need for strategy is linked to the existence of competition, whether to win a war or to conquer the market. But this is a necessary condition and is not sufficient to explain what strategy is.

There is competition among species in nature for survival, but we can't speak of a strategy for natural selection. The random variations produced in species will adapt differently to the environment and only the best adapted will survive. Speaking of the processes of nature, it is interesting to note that Gause's "principle of competitive exclusion" can be verified in experimentation with elementary living beings. According to this principle, when beings of the same species are isolated in an environment with limited resources, none of them survive. However, if there are beings from different species, survival is possible. In other words, two species that compete in an identical manner cannot exist in the same environment. The richer the environment is in terms of resources, the more species there will be, and also more competition (Henderson, 1989).

What differences and similarities are there between what happens in nature and what happens in the business world?

As in nature, in the business environment, there cannot be companies competing in the same way for the same market, even thought this is not evident at the first glance.

Therefore, there is a similarity here.

However competition existed before strategy. But there is a basic difference between natural competition and strategy. Natural competition is evolutionary, governed by the laws of probability; strategy is revolutionary, governed by reason and imagination, aiming at accelerating the pace of change. Revolution-ary here is used in the sense of breaking with the natural course of things, in the sense of making deliberate interventions.

Thus for Henderson (1989), strategy is a deliberate search for a plan of action that will develop a competitive advantage for the business and putting this plan into practice.

This search necessarily begins with an understanding of whom and where you are and that your goal is to increase the scope of the advantage a company will have in competing for the market.

Note that strategy has two perspectives: that of a plan, and also the execution of this plan. This view is also defended by Mintzberg, Ahlstrand, and Lampel (1998). For these authors, strategy is a plan for directing activities toward a future: those who develop it desire to shape favorably for themselves. On the other hand, there is the notion that strategy is equally linked to the execution of the plan, to what really was done. Thus, these authors understand that strategy is a pattern that is followed in a consistent way over time.

Distinguishing What Strategy Is

Some ideas have been confused with the concept of strategy, which makes a discussion about them necessary in order to move ahead with the study proposed in this book.

For Porter (1996), when faced with ever more aggressive competition in ever more rapidly changing markets, companies learn to be flexible, to respond quickly to competition and to changes in the markets. The dissemination of better managerial practices, which seek gains in efficiency, has taken on increasing importance. However, this has led companies to confuse operational efficiency with strategy. Therefore, it is necessary to distinguish between the two.

While operational efficiency is necessary in a competitive scenario, it often becomes a condition for companies to participate in a market, and does not constitute a form of strategy, nor can it replace it. In terms of competitive advantage, the company can surpass its rivals just by managing to establish a difference that it can maintain. To this end, the company should look to deliver value to clients in a different form, to create value for the company at a lower cost, or to do both.

Figure 1.1. Efficiency and effectiveness (adapted from Laurindo, 2002)

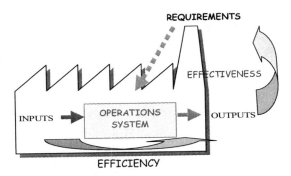

First, before a discussion about operational efficiency and strategy, it is necessary to distinguish efficiency from effectiveness (Figure 1.1).

Efficiency is a measure of the performance of the process of conversion of inputs into outputs, while effectiveness is a measure of the degree to which the outputs satisfy requirements. Efficiency is related with "doing things in the right way", such as using resources well, with a focus internal to activities. Effectiveness is related to "doing the right things" obtaining results in accord with goals, with a focus on the outside environment (Drucker, 1963; Laurindo, Carvalho, and Shimizu, 2003).

For Porter (1996), operational efficiency means executing similar activities better than the competitors. To achieve efficiency, several managerial tools have been developed, for example TQM (total quality management), benchmarking, outsourcing, partnering, and reengineering. These tools are important in a competitive environment; however they are not sufficient to replace a company's strategy.

On the other hand, a strategic position means carrying out activities which are different from those of rivals or to execute similar activities in a different way. One of the problems of focusing just on operational efficiency is the fact that few companies manage to compete successfully for an extended period of time if they base themselves in this aspect. Therefore, operational efficiency is not enough, since there is rapid dissemination of the best practices, which are replicable by other companies and which become commercialized products. A second reason is because the larger the number of companies that adopt practices such as benchmarking and outsourcing or any other tool, the more they become similar, thus making it impossible for some of them to stand out among the rest and thus they leave the field vanquished.

Porter argues that a generalized focus on operational efficiency explains the wave of consolidations and mergers in certain industries. Since the companies lack a strategic vision and base themselves solely on an evaluation of operational performance, they do not find an option for growth other than buying, being bought, or merging.

In turn, Campbell and Alexander (1997) argue that often strategic planning does not result in effective action. For them, this is the result of failing to understand what it means to develop strategy.

First, they argue that there is a failure to differentiate between purposes and constraints. Purposes are the reason for the organization's existence, what the company desires to do. Constraints are what an organization needs to do to survive. Another problem resides in how a company can implement strategy. Finally, there is the expectation that good planning will result in better strategies. For these authors, however, developing a good strategy should be based in a real understanding of the benefits to the company of having well established purposes, as well as in seeking to generate greater value than its competitors.

Another issue that Campbell and Alexander point out is the definition of company goals, which directly affects the development of strategy. Statements about providing shareholders with a higher return; increasing value to clients; higher-than-market-levels salaries and carrier opportunities for their collaborators do not help to define strategy, because they are just new ways of stating the universal goal of all companies to develop and maintain competitive advantage. Many executives erroneously believe that satisfying the stakeholders is a goal that leads to correct strategy; generating value for the stakeholders is not an objective, but an economic constraint on a company's actions. The reason for this is that companies will not have the loyalty of their stakeholders (clients, stockholders, suppliers, and collaborators) if these do not perceive that the company is adding a value at least equal to that provided by its competitors. Achieving objectives depends on managers' ability to develop appropriate strategies, since if they can't establish a strategy, the goals will be discarded as nonviable. Similarly, these authors contend that a strategy is only viable if there are tactical actions that make its implementation possible.

Christensen (1997) stresses that another problem in elaborating strategy lies in the fact that this activity is not usually exercised every day, which means that it is not at the heart of the executives' daily activities. Strategy should be coherent with the environment of the company and company resources should be aligned with executing this strategy. Christensen believes that, in general, there is a deficiency in the connection and alignment between the process of conceiving strategy and the process of implementing it.

Porter's (1996) view that strategy differs fundamentally from the search for operational efficiency is in part corroborated by Hamel (1996), who defends the idea that changes of an incremental nature are not enough for the success of a strategy for the majority of companies. Small cost reductions and marginal improvements in quality and in delivery times are some of Hamel's examples of incrementalism. All these implicitly seek operational efficiency. The author states that making strategy implies assuming more revolutionary postures, which can affect the way companies operate in a more significant manner.

Likewise, there is a similarity between the positions and questioning of Campbell and Alexander (1997) and Christensen (1997) about the need to understand the difference between strategy and strategic planning. Hamel affirms that strategic planning in general is not in fact strategic, since he interprets the traditional processes for developing strategy to obliterate the revolutionary stance which he advocates. Strategy should be a result of "revolutionary" and "subversive" processes that are easier to find in small companies, which are not the traditional market leaders. The leaders define the rules in force for an industry, but revolutionary companies have the potential to reinvent these rules.

It is necessary to distinguish strategy from the quest for operational efficiency, as well as to understand the differences that separate the concepts of strategy and strategic planning processes.

Strategy as a Choice Among Options

For Porter (1996), a competitive strategy means choosing a different arrangement of activities to deliver a package of unique value, thus staking out a strategic position. Strategic positioning can be realized based in three distinct sources that are not mutually exclusive: the variety of products and services, meeting the needs of a certain group of consumers, and the particularities of accessibility of a specific group of consumers.

For positioning based on the variety of products and services, the main idea is to chose a range of products and services to be offered and to develop activities which will allow them to be produced in the best way possible.

When positioning is based on the needs of a group of consumers, differences in terms of obtaining an advantageous positioning only occur when the set of activities that allows specific services is also differentiated. Note that these specific needs can be anything from a greater sensitivity to price, to products with specific characteristics — differentiation in need does not translate into a meaningful position, unless the arrangement of activities to satisfy clients is also different.

Differences in accessibility can lead to strategic positioning, even when consumer needs are not different from those of other customers, but when the means to reach customers demands a differentiated set of activities. This can occur due to geographic factors, the scale of production, or other factors which require a specific manner of accessing customers.

For Porter therefore, within this context, the essence of strategy is the creation of a unique, valuable position, involving the choice of an internal arrangement of activities that allows the company to differentiate itself from its rivals.

In a similar fashion, Markides (1999) understands the essence of strategy to lie in the company's choosing a position that it can sustain as its own. In addition, developing strategy is a process of elaborating questions, generating alternatives, and making choices.

These issues and choices involve three dimensions: which customers to focus on, what products to offer, and how to realize these activities in an efficient manner. The strategic positioning of companies comes from their responses to these three questions, and if they are differentiated, will lead the companies to success.

Choosing a unique position still is not sufficient to guarantee a sustainable advantage, since the competitors can imitate this behavior and aim at the same strategic positioning. However, in assuming some options, the companies have to let go of others, under the risk of not being successful in any of them. Therefore, equilibrium between exclusive alternatives (trade-offs) must be sought, without which the companies will not arrive at a sustainable advantage.

The need for these trade-offs is based in three reasons for Porter: to maintain consistency in image or reputation, compatibility with the nature of the activities themselves, and limitations on internal coordination and in the control of activities.

To maintain a consistent image or reputation, it is important that customers not be confused, but perceive that they always receive the same kind of value.

The compatibility of the characteristics themselves should be preserved to facilitate the more homogenous use of equipment, as well as to meet the demands for capabilities, behavior, and training of employees and managers.

The existence of limits on the internal coordination and control means that the company has to make choices in line with its priorities, under penalty of not achieving adequate performance, if it divides its efforts among many alternatives.

Therefore, a point that is the very essence of strategy is knowing how to choose what to do and what not to do. The development of competitive strategy has a broad nature involving how the company will compete, what its goals should be, and what policies are necessary to achieving these goals.

This spectrum of choices contains two groups of factors that influence decisions: the external competitive environment in which the company is active and its own internal characteristics. In turn, each of these unfolds into two other factors.

Both the threats to companies and their opportunities are to be found in the competitive environment. Internally, the company has both strengths and weaknesses. The SWOT (Strength, Weakness, Opportunities, and Threats) analysis has the objective of recognizing limitations, maximizing the organizations' strong points while monitoring opportunities and threats in the competitive environment. Models, such the Structure Analysis of Industry (Porter, 1979), help to understand the external environment. There are models such as *Core Competencies* (Prahalad & Hamel, 1990) which lend themselves to analyzing the internal situation of companies. Both types of models will be studied in later chapters of this book.

The Alignment of Forces to Build a Good Strategy. Can a Good Strategy Be Replicated or is There a Formula for a Good Strategy?

According to Porter, the choice of an adequate positioning aims at determining which activities the company should carry out and also which it should not. As a consequence, the company should conceive of an internal configuration appropriate for executing these activities and also how the activities will be related amongst themselves. This interrelationship among activities should seek not just compatibilization, but reciprocal reinforcement as well, thus increasing the potential to obtain the competitive advantage desired by the company.

According to this reasoning, Porter considers the existence of three levels of compatibilization, which could sometimes occur simultaneously: consistency of activities with the company's strategy, mutual reinforcement among the activities, and optimization of effort.

Consistency between company strategy and each activity in the functional realm is the first level of compatibilization, which prompts accumulation (and not contradiction) of the competitive advantage of these activities. This creates a single vision of strategy, which improves its implementation as well as facilitating its communication and its transmission to clients, employees, and shareholders. The American airline company, Southwest (the model for the Brazilian GOL), for example, suspended on-board meals and promoted more frequent rotation of planes within its strategy for low cost, marketing to a price-sensitive public looking for convenience.

At the next level, not just consistency is sought, but rather that there be a mutual reinforcement among activities so that they produce mutually reinforcing effects. Software companies put test versions (the so-called beta versions) of their product at the disposal of some users. Testing these versions through use permits errors to be corrected, features to be changed, and also reinforces the intent of the users to use the software.

When compatiblization reaches the third level, there is an optimization of effort. The most basic form of this optimization involves the flow of information and coordination, with a view to eliminating redundancies and minimizing losses. There are more elaborate forms, such as those used in the development of product designs that transfer installation and support activities to the user or the establishment of partnerships with suppliers and distribution channels. For instance, limited menus in fast-food chains allow them to maintain quick service with a standardized operational efficiency consistent with their purposes.

Note that these compatibility factors indicate that the set of activities, and not each activity, is what is important to establishing and maintaining competitive advantage. Concern with the search for excellence in performance of individual activities is a feature of operational efficiency; it is not a strategy. For Porter (1996), it is the totality of the system of activities that emanates competitive advantage and consequently, the success of strategy. Efficiency in individual activities, as we have seen, can be more easily copied than this integration of activities within the company.

Meanwhile, market pressures generate an environment that some call "hyper-competition" and in this circumstance, companies often limit themselves to imitating their rivals, and this alone reinforces competition since it levels the antagonists. Acting in this way, the companies cease to have a strategy, since they stop making the necessary choices.

This scenario favors seeking operational efficiency since it can generate palpable results in little time and the companies are focused on performance measures. It appears to be a more certain route than assuming the risks of making decisions about strategy, which means letting go of some things in favor of others. These choices also can force the company to abdicate some clients and some income, which from the immediate perspective, is not attractive. .

This does not mean that operational efficiency is not desirable; increasing it is a necessary part of managing a company, however, it is not a strategy. Both operational efficiency and strategy are very important, but different due to their different focuses.

Operational efficiency is focused on continuous improvements to all aspects and not making mutually exclusive choices, which is intrinsically different than making trade offs. In this context, there is a search for constant changes, flexibility, and a continuous effort to achieve the best practices. On the other hand, the focus of strategy aims at defining a unique position, making very clear trade-offs and making activities compatible. To accomplish this, ways of reinforcing the company's position are continuously sought and this requires discipline and continuity.

Therefore, strategic continuity does not mean having a static view of the competitive scenario. The company will need to change its strategy if there are significant changes in the structure of the industry. Meanwhile, the choice of a new position should be guided by the ability to make new trade-offs and to develop a new system of complementary activities, (which makes the search for continued improvements more efficacious) to obtain a sustainable advantage.

Campbell and Alexander similarly stress that companies and managers develop "fads" such as TQM (*total quality management*), *benchmarking*, and reengineering, and others, seeking to stay out in front of their competitors. In turn, these adopt the same fads, (in addition to generating others), under the risk of not obtaining the competitive advantage if their rivals do so and are successful. It can be seen then that fads produce better results, but do not resolve issues in the long-term since they do not usually lead to developing strategy.

Markides (1999) complements the above perspectives, warning that unique strategic positions are transitory. More aggressive competitors will seek to imitate these positions if they prove to be attractive, and in fact, no strategic position is truly unique. In addition, given the dynamics of business activities, new strategic positions arise continuously.

New positions occur based on new combinations of responses to three basic questions: who, what, and how to challenge the dominance of the reigning positions. Thus, in reaching a new segment of consumers, by creating a new value proposal or even a new means of producing or distributing a product, the business will be creating a new strategic position.

This process can occur in any industry, if the same apparently inexpugnable strategies can be overthrown by unknown companies that base themselves in the creation and exploration of new strategic positions in an industry.

Markides shows that this process begins with the "dominant" enterprises in industry creating unique strategic positions. "Traditional" companies (perhaps "traditionalist" is better said) imitate these dominant companies, seeking to obtain part of the market. On the other hand, there are more and more "strategic innovators", who conquer large parcels of the market, frequently of the new markets that they help to create. Among examples of this last type of company, the author included, among others, Canon (commented upon in the box above) and Dell (commented upon further along in this chapter).

Note that Hamel (1996) made an analogous classification, dividing companies into three types:

- **Rule makers:** these are the leaders who build an industry, the dominant oligarch. They include large companies such as IBM, United Airlines, Coca Cola, and Hertz, the car rental agency.
- **Rule tailers:** these render tribute to the industry leaders, which for Hamel is very little to serve as a strategy. For examples we can site Fujitsu, McDonnell Douglas, and Avis, the car rental agency.
- **Rule breakers:** companies that rewrite the rules, inverting the order of things in the industries where they are active, these are the discontent, radical, and revolutionary of the industry. Dell computer would fall into this category as well as the watch maker Swatch and Southwest Airlines.

Returning to Markides view, it is not possible to predict what the emerging strategic positions will be. Therefore, in facing market uncertainties, companies have two generic options: innovate or exploit the innovations of another company. Note that both options can be adopted by either established enterprises or by new entrants. Thus strategy is essentially dynamic and, in this context, a business should be guided by the following points:

- Establish a distinctive strategic position in the industry where it is active.
- Compete on the basis of this position in order to be better than the industry competition.
- Constantly be on the lookout for new strategic positions.
- When identifying another viable strategic position in the industry, the company should attempt the difficult task of administering both positions simultaneously. To the extent that the old position matures and begins to decline, the company should gradually make a transition to the new position. The cycle then should be recommenced: when competing in the new position, the search for yet another new viable strategic position should continue.

In this process, the company should eventually make a leap to a new technology or even into another industry. However, in moving to a new industry the company should repeat the process of dynamic strategy.

Thus, for Markides, strategy means that the companies, even those that are presently successful, should continuously revise and challenge their responses to the questions: who, what, and how, in order to remain flexible and ready to adjust their strategies in the eventuality that market responses not be favorable.

Characteristics and Elements of Competitive Strategy

To finalize this chapter which discusses the concept of strategy, it is worth making some final comments about the nature and characteristics of competitive strategy.

In addition, there is a question about who should be concerned with the company's strategy. For several authors, developing strategy is the main objective of the executives of a business.

Hamel (1996) however, has a different opinion, stating that strategy should be a matter disseminated at various levels of the hierarchy, based on his point of view that strategy should be of a revolutionary nature.

In Hamel's view, upper-level executives are impregnated with industry dogma, have more homogenous experiences, and a strong connection to what was done in the past. Thus, it is unlikely that they will become the promoters of the revolution that he preaches must occur for companies to remain competitive. The revolutionaries, however can be found in all companies and at different levels of the hierarchy, and should be engaged in a discussion of the future, thus becoming "strategy activists". The company should change perspective, involving the highest levels of the hierarchy (where the monopoly on allocating resources lies) as well as the mid and lower levels (where there is more imagination and propensity to change). The process of developing strategy in itself should be seen as a strategy involving all levels of the company in such a way as to make possible the changes needed for the survival and success of the company.

Henderson (1989), some basic elements are present in a competitive strategy:

- The ability to understand the competitive environment as an interactive system (competitors, customers, money, people, resources).
- Ability in using this understanding to predict the effects of a strategic move.
- Resources can be committed to new uses even when the benefits are not immediate.
- Ability in foreseeing the risks and returns with sufficient accuracy to justify the new use of resources.
- Disposition for action.

As has been observed, strategy is revolutionary (here used in a less "subversive" sense than in Hamel's view), since it is deliberate, and aimed at rapid changes in competitive relations. According to Henderson (1989), there are factors inhibiting this revolutionary nature — the failure and advantages inherent in the position of an attentive defender.

Over time, one can observe alternating periods of more or less heightened competition. Further, beginning at the end of the 20th century, the periods of calm have become shorter.

Strategy depends on subjective judgments of one's own actions and those of one's rivals. *A posteriori* analysis of events reveals that it is not always the strategy which appears evident that had been previously imagined.

For Mintzberg, Ahlstrand, and Lampel (1998), strategy has the following aspects, present in the different schools they studied:

- **Having to do with the organization as well as the environment:** There is a need for an organization to know itself as well as the environment in which it operates.

- **Its essence is complex:** The process of defining and implementing strategy involves several, often conflicting variables.

- **Affects the overall welfare of the organization:** The impact of a good or bad strategy permeates the entire organization.

- **Involves issues of content as well as process:** A well-thought-out and planned strategy needs adequate implementation. Likewise, one can think of the need for an adequate process to conceive strategy.

- **It is not purely deliberative:** Strategy can be deliberated (planned, the result of will), but it frequently is a result of events and opportunities that appear in the course of a company's activities; in these circumstances, the strategy is called emergent.

- **Exists at several levels:** There is corporate strategy, which determines in which business to be active, and also business strategy, which seeks the best means of competing in a given business area.

- **Involves several thought processes:** Strategy involves work in conceptualizing as well as analyzing the situation. Therefore, the elements present in strategy are there so that one can understand the process of developing business strategy. In the chapters which follow, these factors will be discussed in detail.

Case Studies: Strategy and Decisions in Perspective

Case – A Modern Conflict: Apple vs. IBM, The First Personal Computer War

The 1970s—at that time, the computer market was heavily dominated by IBM and its enormous mainframes, also maintaining the greatest market share, and the largest profits as well.

A new company launched a product that initially had more of an entertainment than a work function. The company was Apple and the product, the microcomputer. Based on the ideas that its buyers liked to work with electronics, it had modular components and several slots that permitted a number of improvements and expansions. Meanwhile, new software for the microcomputer (called Apple II+) introduced the industry to a new course: the electronic spreadsheet. The appearance of the first electronic spreadsheet (Visicalc) showed the enormous potential the microcomputers had for business. Apple II+ sales grew at an amazing rate and other microcomputer manufacturers leapt in to dispute the new market.

At first IBM did not react. But the growth of microcomputer sales began to discomfit the mainframe market. IBM's first attempt at reacting was to deny that the microcomputer had the potential to replace the mainframe. Later, it realized its error and launched the concept of end-user product, which was software for mainframes. This was more user-friendly, which was one of the main arguments in favor of microcomputers. The results were not what IBM had wanted. A new strategy was needed. In an attempt to gain time, IBM sought partners to launch its first microcomputer, in an intense outsourcing process. Its main partners became Intel for the micro processing chip and Microsoft for the software. The IBM PC introduced in 1981 (followed by the PC XT in 1983 and PC AT in 1984) was a big success and became the market standard whose descendents are on the market today.

Later, the PC industry moved on to new victories. For the time being, IBM remained in an advantageous position.

Returning to the story at the beginning of this chapter, one can imagine an analogy with military strategy. Apple attacked IBM's territory with a very innovative strategy. IBM initially insisted on fighting on its own ground, tried guerrilla warfare, and finally attacked Apple on its own territory and managed a victory.

The use of the analogy, especially to military strategy, is very common in the studying of business strategy. Nevertheless, certain caution should be exercised since this is a resource to facilitate understanding and should not be taken literally. As was said regarding von Clausewitz, analogies should be used as a source of inspiration.

Case – Sources of Strategic Positioning: Lojas Yamada

The Grupo Yamada, a chain of stores in the state of Pará, founded by the Japanese immigrant Yoshio Yamada 50 years ago, made a "preferential option for the poor" and became the largest retail chain in its state. Exploiting the peculiarities of local customs and creating stores for the low-income customer in the informal economy (popcorn vendors, open air market vendors, manicurists, domestic employees, and ambulatory vendors), it experienced an extraordinary rate of growth in its sales from 63 million *reais* to 379 million in 1999. To attain this result, it facilitated credit for people without a stable or registered employment, opened up space for those in the informal economy (which absorbs 40% of the economically active population), and 70% of its clientele are low-income customers. The principal credit mechanism is the company's own credit card which is responsible for almost 80% of the chain's income.

Even though these customers had shown themselves to be better payers than was supposed, as a preventive measure, the company created a credit and payment management system unique in the country, that utilizes specialized informants as well as a computerized system of credit analysis. With this, they can evaluate a client's credit application in 15 minutes. However, it overlooks overdue payments when this will lead to customer loyalty and offers life insurance (to ensure payments), permanent disability, and loss of income.

In addition, Yamada knows how to deal with local logistical difficulties and knows its customers' peculiarities, which include the typical local cuisine.

In this way, the company sought a strategic position based in the creation of a differentiated form of access to consumption for low-income clients.

Adapted from Revista Exame (November 15, 2000, Edition 727)

Case – Copying Strategies for Copying?

According to Markides, an illustrative example of seeking a unique strategic position can be found in the photocopying industry. Xerox was the leader in this market in the 1960s with a singular and defined strategy which prioritized corporate clients and focused on the production of large copiers which were rented, not sold, by its own sales force. In the 1970s, weighty rivals such as IBM and Kodak adopted the same or similar strategies but did not manage to achieve similar success. Both sought the same large corporate market and IBM even adopted the practice of rental.

Canon, in turn, came to be the leader (in terms of volume) in the 1980s, serving small and medium companies as well as the end user with smaller copying machines with attractive pricing and quality. The machines were sold — not rented — and their commercialization was done through a network of intermediaries.

Case – The Second PC War: Dell Computer Corporation vs. IBM and COMPAQ

Among the many companies that began to manufacture microcomputers on the PC standard, one presented a new form of working that had a big impact on its results. This is the Dell Computer Corporation.

Founded in 1984, it began by making upgrades of IBM PC clones. Beginning in 1985, it started to produce its own computers.

Dell analyzed the direct competition and perceived that IBM, Compaq, and Hewlett Packard (HP) sold through intermediaries. As a consequence, there was an increase in stock and costs and the response time for final consumers was slow. Michael Dell, founder, president, and CEO of Dell Computer, resolved then to sell directly to end-consumers. This means an intense effort to reconceptualize stock management, logistics, and all the administration of the supply chain. Further, Dell concentrated on selling to companies to whom it could sell machines of higher value.

In fine tune with the supply chain, it was possible to reduce both time and cost of production and distribution.

Even though the basic ideas of this strategy were present from the beginning, the grand catalyst was the advent and dissemination of the Internet, which greatly facilitated its implementation. Before this, Dell had undergone difficulties due to the obsolescence of a lot of existing microprocessors in large quantity in its stock, as well as having tried unsuccessfully to commercialize its PC's through retail outlets.

In Dell's formula, not only are sales direct to clients, but production is only initiated when an order is placed. Further, the company focuses on service delivery and technical assistance, by telephone and house calls. Products, targeted on companies as a priority, include the most recent technological advances and therefore, have a higher added value.

Consistently acting in this way, Dell billed more than 30 billion dollars in 2001, becoming the largest company in the PC sector, still in an intense dispute with HP.

Therefore, in terms of Markides ideas about dynamic strategy, Dell innovated significantly in the "how" to develop its activities and was a revolutionary company.

Adapted from news on the *Portal Exame* and from Reid & Sanders (2002).

Case – Remedies for Strategy and Strategy for Remedies

The Distribuidora de Medicamentos Panarello, of the state of Goiânia, was founded by Paulo Panarello of São Paulo and is the largest Brazilian company in the remedy distribution sector of approximately 300 companies. Its trajectory is of interest to the study of strategy.

The company billed 870 million dollars in 2000 (15.7% of retail medicine sales in the national market) which represents significant growth in relation to the 200 million of six years earlier.

The founder had to help with family finance from the age of eight, selling popsicles made by his mother in open-air markets. Later he had his own businesses, starting with a car mechanic shop, then a fleet of taxis, a restaurant, and a construction firm for low-income clients. At the time he was not yet 25 years old.

A stroke of luck helped to shape his future when a sister-in-law married Emiliano Sanches, the owner of SEM laboratories, a major producer of generic drugs. He then represented EMS in Goiania. In this city, Panarello opened a drug distributor that started small. However, right away he obtained concessions from other laboratories, expanding his business at first to the rest of the state of Goiás and later to the states of Minas Gerais and Rio de Janeiro, finally achieving coverage of 21 states in the northeast, central-western, southeast, and southern regions of the country by the mid-1990s. The northern region, except Tocantins, was left out of his plans due to difficulties and the cost of access.

Thus, the company became the drug distributor with the largest geographic coverage, obtaining a big competitive advantage since there are more than 50,000 pharmacies dispersed throughout Brazil, which makes direct distribution nonviable.

Panarello's team of 900 sales representatives uses telemarketing and electronic commerce. One of the company's strengths is services provided to laboratories (such as when new drugs are launched) and also partnerships with pharmacies (for whom Panarello provides financing and more generous payment terms than the average practice in the sector).

In the 1980s, two circumstances helped drive the growth of the company. First, there were large gains made from the financial markets during the high inflation period prior to the Plano Real economic program, thanks to long-term payment plans with it suppliers. The second factor was obtaining generous financial benefits conceded by the government of Goias. Thus, Panarello was able to begin the new decade with more resources on-hand than the competitors.

In this context, in the mid-1990s, approximately half of the cmpanies in the sector failed, including many of his largest rivals, who did not adapt themselves to the end of the inflationary times. Further, many distributors also had their own pharmacies which caused problems with lack of focus. Panarello then concentrated on serving isolated pharmacies, taking advantage of the spaces not served by competitors.

The company was also concerned with its operational efficiency. It invested more than one million dollars installing computerized conveyors in its Porto Alegre and São Paulo affiliates, which automatically separate orders (accepted up to 100 *reais*—approximately 40 dollars), thus making service quicker. All the lots are registered in a computerized system that identifies individual sales. IT acquired a system for integrated management (the R3 by SAP) that in addition to controlling all activities, also serves as a marketing tool against competition. This is because it makes it possible to collect a large quantity of information about storeowners and this can be used as bargaining power with the laboratories.

For reasons of security, all delivery vehicles are tracked by satellite and radio and have armed escorts.

Finally, it contracted a large consulting firm to develop a plan to professionalize the company.

With these precautions and its integration and infrastructure, the company felt ready to confront both national and foreign competitors. Its proposal is to grow based in generic medicines whose gross margins are larger (20% vs. 16% for conventionals), without ceasing to explore new markets such as distributing cosmetics, which comprise 20% of sales in pharmacies.

The main idea is "to earn less over more units sold."

Adapted from *revista Exame,* May 4, 2001 (Edition 737).

Questions for Reflection and Discussion

1. What is the difference between prescriptive and descriptive approaches to strategy?

Considering the case in the section titled A Modern Conflict: Apple vs. IBM, The First Personal Computer War, answer the following question:

2. For many authors Machiavelli's phrase "the ends justify the means" actually had the sense of "the ends determine the means." Where can this be found in the history of Apple vs. IBM?

Considering the case in the section titled Sources of Strategic Positioning: Lojas Yamada, answer the following questions:

3. Explain how Lojas Yamada constructed its differentiated position.
4. Porter stated that sometimes differentiated positioning derives from more than one source simultaneously. Aside from the one mentioned above, what other source can be present?
5. What trade-offs does a company need to make? For what reasons?
6. Would it be possible for another company to copy this positioning?

Considering the case in the section titled Copying Strategies for Copying?, answer the following questions:

7. Based on Porter and Markides's ideas about positioning, explain the success of Xerox and Canon and the failures of IBM and Kodak.

Considering the case in the section titled The Second PC War: Dell Computer Corporation vs. IBM and COMPAQ, answer the following questions:

8. In what respect was Dell revolutionary?
9. What opportunities did Dell exploit for its success?

10. How did Dell make its activities compatible with its strategy?

11. In what way does Dell differ fundamentally from Apple in terms of strategy?

Considering the case in the section titled The Second PC War: Dell Computer Corporation vs. IBM and COMPAQ, answer the following questions:

12. Does the Panarello case reveal a process of strategy development that is intentional or emerging?

13. From the description of Panarello's trajectory, which are the choices in strategic thinking that best apply?

14. What is the source of the company's positioning?

15. How is its operational efficiency made compatible with its strategy? If competitors copy this efficiency can they threaten the company?

16. Think about Panarello, Dell, Yamada, and even McDonalds. Does their way of acting show a strategy or a search for operational efficiency?

References

Campbell, A., & Alexander, M (1997). What's wrong with strategy. *Harvard Business Review, 75*(6), 42-51.

Christensen, C.M. (1997). Making strategy: Learning by doing. *Harvard Business Review, 75*(6), 141-156.

Christensen, C.M., & Overdorf, M. (2000). Meeting the challenge of disruptive change. *Harvard Business Review, 78*(2), 66-76.

Drucker, P. F. (1963). Managing for business effectiveness. *Harvard Business Review, 41*(3), 53-60.

Drucker, P. F. (1974). *Management: Tasks, responsibilities, practices.* Harper & Row.

Foster, R.N., & Kaplan, S. (2001). *Creative destruction: Why companies that are built to last underperform the market — and how to successfully transform them.* Random House.

Hamel, G. (1996). Strategic as revolution. *Harvard Business* Review, *67*(4), 69-82.

Henderson, B.D. (1989). The origin of strategy. *Harvard Business* Review, *67*(6), 139-143.

Hurst, D.K. (2001). Strategy. *Strategy+*Business, *25*(4), 71-74.

Kaplan, R.S., & Norton, D.P. (1992). The balanced scorecard: Measures that drive performance. *Harvard Business Review, 70*(1), 71-79.

Kaplan, R.S., & Norton, D.P. (1996). Using the balanced scorecard as a strategic management system. *Harvard Business Review, 74*(1), 75-85.

Kaplan, R.S., & Norton, D. P. (2000). Having trouble with your strategy? Then map it. *Harvard Business* Review, *78*(5), 167-176.

Laurindo, F.J.B. (2002). *Tecnologia da informação: eficácia nas organizações*. São Paulo, Editora Futura.

Laurindo, F. J. B., Carvalho, M. M., & Shimizu, T. (2003). Information technology strategy alignment: Brazilian cases. In K. Kangas (Ed.), *Business strategies for information technology management* (pp. 186-199). Hershey, PA: Idea Group Publishing.

Maquiavel, N. (1976). *O príncipe (com comentários de Napoleão Bonaparte)*. Publicações Europa-América, Mira-Sintra.

Markides, C. (1999). A dynamic view of strategy, *Sloan Management Review, 40*(3), 55-63.

Mintzberg, H., Ahlstrand, B., & Lampel, J. (1998). *Strategy safari*. New York: The Free Press.

Mintzberg, H., & Lampel, J. (1999). Reflecting on the strategy process. *Sloan Management Review, 40*(3), 21-30.

Porter, M.E. (1979). How competitive forces shape strategy. *Harvard Business Review, 57*(6), 137-145.

Porter, M.E. (1996). What is strategy? *Harvard Business Review, 74*(6), 61-78.

Prahalad, C.K., & Hamel G. (1990). The core competence of the corporation. *Harvard Business Review, 68(*3), 79-91.

Reid, R.D., & Sanders, N.R. (2002). *Operations management*. New York: John Wiley & Sons.

Tzu, S. (1983). *A arte da guerra*. Adaptação de James Clawell. Editora Record, Rio de Janeiro.

Chapter II

Developing Strategies For Competitive Advantage

Understanding the Competitive Environment

As in any game, the success of competitive strategies depends on knowing the rules as well as the other players. Nevertheless, in the real competitive environment, the rules are not always clear and can change very quickly, demanding quick responses and making it increasingly difficult to map the moves of the main players.

Strong monitoring channels must be maintained to follow changes in the competitive environment and to discern new trends. Changes in the environment can result from emerging technologies or changes in society's behavior, and thus in clients' demands. They can also be the result of competitors' moves in the market.

Thus developing a good competitive strategy depends on mapping the environment and constantly monitoring it to be able to capitalize quickly on opportunities or neutralize threats.

The focus of this chapter is on mapping the environment. It will show the main aspects of the model for industry analysis and explain the process of forming strategic groups and pressure maps.

Industry Analysis

Porter (1979) developed a model to analyze the environment based on mapping five competitive forces in order to better understand the rules of the competitive game and to help companies to find a position in the industry with greater clarity. During the 1990s, it was often remarked that environmental analysis had little to contribute given the turbulent state of the new economy, but Porter (2001) was able to demonstrate how important environmental analysis is, especially when there are a large number of uncertainties.

A good map is most useful during a storm!

To develop a map of an industry, one needs to know how the main players behave and how the battle for greater profitability works. According to Porter (1979), there are five competitive forces that run through an industry: customers, suppliers, current competitors, new entrants, and substitute products or services.

Understanding these five forces is vital to formulating a company's competitive strategy. The model for Industry Analysis is shown in Figure 2.1.

The pressures exercised by these forces are structural determinants both of competition and of an industry's profitability (Porter, 1979). In Figure 2.1, the battle for profitability in the supply chain, i.e., the bargaining power of

Figure 2.1. The five competitive forces (adapted from Porter, 1979)

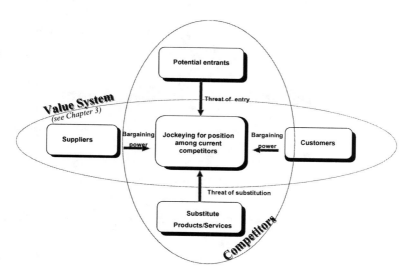

customers and suppliers is laid out along the horizontal axis. The relationship among competitors, whether those are already established, potential entrants, or substitute products, is shown along the vertical axis.

It is important to emphasize that industry, in this context, means an industrial sector and not a single company.

The structure of an industrial sector depends on how the competitive forces are configured. When they are stronger, there is less potential for profitability. It is easy to imagine that within an industry with fierce competition, the rate of return tends to be less. On the outside limit, an industrial structure with all five forces intensified, approaches the economic model of "perfect competition."

On the other hand, there are industries where the five competitive forces are weak, i.e., the rivalry among existing competitors is not intense, the entry barriers for new competitors are difficult to overcome, and there are no substitute products. Allied to this favorable scenario, the sector is the driver of the supply chain, with high bargaining power with the others tiers in the chains, whether customers or suppliers. This type of industrial sector is called "five star" since it shows a high potential for profitability.

Industry analysis allows us to identify which competitive forces most influence the industrial sector. It is common for one force in the competitive industrial environment to stand out and the competitive strategy should focus on it. It is then possible to influence the competitive environment in such a way as to assume a strategic position that can neutralize it, and thus to obtain a sustainable competition advantage, as seen in Chapter I.

It is worth emphasizing that the map of the sector structure is dynamic, since the industry can undergo changes and, depending on the magnitude of the competitive movement of each player, the shape of the five forces can be altered, having an impact on its attractiveness.

Mapping the Competitive Forces in the Supply Chain: Relationships with Customers and Suppliers

Bargaining power in the relationship with customers and suppliers has a decisive impact on both an industry's profitability and attractiveness. Imagine the vehicle assembly plants and their auto parts suppliers seated around the bargaining table. It is east to predict that the scale will tilt toward the side of the assemblers.

When the customers are concentrated and direct large volumes, such as the case of the assembly plants, they manage to bargain for better prices, increasing demands for quality, flexibility in the product mix and the volume of production, as well as access to information via Integrated Management Systems — ERP. They thus diminish the industry's freedom to establish its own rules. This situation is aggravated when the products supplied by the industrial sector are standardized, are not critical to the quality of the customers' production, and can be substituted without generating costs for the change (Carvalho et al., 2003).

Table 2.1 shows some aspects, which determine the bargaining power of an industry, tilting the balance when they are present.

When the forces in the supply chain are intense, it is important to outline a strategy for buyers and suppliers, with criteria for choosing buyers and for selecting target customers and also for developing a buying strategy, paying attention to strategic aspects and not just operational ones.

This matrix proposed by Cox et al. (2001) is a useful tool for analyzing bargaining power between buyers and suppliers. Figure 2.2 shows the matrix, where the horizontal axis shows the dominance of the supplier and the vertical shows the dominance of the buyer, and four quadrants: buyer dominance, interdependence, independence, and supplier dominance.

The quadrants of buyer dominance and supplier dominance indicate who has power over the other. In the independence quadrant, buyers and suppliers have attributes of power, and both must be involved in order to carry out any agreed upon exchanges. In the independence quadrant, neither of the two have attributes of power, nor are they capable of demanding that the other fulfill their requirements, and both have other opportunities for doing business.

Table 2.1. Analysis of customer and supplier bargaining power

Customers	Suppliers
Customers are concentrated or make large volume acquisitions.	Supplier product is a critical input. It is unique or differentiated.
Purchases represent a significant part of their costs.	The group of suppliers is dominated by few companies and is more concentrated than the industry being analyzed.
The industry's products are standardized and/or are not important for the customers' product quality.	The industry analyzed is not an important customer for the group of suppliers.
The customers have all the information.	The suppliers' products are differentiated and do not compete with substitute products.
The customers represent a concrete threat of backward integration.	The suppliers are a concrete threat of forward integration.

Figure 2.2. Buyer×supplier power (adapted from Cox et al., 2001)

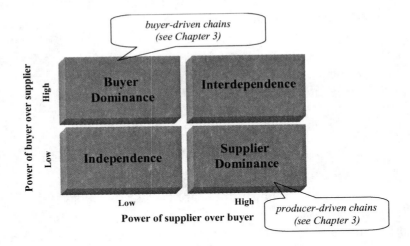

Yet in the more complex supply chains, a more detailed analysis of the relationship among the links must be done. It is necessary to identify which link commands the chain, i.e., dominates the strategic activities which add value. Two aspects take on special importance in this analysis, as we will see in more detail in Chapter III — governance of the chain and the value system.

Analyzing the Competitors: Current, Potential and Substitutions

Competition in a given industry can be a factor that significantly limits profitability. In an industry with an intense rivalry, this can lead to predatory actions, eroding the attractiveness and profitability of the industry as a whole.

It is important to note that rivalry should not be analyzed just in the context of existing competitors, but also in the extended rivalry which includes new entrants and substitute products and services, as illustrated in Figure 2.3. In industries that are threatened by substitute products or have a high potential for new entrants, competition tends to be sharper and often sets off price wars.

There are many aspects that have an impact on the rivalry among established competitors in an industry and in the battle for market share and better competitive positioning. Imagine, for example, a sector where growth is slow or stagnant! For a company to grow, it has to take market shares from the

Figure 2.3. Forces of competition: competitors, entrants and substitutes

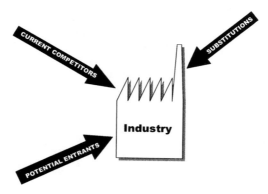

competitors, increasing rivalry among the established competitors, which is not the case when the industry is growing overall.

The main points to be verified in analyzing the forces of competition are:

- Numerous or balanced competitors
- Slow growth of the industry
- High fixed costs
- Absence of differentiation
- Increased capacity in large increments
- Competitors with divergent strategies
- High exit barriers

When rivalry is extensive, the threat of new entrants to an industry is strongly related to the effective entry barriers and the expectation of potential competitors regarding retaliation from already established players.

The main source of entry barriers for new competitors is the economies of scales, whether for production, research, marketing, or services, which require that the entrant operate on a large scale or which place the entrant at a cost disadvantage. In addition to this barrier, there are cost disadvantages, which are independent of scale, such as patent costs, access to raw material, location, official subsidies, and learning curves. For a long time, Xerox took advantage

Figure 2.4. Factors affecting the learning curve (adapted from Heizer and Render, 1999)

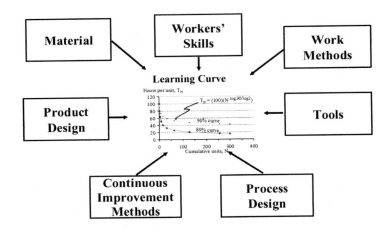

of its patent for the copying machine to remain all alone in the market, however, when the patent expired, a lot of entrants such as Canon, Hewlett Packard, and others came on the scene.

According to Heizer and Render (1999), learning curve models were first observed for the aeronautics industry. It has been calculated that for the period 1925-1957, the number of worker-hours per unit was reduced by 80%.

Learning curves, when applied to the context of strategy, allow us to determine changes in the volume-cost trade-off, and to evaluate performance for the business and the industry. The major restrictions to these models are related to the wide range of variables, which need to be analyzed, as illustrated in Figure 2.4.

Other important sources of barriers are: *product differentiation, capital requirements, change cost* and *access to distribution channels*.

The threat of new entrants can also affect expectations regarding retaliation from already established competitors, especially when excess capacity and/or capital are available to maintain and sustain a direct battle.

Finally, the last force of competition to be analyzed is the pressure of substitute products/services. Substitutes can be defined as those which carry out the same function, even with another technology base (another industry). Substitutes, which are subject to price/performance, trade off with products from the industry and/or those produced by five-star industries merit the most attention.

Taking a Look Inside the Industry

As we saw earlier, even though all the companies within an industry are subject to the same forces of competition, they adopt different strategic positions with different results. Therefore, the analysis of the overall industry can be deepened, extending to a structural analysis within the industry

The steps for doing a structural analysis inside the industry are:

- **First step:** Characterize the strategies of all the significant competitors in all their dimensions.

- **Second step:** Evaluate the dimensions and the composition of the mobility barriers, which protect each group.

- **Third step:** Evaluate the relative bargaining power of each strategic group in the industry *vis-a-vis* their buyers and suppliers.

- **Fourth step:** Evaluate the relative position of each strategic group with regard to substitute products.

- **Fifth step:** Evaluate the patterns of interdependence in the market among the strategic groups and their vulnerability to conflict initiated by other groups.

Dimensions of Competitive Strategy

The breadth of different strategies throughout an industry depends on the nature of the industry. The choice of strategy has repercussions in the strategic dimension, which demands trade-offs. According to Porter (1987) the following dimensions can be identified:

- **Specialization:** The degree to which the company concentrates effort on the breadth of its line, target-client segments, and geographic markets.

- **Brand identification:** The degree to which a company seeks recognition of its trade name through marketing.

- **Channel policy:** The degree to which a company seeks to develop trade-name recognition directly with the end-consumer, or supports the distribution channel in selling its product.

- **Choice of channel:** The choice of distribution channels varying the company's channels, specialized or general.

- **Product quality:** The level of product quality in terms of raw material, specifications, tolerances, and characteristics.

- **Technology leadership:** The degree to which the company seeks technology leadership instead of imitative behavior.

- **Vertical integration:** The amount of value added reflected in the level of integration forward and backward, involving aspects such as captive distribution channels and exclusive retail outlets, among others.

- **Cost position:** The degree to which the company seeks a position of lower cost in manufacture and distribution.

- **Service:** The degree to which auxiliary services are provided for its product line, such as technical assistance, credit, etc.

- **Price policy:** Relative price position on the market, related to cost and quality.

- **Leveraging:** The degree of financial and operational leveraging.

- **Relationship to headquarters:** Demands form headquarters. This can be a department of a diversified conglomerate, a link in the vertical chain, part of a group of businesses related to a general sector, or a subsidiary. It influences goals, resources, and the division of operations.

- **Relationship with governments of the country of origin and the host country:** Multinational companies have a relationship with home country governments and those of the countries in which they operate, in terms of supplying resources, regulations, and other types of aid.

Strategic Groups

Strategic groups allow clustering the firms in groups of similar companies, consisting in an analytical tool that makes easier the industry's analysis. Strategic-groups method assumes that similar firms react similarly in the some external disturbances (Feka et al., 1997).

Strategic groups cluster firms in groups of similar companies, forming an analytical tool that makes it easier to analyze the industry. The strategic-group method assumes that similar firms react in a similar way to external disturbances (Feka et al., 1997). While the company should stake out a singular position, it is possible to identify strategic groups that are following the same or a similar strategy within an industry (see the section titled Dimensions of Competitive Strategy). These strategic groups usually diverge in their approaches to the product or to marketing. Even though there could be cases of a single strategic group in an industry, these are rare.

An industry's historical development explains differences in strategy and the barriers to mobility, which follows the players' different resources and potentials, as well as their differences in terms of goals and positioning with regard to risk. This leads to the formation of strategic groups within the industry. Yet, changes in the industry's structure can facilitate the formation of new strategic groups or make the groups homogenous.

Strategic groups affect the barriers to mobility, bargaining power up and down the supply chain, the threat of substitutions and rivalry within the industry. Global barriers to entry differ greatly depending on the specific strategic group the newcomer intends to join, as well as creating barriers to changes of position from one strategic group to another. These barriers to mobility end up discouraging changing strategic position. High barriers explain differences in profitability between companies.

Strategic groups can also affect bargaining power in the chain, since they confer different degrees of vulnerability on common buyers and suppliers. Strategic groups permit one to focus on different parts of the product line, to serve different customers, to operate with different levels of quality and technological innovation, and to have different cost positions, minimizing the level of exposure to competition from substitute products.

The presence of several strategic groups almost always affects the level of rivalry inside the industry, since there can be interdependence among the groups in the market or in their degree of overlap in targeting customers. The possibility of product differentiation achieved by the groups, the number and relative size of the strategic groups, strategic distancing between groups, or the degree of divergence of strategy are other factors that have impact on the global rivalry of the industry.

A company's viability, as a function of its chosen strategic group, is affected by the structural analysis within the industry, as we have seen. Still, other factors affect the profitability of a company or group, such as the position of the company inside its group, the degree of competition within the group, the scale of the company in relation to others in the group, the cost of entry into the group, and the company's ability to execute and implement its chosen strategy in operational terms.

It is worth stressing that it is not always true that a company with a larger market share is more viable. Larger companies will be more viable if they compete in strategic groups more protected by barriers to mobility and with a stronger position in the chain, and the smaller companies will be more viable if there are no large economies of scale and if they adopt differentiated strategies for service and technological innovation. This exception should not be taken as a rule, since that could lead to a commodity trap. The view that cost position is the sole sustainable factor on which a competitive strategy can be built, which can invade the territory of other areas of strategy, is not easily sustainable, an, in global low-cost positioning, is not always necessarily important.

SWOT Analysis and Strategic Groups

The analysis and choice of which strategic groups one should compete in has implications in formulating strategy. Hence, these decisions have to take into consideration the comparison between a company's strengths and weaknesses, whether they are structural or related to implementing the selected strategy, and they must highlight distinctive competencies in order to maximize opportunities and minimize threats arising from the competitive environment. The SWOT analysis seen in Chapter I, allows us to visualize the impact of strategic groups on strategy in a structured way as illustrated in Table 2.1.

Strategic Groups Map

The map of strategic groups presents a graphic demonstration of competition in an industry, identifying the relative position of the diverse adversaries within it.

The map of strategic groups is laid out along two axes, which contain the critical dimensions for industry analysis, usually dealt with at two levels, high and low, as illustrated in Figure 2.5. Hence, the first step in mapping is to select the strategic variables that will be used along the axes. In order to do so, one needs to decide which variables determine the most important barriers to mobility for the industry.

An analysis using maps of the strategic groups permits:

- Identification of barriers to mobility
- Identification of the marginal groups

Table 2.1. SWOT analysis and strategic groups

S Strengths	W Weaknesses
Factors that build barriers to mobility	Factors that weaken barriers to mobility
Factors that reinforce bargaining power of the group with buyers and suppliers	Factors that weaken the bargaining power of its group with buyers and suppliers
Factors that isolate the group from the rivalry of other companies	Factors that expose its group to rivalry of other companies
Larger scale in relation to the strategic group	Smaller scale in relation to its strategic group
Factors allowing for lower costs for entry into its strategic group	Factors provoking higher costs for entry into its strategic group
Strong ability to implement strategy in relation to competitors	Much lower capacity to implement its strategy in relation to competitors
Resources and abilities which allow it to overcome barriers to mobility and penetrate more interesting strategic groups	Lack of resources and ability that allow it to overcome barriers to mobility and penetrate more interesting strategic groups
O Opportunities	**T Threats**
Creating a new strategic group	Other companies join its strategic group
Move to a strategic group in a more favorable position	Factors that reduce barriers to mobility of the strategic group, diminishing its power in relation to buyers and suppliers, worsening its position in relation to substitute products or increasing its exposure to greater rivalry
Strengthening of the structural position of the existing group or the company's position in the group Move to a new group and strengthening of this strategic group's structural position	Investments that aim to improve the company's position increasing barriers to mobility
	Attempts to overcome barriers to mobility to join more interesting or entirely new strategic groups

Figure 2.5. Division of the industry in homogeneous groups (adapted from Scaranello, 2004)

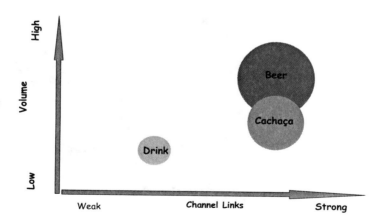

- Graphic representation of the direction of strategic moves
- Trend analysis
- Forecast of reactions

Feka et al. (1997) state that total revenue can measure the size of each company, while its business focus can be seen in the percentage of sales in relation to the company's total revenue. The market share of the analyzed company's product in relation to its competitors determines its market positioning. However, it is important to stress that other measurements could be used to represent better the competitive environment in a specific industry.

Competitive Pressure Diagram

Another instrument to map the competitive environment is the competitive pressure diagram (D'Aveni, 2002). According to this author: "The more two firms' products or geographic markets overlap, the more pressure they exert on each other. The pressure is proportional to the importance of markets to each firm and their degree of penetration. This simple concept enables organizations to quantify the degree of pressure that one rival puts on another." As D'Aveni writes, pressure systems can never be frozen; the best that can be achieved is a kind of 'dynamic stability'.

D'Aveni (2002) states that the competitive pressure from a given incursion into a rival's geographical or product market can be measured by two factors: the importance of the market (I.M.) and the size of the incursion (S.I.). This pressure is given by the formula:

$$\text{Competitive Pressure} = \text{I.M.} \times \text{S.I.} \tag{1}$$

Where:

- **I.M.:** The percentage of the targeted firm's total revenue represented by the market;
- **S.I.:** The market share achieved by the invading firm.

Similarly, to the strategic groups, the pressures map is valid just for a short period. In this diagram, each circle represents one of the market players and arrows represent the pressure each player is exercising on the others. The diameters of the companies' representative circles mean the size of the respective market share at that moment. The width of the arrows in the diagram indicates the intensity of the pressures.

These pressure maps can be also useful to take decisions about, offensive or defensive moves, in conjunction with other decision-making tools like the rivalry matrix, decision trees, and Game Theory. However, Furrer and Thomas (2000) warn that the analyzed market should have few decision variables and a predictable environment.

In both kinds of competitive environment maps, data about the market should be obtained from secondary sources in order to construct these diagrams.

Internal Analysis of the Company to Adequate Positioning

Identifying the competencies a company needs in order to gain competitive advantage in a market which is in constant mutation is an arduous task. However, the capacity for knowing its potential and developing it in a consistent way can be decisive for a successful positioning on the competitive scene.

As we saw in Chapter I, self-knowledge propounded by Sun Tzu and other philosophers is a decisive weapon in the competitive game.

The focus of this chapter is to discuss how a company should position its competitive strategy in order to maximize its competencies, but without losing sight of the competitive state of the industry overall.

Core Competencies

The word competence comes from the Latin, *competere*. The derivation of the concept of competencies can be seen by taking apart the Latin word: *com*, which means *together* and *petere*, which means *effort*. Identifying the set of forces that will be able to lead the organization to build a sustainable competitive advantage is vital in the context of strategy. (Rabechini Jr. & Carvalho, 2003).

Prahalad and Hamel (1990) relate the competitive success of a corporation to its ability to identify, cultivate, and exploit its core competencies.

For these authors, competitiveness in the long-run derives from the ability to build core competencies more rapidly and at a lower cost than the competition. To build them, it is necessary to meld a broad range of abilities in production and technology with competencies the enable individual deals and adapt rapidly to new opportunities, generating competitive advantage for the corporation.

In cultivating core competencies, the corporation manages to share costs, without needing to invest more than the competition in research and development.

Figure 2.6 represents the diversified corporation as a large tree. The trunk and larger branches are the core products, the smaller branches are the business units; the leaves, flowers, and fruits are the final product. The roots are core competencies, whose function is to distribute nutrients and provide stability to the tree.

Each part of the tree determines a different plane of competition: core competencies, core products, and final products. The battles for market partners are engaged at each of these levels, and leadership in final products does not imply leadership at the other levels. Being given a dominant position in relation to core products allows a company to mold the evolution of application and finals markets and managing to achieve economies of scale and of scope, since the market share of core products can come from multiple industries.

Figure 2.6. The Tree : a diversified corporation (adapted from Prahalad and Hamel, 1990)

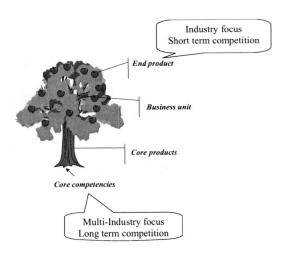

Core products incorporate one or more core competencies, making the link between core competencies and final products. These products are the key components of various final products and contribute to generating value in the final product, materializing core competencies. According to Prahalad and Hamel (1990), Matsushita holds 45% of the market in the manufacturing of key components for VCRs (core product), while its brands participation in the final product (Panasonic, JVC) represents 20% of the market. Another of Matsushita's core products is the compressor, with 40% of the world market, while its participation in air conditioners and refrigerators is quite small.

The concept of core competencies is decisive both for services and manufacturing. In contrast to final products that are consumed upon use, core competencies are enhanced when applied or shared, even though if they are not well-constructed, they can be lost since knowledge also deteriorates.

Core competencies require a commitment to working on organizational frontiers, involving different business units, several levels of hierarchy and different functions. Consequently, the traditional concept of a corporation unnecessarily limits individuals' abilities by making functional cut-offs that patchwork the corporation into autonomous business units, makes core competencies more difficult to achieve.

Identifying Core Competencies

According to Prahalad and Hamel (1990), it is hard to build world leadership when based in more than five or six core competencies. Consequently, if a corporation has not yet managed to achieve a lean list of competencies, it can apply at least three tests to identify them, as follows:

- **First test:** Provides access to a broad variety of markets;
- **Second test:** Makes a significant contribution to the benefits perceived by consumers in the final product;
- **Third test:** It is hard for competitors to imitate.

To aid in this process, it is interesting to have recourse to the idea of the tree, extending the concept of core competencies to core products, and finally, to end products. To make this extension in a consistent way, it is suggested that the company reflect on the following questions:

- How long can competitiveness in business survive if the core competencies are not controlled?
- How central are these core competencies, in terms of generating value for the client?
- What future opportunities will be lost if these particular competencies are lost?

It is important to keep in mind that the complex harmonization of individual technologies and abilities needed to build core competencies cannot be simply acquired by a competitor. It might even acquire some of the technology, but would not be able to duplicate the pattern of internal coordination and learning.

Another important component for self-knowledge is to identify which generic strategies will permit a more adequate positioning in order to construct sustainable competitive advantages.

Generic Competitive Strategies and Positioning

As Porter (1979) suggests, the development of any company in a given industry can be broken down into two parts, the first deriving from the average performance of all its competitors, and the second to the company's performance relative to the sector.

The issue to be discussed in this chapter is the company's positioning in order to obtain sustainable competitive advantage. This advantage should guarantee the company greater income that the average of the sector where it is active.

According to Porter (1979), there are two basic kinds of competitive advantage: leadership in cost or differentiation. Besides, the scope of strategic action should be defined. The target can be a broader market as a target, with several or restricted, acting only in a specific segment.

Based in these two dimensions, there are four possible generic strategies, as illustrated in the quadrants of Figure 2.7. The generic strategies are: leadership in cost, differentiation, focus on cost, and focus on differentiation.

Defining a generic competitive strategy aims at establishing a favorable, profitable, and sustainable competitive position, against the forces that comprise the competition in an industry. Not doing clear positioning in one of these strategies can result in inferior performance, with a high risk that the company

Figure 2.7. Generic strategies (adapted from Porter, 1987)

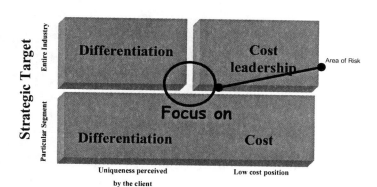

has an average performance because of the different trade-off of these two kinds of strategies.

In addition, the company disposes itself to deliver two distinct types of value packages for the client (cost and differentiation) or to oscillate between them over time, and this can confuse its image to customers and cause it to lose credibility and its reputation.

The alignment of all an organization's activities around a generic strategy makes its implementation easier, as well as its communication with customers, employees, and stockholders. Finally, when the strategic positioning is not clear and the trade-offs are not made explicit, it is hard to build the needed resources, creating problems with internal coordination Porter (1996). In this manner, the most critical position in terms of strategic positioning is the central region, as highlighted in Figure 2.7.

Nonetheless Deschamps and Nayak (1995) warn that this or-or type proposition can lead to errors of interpretation called the Commodity Trap. The Commodity Trap comes from an error of interpretation that associates strategies of differentiation to small, specialized companies active in segments or niches of the market, leaving it to the large companies to adopt strategies of low cost.

Before defining the generic strategy, it is important to verify the positioning of the competitors, by making a detailed structural analysis inside the industry, highlighting the major strategic groups and their dimensions. Remember that the essence of good strategic positioning is selecting activities that distinguish the company from its competitors.

We stress that, in principle, the strategy of cost leadership is not intrinsically better than that of differentiation or vice versa. Everything depends on the external context and the unique conditions of each company!

Cost Leadership

The company that seeks leadership in cost has to focus the entire organization to achieve this objective, creating a culture of low costs, working constantly to reduce waste and remaining constantly attentive to the cost positions of its competitors.

In order to obtain this advantage, the company needs to make trade-offs, such as letting go of greater variety and flexibility in favor of lower costs. On the other hand, this does not mean that the company that adopts this strategy will have poor-quality products.

The corporation that competes in this strategy has to create a gap in cost performance in relation to other competitors in the industry, which allows it to increase margins of profit, as illustrated in Figure 2.8. If the company manages to establish a level for costs which is much lower than the competition, but at the same time sets off a price war, this will reduce the margins and consequently its profitability. The goal is to work with costs well below average for the industry but to set prices only slightly lower than the competition.

Figure 2.8. Generic strategies: cost leadership

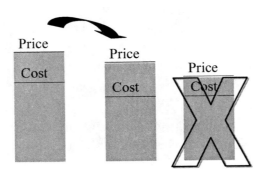

Companies such as the airline GOL, are always searching in different areas, involving quick in flight service, that doesn't require preparation and facilitates the later cleaning of the airplane, quick boarding and debarking procedures, making equipment available more rapidly for new flights, as well as investing in technology and maintenance focused on operational efficiency.

The bases for competition in this strategy are shaken up when competitors are able to quickly overcome the gap, eroding the bases for cost leadership, or when technology changes, eliminating advantages of scale, for example.

Differentiation

The rationale for a generic strategy of differentiation is also to increase the company margin starting from the price variable, not the cost variable

The goal of the companies that compete for differentiation is to identify and satisfy customers' needs, but those needs for which the client is inclined to pay a premium price. Therefore, the greater viability obtained in this business profile derives form the price premium. This does not mean, however, that companies that compete with this generic strategy can disregard the price variable. Once the target for differentiation has been defined, only costs associated to differentiation can be absorbed. In other aspects, the company should also exercise careful daily cost management, if it doesn't, it will be eliminating the margin obtained from the premium price with excessive costs as illustrated in Figure 2.9.

Companies such as the Brazilian airline TAM seek out added value by offering differentiated services to the client which allows it to charge more, and it clearly communicates the difference to the client — "TAM's way of flying". To add

Figure 2.9. Generic strategies: differentiation

value, it offers a more customized service in the air as well as on land. In opting for this approach, the trade-offs with the lower-cost positioning are explicit.

Results of competitive advantage in differentiation usually lead to investments in innovation and technology, always with the focus on the specific needs of the customers which add value, as well as the use of more specialized labor who in counterpart obtain higher remuneration.

The bases for competition in this strategy are shaken when the competitors are able to quickly manage to imitate the target of differentiation offering very similar packages of value or the differentiated object loses importance due to changes in the environment. For this reason, these companies have to be always in motion, improving performance and innovating more rapidly than their competitors.

This strategy implies higher risks, since the target of differentiation chosen by the company will not be able to obtain a premium price. In this case, the company will have costs higher than the industry average, without being able to charge more for its extra costs, since customers don't see value in the package offered. This happened with several retail companies that decided to differentiate their products through selling on the Internet, but didn't manage to add value, since the average consumer hasn't even got a computer, and they suffered losses with B2C (business-to-consumer).

Focus

The generic strategy of focus, on cost as well as differentiation, has many things in common with the strategies of cost leadership and differentiation, respectively. Basically, they differ in competitive scope.

The key to this strategy is to find the lucrative, sustainable target segment to exercise the strategy, whether of cost or differentiation. This focus on a segment allows the company to develop performance superior to its competitors, who have multiple targets. This segmentation can be a function of a geographic cut, or of scale, or an activity that reaches a specific type of consumer.

Once the target segment has been selected, the company has to devote all its efforts consistently in this direction, clearly communicating its option to the market. To have greater success in selecting the segment to implement the strategy of focus, segments that are more needy than others must be prioritized.

As with the strategy of differentiation, here the risks are also high since in addition to the specific trade-offs of strategy of cost or differentiation, there are trade-offs related to the target segment, for example, abandoning distribution channels. In case the trade-offs made do not result in value for the customers, these choices end up generating performance inferior to the industry average.

Defining generic strategy has a decisive impact on manufacturing strategy and the definition of competitive criteria that orient it, as we will see shortly.

Case Study: Strategy and Decisions in Perspective

Case – Competition in the Automobile Industry

Auto assembly plants engaged in much more respectful competition in the past than now. Partnerships such as Autolatina in Brazil, shared between Volkswagen and Ford, from 1987 to 1995, were viable in the closed market, but ceased to be so with the opening of commerce. The number of competitors with plants in the country multiplied, from those already installed before the opening, GM, Fiat, and Toyota, to those of the French – Renault, Peugeot, and Citroën; and the Japanese with Honda. Presently the majority of models produced in Brazil are of European origin.

To aggravate the situation, the automotive industry began to experience slow growth during that period, which led to even sharper competition.

The assemblers depended more on the supply of components produced and supplied by the first tier suppliers, with higher added value, which related to second and third level tiers in the supply chain, who manufactured sub-sets and individual components.

Case – Analysis of Competition in Belem

The absence of large Brazilian retail chains in the city of Belém, in the Amazon State, is due to difficulties in meeting the specifics of the local market and the complexity of supplying it.

In the 1980s, the Pão de Açúcar Group, the largest supermarket chain in Brazil, was the largest major supermarket chain present in Belém, but ended up beating a retreat during the group's restructuring. The Bom-Preço channel also gave up fighting over Belem's consumers, closing 10 stores in 1993.

Local groups were very aggressive in defending their territory, balancing modernizing of their stores with their regional roots. Peculiarities of local demand are very marked. Regional customs make the residents of Belem very particular consumers of things such as vegetables typical of the region, such as jambu, bacuri, cupuaçu, teperebá, or uxi, and the substitution of fresh milk with powdered milk. Imagine the effort needed to supply customized products for department stores or supermarkets in this city!

Due to their good knowledge of the characteristics of the local market, the local retail groups, such as Yamada, Leader, and Visão have managed to hold their own. Among the major retail chains in the country, only C&A, Arapuã, Riachuelo, and Lojas Americanas dispute the local market.

Source: Adapted from *Revista Exame* (2000).

Case – Bologna Competitive Market

The bologna market in metropolitan São Paulo, Brazil, is highly competitive. The main players are six high competitive companies with strong local brands: Cardeal, Ceratti, Marba, Rezende, Sadia, and Perdigão.

Two pressure maps were drawn and each diagram is a picture of the São Paulo's bologna market for each period analyzed. For the studied industry, it was assumed that the importance of the market (I.M.) was the percentage of bologna in the company's total revenue and the size of the incursion (S.I.) was the market share achieved reached by each analyzed player.

The strongest pressure ordinarily gets the quickest or the most effective response. Figure 2.10 shows a competitive pressures map, which represents the beginning of a great offensive movement of Ceratti over its stronger competitor, Marba, with significant reflexes on the others. It seems that Marba did not make any effort to avoid the imminent aggression from Ceratti.

Figure 2.11 shows a significant expressive retaliation by Marba over Ceratti for the purpose of recovering its market share. Cardeal also made sales efforts to gain market shares from Ceratti, Sadia, and Perdigão. Apparently, Perdigão

Figure 2.10. Competitive pressures map in moment 2 (2001)

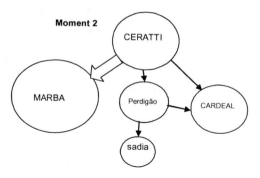

Figure 2.11. Competitive pressures map in moment 3 (2002)

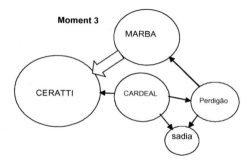

had directed its efforts to other regions in Brazil, and maintained its margins in São Paulo.

Source: Adapted from Pereira, Carvalho and Laurindo (2004).

Case – Building Competencies at NEC

At the end of the 1980s, NEC emerged as a leader in the area of semiconductors and as one of the major competitors in producing telecommunications and computers. In addition to consolidating its position in mainframes for computers and acting in the areas of public commuters and transmitters, it began to produce products for everyday use such as cell phones, faxes, laptops — linking telecommunications and office automation.

NEC is the only company among the five major revenues in telecommunications, semiconductors, and mainframes industries.

In the beginning of the 1970s, NEC articulated a strategy to explore the convergence of computers with communications, which was called "C&C." The success of this management strategy resulted in the acquisition of competencies, especially in semiconductors. NEC formed the "C&C Committee" composed of high-level executives to supervise the development of its core products and core competencies alongside its individual business interests. In accordance with its strategic structure, NEC transferred enormous resources to fortify its position in components and central processors. By employing collaborative arrangements to multiply its internal resources, NEC was ready to accumulate a vast range of core competencies.

NEC carefully identified three channels for technological evolution and interrelated markets, involving things from its large mainframes to distribution processes, components from simple ICs to VSLI, and communications from mechanical exchange bars to complex digital systems that we now call ISDN. Finally, NEC determined that semiconductors would be its most important product.

To build up its competencies rapidly and at low cost, NEC got involved in numerous numbers of strategic alliances, which numbered over 100 just in 1987. In mainframes, the best-known alliance was with Honeywell and Bull. Almost all the arrangements in the area of semiconductors and components were oriented toward access to technology. The research director at NEC summed up this acquisition of competencies during the 1970s and 1980s thusly, "From the point of view of investment, it was much cheaper and quicker to use outside technology. There was no need for us to develop new ideas."

Source: Adapted from Prahalad and Hamel (1990).

Case – In Search of a Generic Strategy at Bunge

The Bunge group, the third largest processor of soy in the world, with billing of 10 billion dollars per year, is active in Brazil, Argentina, and the United States.

Brazil is responsible for about half of world sales, and it is only here that the group has a consumer goods division, Santista Foods, with 20 factories and over 100 brand names that range from breads to margarines.

About three years ago, the Bunge stockholders resolved to focus on the agricultural commodities market to compete with the Americans, Cargill and ADM, the two largest corporations in the sector.

Based on this decision, several business units were sold, but Santista, which had been put up for sale in 1998, remained. According to a former Santista executive: "the consumer area always represents the least part of Bunge's billing and 90% of its headaches," constituting a kind of foreign body in the Bunge organism, since the integration of this company into the global strategy has required major efforts by its executives.

Santista has been devalued by about 10 million dollars since its acquisition by the Bunge group, with significant liquid losses in 2000, causing Bunge's entire Brazil operation to close in the red.

The total profit on other operations — pulled by the fertilizer area — was about 60 million dollars "Despite the slips in the consumer areas, the group has been very successful with its strategy in the area of commodities and fertilizers," says Luciana Massaad, investment analyst for the Itaú Bank.

The solution to problems caused by maintaining a division foreign to Bunge's focus has to do with the challenge of valorizing Santista Foods and Sears, separating out the businesses that are of interest to the group, integrating them into the global strategy, and selling off the rest, preferably for a good price.

Many of Bunge's difficulties with the consumer area come from the group's traditional vocation in the area of agricultural commodities. This has been the group's area of competency since 1818, when it founded the Koninklijke Bunge in Amsterdam to import grain from the Dutch colonies. Looking for wheat, Bunge arrived in Argentina in 1874. In 1906 it landed in Brazil, acquiring Moinho Santista. During periods of prosperity for wheat, the food group began to develop around these mills, which became accustomed to large volume business. The executives trained at Bunge were never close to the consumer market as were the teams from companies such as Unilever, one of the principals of Santista Alimentos in the area of margarine and mayonnaise. Until a short while ago, sales personnel spoke of tons of bread sold and not in units, as this is normally referred to in other consumer goods companies. "We will never be like a Unilever or Nestlé in terms of brand name management," says Weisser.

The strategy of the team led by Weisser, at least up until now, has been to eliminate the less profitable brands from Santista Alimentos. Some products have also bee redirected to large institutional clients, such as bakeries. "Publicity efforts are not needed in order to serve this market," says analyst/Luciana, from Itaú. "What is important is volume. And Bunge understands volume."

The idea is to integrate Santista more and more into Bunge Foods, Bunge's Food Company in the United States, which does not have consumer brand names and is totally dedicated to the sales segment for bakeries, industries and to the area of its own brand names in supermarket chains. The group is seeking to create synergy between the two operations.

Source: Adapted from Mano (2001).

Questions for Discussion and Reflection

1. What is the impact of B2B (Business-to-Business) relationships on bargaining power in the links of the chain?

2. The merger of Brahma and Antarctica, which created AmBev, aimed to adapt the two national capital companies to the commercial blocks of the Americas, in order to confront the commercial opening. Given the asymmetry of the companies, the market was concerned Brahma would swallow Antarctica with the merger. What has been the impact of the merger that created AmBev on the shape of the beer industry? Which force was most affected?

3. Name a war of substitute industries that has been broadcast in the media.

4. What are generic strategies? Cite an example of each type of strategy.

5. What are core competencies? How can they be identified?

6. Considering the case in the section titled Competition in the Automobile Industry, answer the following question:

   - Analyze the five forces of competition in this industry.
   - Did the changes in the patterns of growth in this industry affect the intensity of the forces of competition? Which ones?

7. Considering the case in the section titled Analysis of Competition in Belem, answer the following questions:

   - Which strategic dimensions would represent well an analysis inside the industry in this case?
   - Which would be more adequate for an analysis of strategic groups?
   - Make an analysis of competition in this context.

8. Considering the case in the section titled Bologna Competitive Market, answer the following questions:

    - Compare the strategic groups map and competitive pressures map.
    - Make an analysis of the competition in this context.

9. Considering the case in the section titled Building Completencies at NEC, answer the following questions:

    - What are NEC's core competencies and products?
    - What are its final products? Comment on the range of markets reached by each of these products.
    - How was the concept of competence implemented at NEC?

10. Considering the case in the section titled In Search of a Generic Strategy at Bunge, answer the following questions:

    - Using Figure 2.7 as a reference, locate Bunge Foods and Santista in one of the quadrants.
    - Bunge Food has to harmonize its companies with disparate generic strategies, what are the main points that need to be balanced? What generic strategy should be adopted?

References

Carvalho, M. M., Laurindo, F. J. B., & Pessôa, M. S. De P. (2003). Information technology project management to achieve efficiency in Brazilian Companies. In S. Kamel (Ed.), *Managing globally with information technology* (pp. 260-271). Hershey, PA: IRM Press.

Cox, A., Sanderson, J. E., & Watson, G. (2001). Supply chains and power regimes: Toward an analytic framework for managing extended networks of buyer and supplier relationships. *The Journal of Supply Chain Management, 37*(2), 28-35.

D'Aveni, R. A. (2002, Fall). Competitive pressure systems: Mapping and managing multimarket contact. *Harvard Business Review*.

Deschamps & Nayak (1995). Product juggernauts. *Harvard Business School*.

Feka, V., Xouris, D., & Tsiotras, G. (1997). Mapping strategic groups: An international example. *Journal of Business & Industrial Marketing, 12*(1), 66-75.

Furrer, O., & Thomas, H. (2000, December). The rivarly matrix: Understanding rivarly and competitive dynamics. *European Management Journal, 18*(6).

Heizer & Render (1999). *Operations management*. Upper Saddle River, NJ: Prentice-Hall.

Mano, C. (2001). Não sei se caso ou compro uma bicicleta. *Revista Exame, 1*, 735.

Na terra do açaí. (2000, November). *Revista Exame*. São Paulo.

Pereira, P.L.S., Carvalho, M.M., & Laurindo, F.J.B. (2004). Competitive mapping in a Brazilian food industry. In EUROMA2004 — European Operations Management Association International Conference, Fontainebleau. *Proceedings of EurOMA2004* (vol. 1, pp. 247-256).

Porter, M. E. (1979, November/December). How competitive forces shape strategy. *Harvard Business Review*, 137-145.

Porter, M. E. (1987, May/June). From competitive advantage to corporate strategy. *Harvard Business Review*.

Porter, M. E. (1996, November/December). What is strategy? *Harvard Business Review,* 61-78.

Porter, M. E. (2001, March). Strategy and the Internet. *Harvard Business Review*, 63-78.

Prahalad, C.K., & Hamel, G. (1990, May/June). The core competence of the corporation. *Harvard Business Review*, 79-91.

Rabechini, R. Jr., & Carvalho, M.M. (2003). *O perfil das competências em equipes de projeto*. *Revista de Administração de Empresas* — RAE Eletrônica – FGV.

Scaranello, B.M. (2004). *Análise da concorrência: Um estudo de caso do setor de bebidas*. Trabalho de Formatura. Escola Politécnica da USP. Orientadora: Marly Monteiro de Carvalho. São Paulo.

Chapter III

An Overview Of Value Chains, Supply Chains And Strategic Alliances Issues

Introduction

In the competitive scenario unfolding at the beginning of the 21st century, characterized by the fast pace of technologic changes and opening and volatilization of global markets, an understanding of global value chains is of critical importance to outlining strategy.

As shown in Chapter II, in the most complex production chains, assessing bargaining power in relation to customers and suppliers may not be enough to understand the power relationships in the global competitive market. Imagine a semiconductors industry, whose clients may be the PC industry, but also be in telecommunications, electronics end users, and new areas such as *smart cards*. How can one discuss bargaining power based only on the elements introduced on Chapter II?

On the other hand, the process of decentralizing production activities, very often marked by globally-based outsourcing and by the streamlining of yesterday's large corporate structures, created the so-called "network-companies." According to Chesnais (1996), large companies operating on a global basis gave priority to some functions considered strategic, leading a global chain of suppliers and distributors, performing activities previously performed by verticalized companies.

This process of "de-verticalization" presents some risks. However, when a company takes over value activities, it is possible to enforce its interests over other chain links by using its economic power.

For small companies, which are part of these large chains, the understanding of power dynamics and relations is decisive for their survival and development, and to outline defensive strategies enabling them to increase their relative power in the chain by means of partnerships and networks of cooperation.

The issues discussed are vital for strategy definition, since they bring a more detailed understanding of the game rules of the global value chains and of how to take advantage of its configuration, using networks and partnerships, or making use of location.

This chapter intends to present a more in-depth discussion of the supply chain, introducing issues such as location, networks of cooperation, and the study of governance, both of local and global scope. The concept of value chains, both in product-based and in service-based industries, are addressed.

How to Define the Term Chains

You are certainly familiar with the concepts of value chain, supply chain and global value chains. Are these expressions synonymous or is there a difference in concept among them?

The first source of confusion is the fact that different research areas study the same phenomenon: the connection of several linkages in a chain, deployed in several tiers, from input to selling in global markets. These academic approaches are from the areas of strategy, logistics and operations, in addition to the economists, geographers, and social scientists.

Although there are several similarities between these approaches, each area emphasizes different features of this phenomenon, as presented in the following sections.

The Value Chain

For Porter and Millar (1985, p. 3), the value chain "is system of interdependent activities, which are connected by linkages," and could be divided in technologically and economically distinct activities that a company uses to do business, which affect cost or efficiency of other activities. Each of these activities would be a value activity.

Nine generic activities have been identified by these authors, and classified in two groups: support activities and primary activities, as shown in Figure 3.1. The four support activities are: firm infrastructure, human resources management, technology development, and procurement. The five primary activities are: inbound logistics, operations, outbound logistics, marketing and sales, and services. To be performed, each one of these activities requires a physical and a data processing component, which is the reason why information technology (IT) has such a large impact on the value chain, as shown on Chapter VII.

The *value system* concept is an enlargement of the *value chain* concept, contemplating an industry's value chains from suppliers to end-consumers. Figure 3.2 shows the connections between activities within this value system.

Figure 3.1. The value chain (adapted from Porter & Millar, 1985)

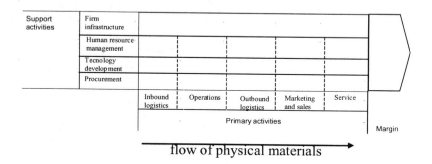

Figure 3.2. The value system (adapted from Porter & Millar, 1985)

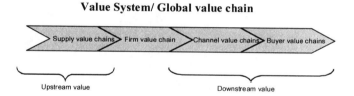

It should be stressed that the *value chain* concept coined by Porter and Millar (1985) is contained within the firm bonders, and that the *value system* concept is the one bearing more similarity to the themes discussed in the next section, that is, supply chains and global value chains.

Duhan et al. (2001), however, argue that in knowledge-based companies there are difficulties in using value-chain analysis, as shown in Table 3.1. In this kind of company, the value chain is less evident, due to the process's interactive nature, making it difficult to discriminate the added value of a single step. On the other hand, in knowledge-based companies, human resources are essential in achieving competitive advantage, which requires competence to extract individual knowledge from experts through collaboration, managing a relevant amount of informality.

Quinn et al. (1990) also emphasize the knowledge assets in companies, especially in so-called intelligent enterprises, such as biotechnology, semiconductor and electronics industry. In these industries, these authors identify a loosely structured network around specialized core competencies, with a service-based strategy.

Table 3.1. Value chain analysis applied to knowledge-based companies

Characteristics of value chain analysis	Characteristics of knowledge-based firms
Orientated towards the production of goods rather than services.	Produce intangible services based on knowledge and experience.
Implicit primacy of primary activities over support activities.	Support activities have a much greater importance, directly adding value through human creativity.
Uni-directional, following the flow of physical materials.	Operate a feedback-loop mechanism, continually gathering information, developing skills, and using experience to enhance the service product.
Reflects capital investment priorities of plant and machinery.	Human assets are more important than capital assets.

Figure 3.3. The service-profit chain (adapted from Schlesinger & Heskett, 1991)

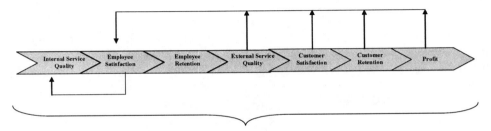

Focus on intangible services based on knowledge and experience.

Schlesinger and Heskett (1991) also argue that human resources are a critical resource in service activities and propose a service-profit chain, as shown in Figure 3.3. These authors argue that if the company just has employee satisfaction and retention it could be possible to achieve customer satisfaction and retention and, in consequence, a competitive advantage. A similar idea was proposed by Rucci et al. (1994) that highlights employee importance in the service value chain, so-called employee-customer profit chain.

Heskett et al. (1994) also propose a service-profit chain audit, which allows making a diagnosis through 25 questions classified in the following categories: *profit and growth, customer satisfaction, external service value, employee productivity, employee satisfaction, employee loyalty, internal service quality, leadership,* and *relating the measures.*

Supply Chain

Several researchers, especially in the logistics area, use the expression supply chain. According to Bowersox and Closs (2001), supply-chain management is the integration of the company's essential business processes, from raw materials to end-users.

Although this definition bears some similarity to the *value system*, in this case there is no concern with differentiating between support and primary activities, emphasizing the same primary activities, i.e., logistics.

With the increase of outsourcing, logistic alliances took on a more relevant role in the formulation of corporate strategies. According to Bowersox (1990), the concept of logistic alliances characterized by cooperation, often based on informal agreements, forms a business pact where each part seeks the benefits of synergy brought on by joint work. Logistic partnerships are distinguished from other business cooperation models by the very strong connection between the participants, who, in practice, create an extended organization with its own role, rules, values, and goals.

The most common forms of logistic alliance involve a *producer and a service supplier,* such as storage or transport company, and it can also combine service suppliers' resources.

Other common forms of logistic alliance are *vertical alignment between two or more producers,* and *horizontal alignment.* The former is usually marked by inventory transfer and the latter sells to the same customer base. Both may include a service provider.

For researchers in the operations-management area, the emphasis is on supply-chain management, originating from the study of customer-suppliers cooperation networks typical of Japanese companies, know as *keiretsu*, which display very distinctive collaboration and partnership patterns. An example of these networks is the one headed by Japanese assemblers that guides suppliers, not only of the first tier, but also of the other tiers, transferring technology so as to avoid loss and lack of efficiency, so that the added value can be transferred to consumers. In this context, the concept is very similar to the *value system* concept presented in the section above.

The main issues referring to *supply-chain management*, in this scope, have been discussed in Chapter II.

Global Value Chains

Finally, according to Gereffi (1994), the expression global value chains, found throughout the literature in several areas, can be characterized by the production and marketing of goods involving strategic decisions and the forming of international networks.

For Gereffi (1994), there are two basic shapes of global value chains: *producer-driven chains* and *buyer-driven chains.*

In *producer-driven chains*, the key assets are productive, enabling large manufacturers to coordinate inter-organizational networks, making intensive use of capital and technology, such as those of the automobile and airplane industries.

As for *buyer-driven chains,* the key assets are commercial, such as brand names, or marketing channels. The coordinators of the chain are the large retailers, designers and trading networks, which control how, when, and where the production will take place and what profit share should be attained at each step of the chain, though they have no productive devices. These chains usually involve third-world suppliers, such as shoes and toys (Gereffi, 1999). The main differences between these chains are summarized in Table 3.2.

In more recent papers, Gereffi (2001) introduces a new chain configuration called the internet-oriented chain, i.e., production chains driven by the Internet. This configuration is detailed in Chapter X.

Although the production chain description bears similarities to the previous definitions, here there is more stress on four dimensions, namely:

Table 3.2. Governance structures in global value chains (adapted from Gereffi, 2001, p.34)

Global Value chain	Leading industries	Main drivers	Form & dominant principles of value chain integration	Institutional & organizational innovations
Producer-driven chains	• Natural resources • Capital goods & consumer durables	Transnational manufacturers	Vertical integration (*ownership and control*)	• Vertical integrated TNCs with international production networks • Mass production • Lean Production
Buyer-driven chains	• Non-durable consumer goods	Retailers and marketers	Network integration (*logistics and trust*)	• Growth of export processing zones • Global sourcing by retailers. • Rise of pure marketers • Rise of specialist retailers • Growth of private labels (store brands) • Lean retailing

1. A value chain of goods, services and resources in one or more industrial sector. In this context, it should be stressed that the meaning of *value chain* in Gereffi (2001) is different from the nomenclature proposed by Porter and Millar (1985), in which *global value chain* means *value system*.

2. Geographic dispersion of chains on the regional, national, and global levels.

3. Governance structure along the global value chain (value system), "which refers to the key-actors in the chain that determine the inter-firm division of labor, and shape the capacities of participants to upgrade their activities." (Gereffi, 2001, p. 30)

4. Institutional framework.

Other authors, such as Storper and Harrison, (1991) use the *production system* concept, which has some similarities to the *value system* concept, and is defined as the coordination structure of the chain, with vertical and horizontal relations among companies, that can be governed by market mechanisms or relations between the links.

These authors emphasize, as a relevant dimension, besides the governance structure and productions system features, the existence of clusters of companies. Storper and Harrison, (1991) stress the importance of local issues, especially cluster environment, in the competitive environmental analysis.

Thus, in order to have a better understanding of the competitive environment, the issues of location and clusters of companies are essential to make a good map of the competitive environment and will be detailed below.

Location: The Role of Clusters in Competitiveness

Studies of clusters or local production systems, among other names, originated from several areas, such as economic geography, regional development, competitive strategy studies, and technology development and innovation.

A cluster can be defined as a geographic or sector concentration of companies, originating from external economies (externalities) and joint collaborative actions, enabling collective efficiency gains and entrance to global markets, which individual companies would not attain.

Incidental external economies involve qualified labor, specialized suppliers of goods and services, and the overflow of knowledge and technology.

Joint actions, achieved by deliberate and conscious effort, can be divided into two kinds: cooperation between companies (e.g., sharing equipment) and groups of companies organized into associations or consortia, as for exportation. These joint cooperation actions can be horizontal (among competitors) or vertical (among chain tiers).

Thus, the emphasis lies not only on the incidental aspects resulting from externalities and historical aspects, but also on those related to forming a network relationship between companies and other institutions important for competition, capable of generating joint actions.

The forming of clusters has an impact on productivity and scale, on innovation and new business. In this sense, companies entering a cluster and getting benefits from concentration and specialization have a competitive advantage. These benefits usually enable the locality to compete in the global market by entering production chains.

Being in a cluster enables a company easy access to qualified manpower, minimizing expenses for training, and appropriating knowledge and technology by the overflow effect. Information and knowledge transmission flow either by a formal or informal learning process. Highlighted, however, is the role of cooperative joint actions which allow risk reduction, increase of increase and resources sharing, as stated above.

The negative points could be blocking effects and asymmetries. Blocking effects, due to the excess of external economies, tend to dissuade the concentration of companies, generating, for instance, high transport and rental costs, canceling out part of the mentioned advantages. Asymmetries appear when the leading companies have a strong influence over the strategy of other cluster companies and inhibit joint cooperation actions.

In summary, three aspects contribute to the analysis of local concentration: *competitive market, cluster collaborative environment,* and *cluster collective competencies* as shown in Figure 3.4.

The kind of governance structure in the chain where the cluster seen is inserted, has a strong influence on the possibilities for industrial upgrading and the kind of local or global markets reached, i.e., in *competitive market.*

The kind of local governance seeks to identity the existence of a leading company that conditions the strategy of the other companies in the cluster and the potential for joint action, i.e., affect *cluster collaborative environment.*

Finally, the *cluster collective competencies* also has an impact on the competitiveness of the cluster, investigating the degree of rootedness of technology knowledge, and discussing the stages of technology maturity.

Collective competence can be seen as the ability to attain competitive advantages, shared by companies included in geographically concentrated complexes, or clusters, that an isolated company could not have.

Figure 3.4. Dimensions for cluster analysis

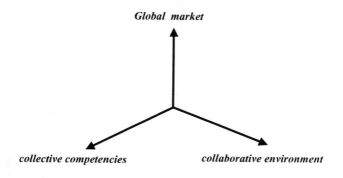

Cluster or Industrial Districts: A Summary of the Theoretical Discussion

Geographic proximity appears as an inductor of externalities (such as qualified labor and access to raw materials) by agglomeration from the time of the first industrial districts formed at the end of the 19th century, generating increasing earnings, as suggested by Krugman (1995).

Heizer and Render (1999) show high concentrations of a specialized labor workforce such as those for cartooning in the Philippines and the perfume industry in France as factors attracting global industries in these sectors to these areas, generating competitive advantages.

The literature reveals several approaches to the treatment of this theme. In this project, the main conceptual focus is on issues related to the strategic impact and to governance, as well as location factors and innovation inducers.

One of the major exponents of the strategic approach to clusters is the researcher Michael Porter, especially the papers of Porter (1998) and Porter and Stern (2001), where the author/s discusses the strategic impact of clusters on corporate competition and on countries.

Porter (1998) dissects the anatomy of some of the main clusters in search of the main players and their relationship concerning competition and cooperation. According to the author, it is possible to identify a network of relations between companies and other agencies related to competition, geographically concentrated and acting in a given field. This network includes suppliers specialized in raw materials, equipment and services, as well as adequate infrastructure and access to distribution channels and consumers. And finally, there are, in several clusters, government agencies and other institutions such as universities, technical training services, standards association, commercial associations, and trade unions.

In summary, Porter's study (1998) presents clusters as a competitive advantage for regions, resulting from the harmony between competition and cooperation, enabling the use of local competencies. Three aspects related with the forming of clusters are stressed by the author in leveraging competitiveness: the impact on productivity and scale, on innovation, and in forming new business. These impacts generated by the forming of clusters are capable of changing the composition of the five forces of competition in relation to the structural analysis of the industry (Porter, 1979).

The existing literature on the impact of industrial clusters on regional development is extensive, encompassing the industrial districts in Italy and in other countries and its impact on economic growth, which is mostly attributed to the effectiveness of small and midsized enterprises (SME) networks, as well as to local level cooperation achieved in the industrial districts of that country and to their inclusion in global chains (Scott & Storper, 1988; Porter, 1998; Porter & Stern, 2001; Ghemawat, 2001).

Schmitz (1992) reports on a flexible specialization, based on a division and organization of production where SMC divided the different production phases of a single product among themselves. The creation of this form would be based on the following features: (a) geographic concentration of companies acting in the same industrial sector; (b) presence of companies of different sizes but with more participation of SMC; (c) production specialization between different companies on the vertical division level, involving producers and suppliers of all kinds of products and services and technological support; (d) large quantity and flexible variety; (e) different companies share horizontal-level production, by outsourcing and complementarities; (f) the most successful complexes compete on other dimensions besides price; (g) ease of entry for new companies; (h) access to information and service networks (Ruas et al., 1994).

Courlet (1993) argues that the industrial location of a small company is done following a different rationale from the large corporations, and proposed the study of their location according to the *local industrial systems*. These systems can be seen as companies concentrated around one or several industrial sectors, interacting among them and with the socio-cultural environment, generating productive externalities for all the companies. Thus, these systems' focus is not exclusively economics, but also historic, cultural, and social.

This author stresses, as location factors, the totality of technical capabilities and the preexisting industrial sectors, the population's cultural identity and habits, quality of life, education, low crime rates, and good elementary and technical schools, that complete the framework for attracting investments and growth for these systems.

The large corporation is usually present in technology transfer, in managerial assistance, in training businesspeople and workers and especially in coordinating the production and distribution system, which encompasses a park of small companies. This kind of configuration, with a large corporation organizing a network of smaller companies, can be found in areas of the Silicon Valley in

California and along route 128 in Massachusetts. A similar situation can also be found in the industrial organization of the Emilia Romagna area, in Italy.

On the other hand, a large corporation or a lead company can bring a strong asymmetry to local companies, as shown by Belussi (1999) in his analysis of the Italian industrial districts. This author found that asymmetric relations between the companies located on the Italian districts have been increasing, forming strongly hierarchic governance structures headed by the large corporations.

However, it is noteworthy that the trends towards specialization and innovation depend on the kind of goods produced and the dynamics of the market where the companies are installed. Under conditions where cost-based competition strategies predominate, these features are not found, characterizing what Segenberger and Pyke (1990) called *low-road* strategies.

Governance Analysis: Global and Local

The concept of governance was discussed by Williamson (1985), and later developed by Hollingsworth and Lindberg (1986), Jessop (1998), Humphrey and Schmitz (2000), and others, to address the process of coordinating the economic players at the public and private, local, and global levels.

Fleury and Fleury (2000) stress that the main idea of production-chain analysis is the identification of power structures or governance, where one or more corporations coordinate and control geographically separate economic activities.

Humphrey and Schmitz (2000, 2001) compiled literature on governance and distinguished four kinds of governance: arm's-length market relationships, networks, quasi-hierarchy, and hierarchy. For these authors, there are intermediate governance structures, where both market-relations as well as hierarchies yield to horizontal structures between the involved parties, resulting in more frequent interactions, with a higher degree of collaboration and cooperation among the companies. It should be stressed, however, that intermediate structures do not necessarily mean an absence of asymmetries.

The relevance of considering different kinds of governance is in the fact that the differences in the coordination patterns of the players has direct influence on their ability of upgrading possibilities of the actors along the chain, and could also have a bearing on their response to fast changes in today's context. Governance structures characterized by strong hierarchies, evolving from the

Table 3.3. Forms of joint action in clusters (adapted from Schmitz, 1997)

	Bilateral	**Multilateral**
Horizontal	Sharing Equipment	Sectoral Association
Vertical	Producer and user improving components	Alliance across value added chain

unequal bargaining power held by the companies involved in the process, represent the greatest threats to the power connections.

For the corporation, identifying the kind of governance held by the chain's players enables it to avoid such threats, by planning neutralizing strategies, turning the tables, and creating opportunities by means of alliances, partnerships, and networks.

Another relevant component in this analysis is local governance, which has an important role in coordinating joint actions among a cluster's companies. This local-level governance does not necessarily replicate the global value chain relations, since very often this locality represents only one link in a large global chain. Schmitz (1997) distinguishs between horizontal cooperation and vertical cooperation, as well as bilateral and multilateral, as shown in Table 3.3.

The main players in this kind of governance are local development agencies and trade associations, who catalyze joint actions of local enterprises, promoting local development and the dynamism of this group of companies. On the other hand, the lead firm's role in conditioning the cluster's dynamics is also an important issue to be stressed, since the other companies also benefit from the leader's development, even if unbalanced.

There are also forms of public local governance that can be coordinated by local government, through the establishment and maintenance of institutions which support local companies, such as training centers, technology services suppliers, and governmental development agencies, among others. According to Porter (1998), clusters enable a new kind of dialogue between the private and public sectors. Government, in its various spheres, should provide educated citizens and high-quality infrastructure. But in this context, there is an important government role: the legislature, both in terms of the rules of competition (laws protecting intellectual property, antitrust, etc.), and to the definition of an industrial policy, which fosters the creation, and growth of clusters (tax reductions, etc.). It is important to stress the role of funding by agencies and banks.

Decision-Making Tool Applied to Environment Analysis

Besides the environment analysis presented in this chapter, there are several decision-making tools that could help the strategist to make a good map.

The Rivalry Matrix, proposed by Furrer and Thomas (2000), is a focusing tool for several analysis models of the competitive environment. Its function is to shown the analyst which is the best model to use in a given market situation. It presupposes that each of the existing models is only effective when applied in a more specific situation, and that the combined use of four models can encompass most of the possible situations.

The Rivalry Matrix includes the two following dimensions, which are used to classify the market under study and to recommend which model should be used: *the number of decision variables and the nature of the environment* (Figure 3.5).

According to Furrer and Thomas (2000), the *number of decision variables* is related to the complexity of the problem under analysis. In more focused cases, such as the launching of a new product, all external variables are taken as constants, while in more complex cases, when the company must decide between several alternatives, the number of variables increases. A typical example of a case with several variables, presented by the authors, is when a

Figure 3.5. Rivalry matrix (adapted from Furrer & Thomas, 2000)

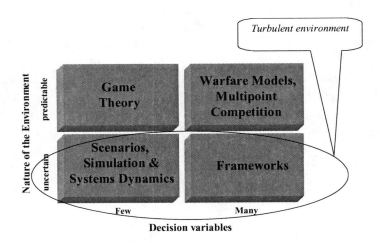

company tries to fight a competitor's price reduction, and has several different strategies, such as to reduce price, launch a new product, improve its own product, enter a new market, or any combination of these alternatives. The authors state that as the problem becomes more complex, and the number of variables increases, the more difficult it becomes to model the situation and the player's competitive movements.

Another dimension used in the Rivalry matrix is the *nature of the environment.* In order to be able to tell which environment is foreseeable or not, it is important to study the market and its evolution. In predictable environments, market variations are very small, or show a constant and organic evolution. On the other hand, turbulent and unpredictable markets are historically characterized by creation of new substitute technologies or by the entrance of a new competitor coming from a totally different industry, causing unbalance and leading to sudden changes in the player's movements (Furred & Thomas, 2000).

The combination of the two dimensions — the *number of decision variables* and *nature of the environment* — comprise the four quadrants of the Rivalry matrix (see Figure 3.5). The analyst must classify the market under study on one of the two quadrants, selecting the best model for his study.

The models analyzed and classified by Furrer and Thomas (2000) according to the main authors in the rivalry matrix are the following:

- **Game Theory Modeling** (e.g., Camerer, 1991; Oster,1999)
- **Scenarios, Simulations, and System Dynamic Modeling** (e.g., Porter & Spence, 1982; Mezias & Eisner,1997)
- **Warfare and multipoint competition** (e.g., Karnani & Wernerfet, 1985; Chen,1996; DÁveni, 1994)
- **Frameworks** (e.g., Porter, 1980, 1991)

The *frameworks* were presented in Chapters II and III, and the others models will be discussed in the second part of this book.

Case Study: Strategy and Decisions in Perspective

Case – Fashion Design Networks

Of all the links of this chain, the clothing sector has great importance in the foreign market, since it represented 45.4% of the total in 2000. It should thus be stressed that the clothing industry responds for almost half of total exports resulting from other links in the chain.

Management of trademarks, development of fashion design and product concept, quality, and marketing became more and more important as critical factors for the success of the brazilian textile industry. Companies adopting the fashion vanguard as a competitive strategy try to distinguish their products, responding rapidly to market signals and fostering creativity, innovation and supply-chain management.

Each season, new collections with new fabrics, patterns, colors, and models are introduced, affecting the whole textile and clothing supply chain. The shorter the development cycle for new products, the greater the need to intensify the relations along the supply chain, so as to make the sector aware of the consumers' needs.

Thus, there is a need to be more flexible. However, it should also be stressed that vanguard companies require that these chain linkages be willing to form long-term partnerships, providing exclusive patterns and finishing in small lots for each season, and trust and confidentiality are essential. These are mid to large-sized companies that maintain a quite balanced and close relationship with the hub company, involving joint development of new products (co-design).

Although patterns of competition present great variation according to the sector and consumer profile, it can be observed that the fashion vanguard companies have been strengthening their own brands or licensing foreign brands trying to obtain overseas markets. At the same time, these companies articulate a wide outsourced network of companies and retail stores, supported by information technology, with effective control of quality and delivery time. These companies, considered vanguard, are responsible for the quick introduction of product innovation in the brazilian market, in tune with the main fashion centers.

The hub companies give priority to product design, brand name, and marketing, and the rest of the production process is done according to an outsourcing system typical of this sector. In this system, there is a service supplier without its own product line, working only under order for third parties. This service supplier makes available facilities, equipments, and workforce, while the hub firm provides all inputs and manufacture procedures. This kind of operation is very common in the cut-and-sew phase that can be done by different service suppliers. These suppliers are usually small, with close but standardized relationships, with a high degree of asymmetry in their relationships with hub firm and low bargaining power. The information system is basically done via the Internet, since these companies have a low degree of information technology.

The selling is done by brand stores, with intensive use of franchising systems. The brand is really a relevant issue for companies working with strategies. It must give to the chosen market segment a strong identification, the feeling of belonging to a given lifestyle *(street, club, surfwear, etc.).* Retailers play an important role, since both architecture and decoration must impart the same concept. Along with these factors, there is also the availability of a full line of products, including products and accessories, promotional items, distinctive packages, and media-covered events. Just as in the case of the service suppliers, the franchise-holding companies receive the complete detailed retailer project and are interconnected by an EDI information system. Franchisers have frequent relations with the hub company, but it seems more like a partnership, since they are important channels that should be kept close to the

Figure 3.6. Network of companies around the fashion design firm

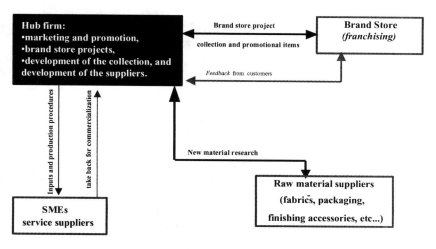

target-market, working as a sensor of market needs and as disseminators of the hub companies' concept.

The activities developed by the hub firm can be divided as follows: marketing and promotion, brand store projects, development of the collection, and suppliers. Figure 3.6 shows the relationship between companies articulated by a vanguard hub company. The width of the arrows represents the intensity of interactions among the networks companies and the shape of the arrow — full or striped — represents the nature of the relationship, standardized and asymmetric relationship, or balanced partnership.

Source: Adapted from Carvalho and Serra (1999).

Questions for Discussion and Reflection

1.   Explain the different approaches to "chain"?
2.   What is the difference between value chain and value system?
3.   What is governance? What is the difference between global and local governance?
4.   Define cluster.
5.   Which are the elements of a structure of innovation capacity?
6.   Considering the case in the section titled Fashion Design Networks, answer the following questions:

   •   Discuss this corporate network according to the various chain approaches presented.
   •   Which is the role of the vanguard company in this context? How does it affect the outsourced companies' strategy?

References

Belussi, F. (1999). Policies for development of knowledge-intensive local production system. *Cambridge Journal of Economics, 23*, 729-747.

Bowersox, D. (1990, July/August). The strategic benefit of logistic. *Harvard Business Review.*

Bowersox, D. J. E., & Closs, D. J. (2001). *Logística empresarial.* Ed. São Paulo: Atlas.

Carvalho, M.M., & Serra, N. (1999). Competitive strategies: The Brazilian textile & garment industries. In Portland International Conference on Management of Engineering and Technology, Portland. *Proceedings in CD, Portland: IEEE (PICMET'99).*

Chesnais, F. (1996). *A mundialização do capital.* São Paulo: Xamã.

Courlet, C. (1993). *Novas dinâmicas de desenvolvimento e sistemas industriais localizados.* In Industrial Districts and Inter-Firm Co-Operation in Italy. Geneva, Switzerland: International Labour Organisation.

Duhan, S., Levy, M., & Powell, P. (2001). Information systems strategies in knowledge-based SMEs: The role of core competencies. *European Journal of Information Systems, 10,* 25-40.

Fleury, A.C.C., & Fleury, M.T.L. (2000). *Estratégias empresariais e formação de competências*: *Um quebra-cabeça caleidoscópico da indústria brasileira.* São Paulo: Ed. Atlas, 2A ed.

Furrer, O., & Thomas, H. (2000, December). The rivalry matrix: Understanding rivalry and competitive dynamics. *European Management Journal, 18*(6).

Gereffi, G. (1994). *The organization of buyer-driven global commodity chains: How U.S. retailers shape overseas production networks.* In GEREFFI, G.; KORZENIEWICZ, M. Commodity chains and global capitalism. Westport: Praeger.

Gereffi, G. (1999). International trade and industrial upgrading in the apparel commodity chain. *Journal of International Economics, 48,* 31-70.

Gereffi, G. (2001). Beyond the producer-driven / buyer-driven dichotomy: The evolution of global value chains in the internet era. *IDS Bulletin, 32*(3).

Ghemawat, P. (2001, September). Distance still matters: the hard rality of global expansion. *Harvard Business Review,* 137-147.

Heizer & Render (1999). *Operations management.* Prentice-Hall.

Heskett, J.L., Jones, T.O., Loverman, G.W., Sasser, W.E., & Schlesinger, L.A. (1994, March/April). Putting the service-profit chain to work. *Harvard Business Review,* 164-174.

Hollingsworth & Lindberg (1986). *The governance of the american economy: markets, clans, hierarchis and associative behavior.* In Streeck & Schimitter, Private Interest Government. New York: University Press.

Humphrey, J., & Schmitz, H. (2000). *Governance and upgrading: Linking industrial cluster and global value chain research.* IDS Working Paper No. 120, p.1-37, Institute of Development Studies, University of Sussex, Brighton.

Humphrey, J., & Schmitz, H. (2001). *Governance in global value chains.* IDS Bulletin 32, 19-29.

Jessop, B. (1998). The rise of governance and the risks of failure: the case of economic development. *International Social Science Journal, 155,* 29-45.

Krugman, P. (1995). *Development, geography and economic theory.* Cambridge, MA: MIT Press.

Porter, M., & Stern, S. (2001, Summer). Innovation: Location matters. *MIT Sloan Management Review,* 28-36.

Porter, M.E. (1979, November/December). How Competitive forces shape strategy. *Harvard Business Review,* 137-145.

Porter, M.E. (1998, November/December). Clusters and the new economics competitions. *Harvard Business Review,* 77-90.

Porter, M.E., & Millar, V. (1985, July/August). How information gives you competitive advantage. *Harvard Business Review,* 149-160.

Quinn, J.B., Doorley, T.L., & Paquette, P.C. (1990, March/April). Beyond products: Service-based strategy. *Harvard Business Review,* 1-20.

Ruas, R. L., Gitahy, L., Rabelo, F., & Antunes, E. (1994, March). *Inter-firm relations, collective efficiency and employment in two Brazilian clusters.* International Labour Office. Working Paper n. 242.

Rucci, A.J., Kirn, S.P., & Quinn, R.T. (1998, January-February). The employee-customer profit chain at Sears. *Harvard Business Review,* 82-97.

Schlesinger, L.A., & Heskett, J.L. (1991, September/October). The service-driven service company. *Harvard Business Review,* 1-20.

Schmitz, H. (1992, July). *On the clustering of small firms.* IDS Bulletin, *23*(3).

Schmitz, H. (1997, March). *Collective efficiency and increasing returns.* IDS Working Paper, Brighton, IDS, n. 50.

Schmitz, H. (1999). Global competition and local cooperation in the Sinos Valley, Brazil. *World Development, 27*(9).

Scott, A J., & Storper, M. (1988). *Indústria de alta tecnologia e desenvolvimento regional: uma crítica e reconstrução.*

Segenberger & Pyke (1990). *Industrial districts and local economic regeneration: Research and policy issues.* in PYKE, F. et alii. Geneva, International Labour Office.

Storper, M., & Harrison, B. (1991). Flexibility, hierarchy and regional developments: the changing structure of industrial production systems and their forms of governance in the 1990s. *Research Policy, North-Holland, 20*(5).

Williamson, O. E. (1985). *The economic institutions of capitalism.* New York: Free Press.

Chapter IV

Aligning Strategy With Organizational Structures And Project Deployment

Introduction

Companies have undergone a process of transformation, organizing themselves to be able to make effective and agile responses to environmental problems and, especially, those having to do with competition and positioning in the market. These responses constitute a set of actions or activities that reflect the company's competence in taking advantage of opportunities, and their capacity for rapid action, respecting time and cost limits and specifications (Rabechini & Carvalho, 2003). To do so, constructing project-oriented organizations and investing in management design tools and techniques is fundamental, and this has become a growing concern of companies.

Handy (1995) points out that organizations in the postindustrial era will be configured like "condominiums", with groups of projects housed together, since what adds the most value to products and services are intelligent, rather than routine, activities (Fleury & Fleury, 2000).

According to Frame (1999), project management practices have consolidated since the 1990s, and several researchers cite this as an obligatory subject matter for companies that seek to develop and maintain competitive advantages. A good indicator of this growth is the presence of the PMI (*Project Management Institute*) in over 100 countries; it has certified around 25,000 project managers since the beginning of 2002 (Rabechini and Carvalho, 2003).

However, studies based in Brazilian companies show that few have formalized development of a management model for the process of innovation and projects (Rabechini et al., 2002).

The main concepts related to project management and the ways that a company can structure itself to reach maturity in its projects will be discussed in this chapter. The alignment between strategy and project management structure is also addressed.

The Project Concept

For Rabechini, Jr. and Carvalho (1999), the concept of projects has been refined in recent years in order to establish a common understanding in organizations that work with this kind of undertaking.

There are several definitions of "project" available in the literature. *ISO 10006 (1997) define project as a single process consisting of a group of coordinated and controlled activities with a beginning and end date, undertaken to achieve an objective, according to specific requirements, including time, cost, and resource limitations. For Tuman (1983), a project is an organization of dedicated people aiming to reach a specific purpose and goal that usually involves costs, single actions, or high risk undertakings which have to be complete by a certain date for an amount of money, within some expectation for performance. Finally, PMI (2000) defines project as "a temporary endeavor undertaken to create a unique product, service or a result."*

Two intrinsic concepts are perceptible in these definitions (Rabechine & Carvalho, 2003): *the first one refers to temporality*, i.e., all projects have a well-determined beginning and end; the second one refers to their *uniqueness* or *singularity*, i.e., that the product or service, *in some way be different than all those similar, accomplished earlier.*

Even though not so explicit in all the definitions in Chart 1, the uncertainty and complexity inherent to projects are also fundamental issues to comprehending this concept. In this sense, Maximiano (1997) and Sabbag (1999) present models which incorporate these issues.

In the model proposed by Sabbag (1999), these questions are dealt with by the Cube of Uncertainty, which is comprised of three variables: complexity, singularity, and precise objectives.

This model evaluates and proposes distinct management strategies depending on the type of project. According to Sabbag (1999), "different projects result in different cubes. For example, a road building project or a typical building construction, normally demonstrates high narrowness with regard to objectives and lower complexity and singularity." On the other hand, "A typical research and development project or one to develop new software, can instead display high singularity and complexity, but show low narrowness of objectives" (Rabechini & Carvalho, 2003).

For Maximiano (1997), projects can be divided into four large categories according to their uncertainty and complexity. The higher degree of unknown, the greater the uncertainty and the greater the associated risk. Complexity can be evaluated through the degree of multi-disciplinarily needed for project execution, the diversity and volume of information to be processed, and the number of organizations involved, among other aspects.

Organizational Structures and the Project

Organizational Structures

According to Patah and Carvalho (2002), organizational structure should be dynamic, i.e., capable of rapid changes if the environment demands them. External factors involved can be an increase in competition in the market niche, a change in technology, or even the unpredictability of demand.

The traditional organization, called functional, is marked by divisions by departments, and displays some positive aspects, such as greater controllability and minimal internal conflict. Each department displays high technical dominion and facilitated internal communications, since each functionary reports to a director. Nevertheless, with the growing diversification demanded by the market, it has become ever more difficult to manage projects inside companies with functional organization, since this system tends to serve the point of view of a department and not the point of view of the client.

Projectized and matrix structures arose as an alternative to the rigidity of the functional organizational structure. The matrix structure is a combination of the functional and project structures and can be divided into weak, balanced, and strong matrix (Patah & Carvalho, 2002). The main advantages and disadvantages of these two structures are summarized in Table 4.1.

Source: Adapted from Meredith and Mantel (2000)

Table 4.1. Advantages and disadvantages of the projectized and matrix structures

Projectized Structure	
Advantages	**Disadvantages**
• project manager has total authority over the project; • all project members are under the responsibility of the project manager; • communications are facilitated and compared to the functional structure; • project team members have a strong identity of their own and thus tend to display a high level of commitment to the project; • there is greater opportunity to make quick decisions; • there is a command unit inside the project; • project structures are structurally simple and flexible and relatively easy to understand and implement; • this organizational structure tends to favor a holistic approach to the project.	• when an organization has several projects, it is usual that several new groups be created and this can cause duplication of effort; • people with specific knowledge about certain matters tend to be allocated to projects when they are available rather than when they are needed by the project; • for high technology projects, the fact that experts "belong" to functional sectors is a big problem for the project manager, since he constantly needs work from these specialists. • project structures tend to show a certain inconsistency in the way they implement policies and internal procedures of the company; • there is considerable uncertainty about what will happen to the project team members when the project ends.
Matrix Structure	
Advantages	**Disadvantages**
• the project manager is responsible for the project overall; • due to the project being distributed throughout the company divisions, it can utilize all their technical capacity; • there is less anxiety about what will happen to project personnel when the project ends; • response to client needs is rapid; • the matrix structure is flexible; • the project has a representative in the company's administrative units; • since there are usually several projects on going simultaneously in the companies, the matrix structure permits the optimization of company resources.	• there can be questions about responsibility for project decision-making and this can delay its implementation; • different project managers can "compete" for available technical resources, and they might not be used in the best manner possible; • in strong matrix structures, the problem of concluding projects on time is as serious as in the project structure; • the project manager needs to have special ability in negotiating resources with the functional managers; • the matrix structure violates the principle of command for the unit; company employees have two bosses: the project manager and the functional manager.

According to Kerzner (2001), in order to choose the most appropriate organizational structure to organize project activity, some factors that influence the decision should be considered: project size, duration, the organization's experience in managing projects, the philosophy of the company's upper management regarding project management, the physical location of the project, available resources, and specific project aspects.

Meredith and Mantel (2000) summed up the process of choosing an organizational structure for a project in six steps:

1.   Define the specific results desired from the project;
2.   Determine the key tasks for achieving the defined results and identify which company departments need to be involved;
3.   Sequence and group key tasks in a logical fashion;
4.   Determine to which project subsystem the task groups will be allocated;
5.   Identify special project and company features that affect the manner in which the project should be organized;
6.   Consider the above information in making the final decision in relation to the pros and cons of each type of organizational structure.

When the organizational structure is not selected in an appropriate manner, several problems can be diagnosed. According to Patah and Carvalho (2002b) some factors are indicative of problems, such as: projects don't manage to meet time, cost, and other requirements; experts feel under-utilized; no one takes responsibility when the project tends toward failure; among others.

Mintzberg and Heyden (1999) warn, however, that organizational charts sometimes do not adequately reflect how people really organize at work. These authors present a new kind of organizational mapping called the *organigraph* which introduces new components called *hubs* and *webs*, in addition to the already used *set* and *chain*, as described in Figure 4.1.

For these authors, the new components — *hubs* and *webs* — can be defined in the following way:

> *"A hub serves as a coordinating center. It is any physical or conceptual point at which people, things, or information move."*

Figure 4.1. Organigraph: hubs and webs (adapted from Mintzberg & Heyden, 1999)

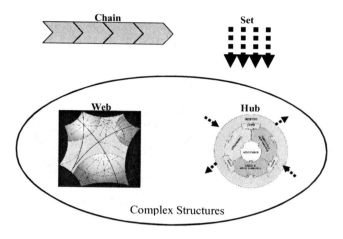

"*Webs...are grids with no center; they allow open-ended communication and continuous movement of people and ideas.*" (Mintzberg & Heyden, 1999, p. 5)

Project Management Office (PMO)

In addition to thinking about structure in the context of each project, the PMO (*Project Management Office*) is a structure intended to apply project management concepts within the organization and can take on various functions. The PMO can greatly aid the transformation of a company's strategies into project management. Rollins (2003a) estimates that there are more than 50,000 PMOs of some type in the USA.

The PMO can be defined as an organizational entity established to aid project managers and organizational teams in implementing principles, practices, methodologies, tools, and techniques for project management (Daí, 2001).

Verzuh (1999) argues that if an organization only occasionally manages projects, there is no need to develop systematic abilities for project efforts. However, if an organization devotes a large part of its energy to project implementation, an inconsequential approach to project management leads to inefficiencies and can even be dangerous. With a larger number of projects being managed, the need for a PMO becomes more evident.

Four evolutions of the PMO model are proposed by Dinsmore (1998), Project Support Office (PSO), Project Management Center of Excellence (PMCOE), Program Management Office (PrgMO) and the Chief Project Officer (CPO). These models run from a simple sector to help project control (PSO) to a company department where all projects managed by the organization pass through (Patah et al., 2003).

When an organization undertakes autonomous projects, the project management function stays within the project itself. The source of information on project-management practices, in this case, comes from earlier experience and that of the project leaders. All costs for the project team are allocated to the project. The organization does not provide support and all project management functions are realized by the project team itself. The function of this kind of PMO is to manage the project in all its integrity. Thus, total responsibility for project success resides with the project manager.

The PSO provides technical and administrative support, tools and services to various project managers simultaneously, aiding in planning, programming, and dealing with changes of scope and in managing costs of the projects. The resources involved, both internal and external, are allocated to the projects depending on the nature and contractual structure of each. Sometimes PSO personnel are loaned to a project during its start up phase or even for the long-term. Responsibility for project success does not lie with the PSO, but with the project managers who use its services.

The Project Management Center of Excellence is a focal point for project experience, but does not take on responsibility for results. It appears as a general overhead expense, which is not allocated directly to projects. To a large extent, the task of the PMCOE is of a missionary nature: to disseminate ideas, convert non-believers, and transform followers into professionals, who are imbued with the methodologies. The center keeps the channels of communication open between the projects and the community outside of project management.

The Program Management Office manages the project managers and is, in the last instance, responsible for project results. In large corporations, the PrgMO concentrates its efforts on the priority projects. Other projects are managed by departments or units, and receive support from the PrgMO as needed. By nature, the PrgMO encompasses the functions of the PMCOE and, in some cases, of the PSO. For a PrgMO to function adequately, power, corporate priority, and control over the business environment are necessary.

The CPO's responsibility is to care for and nourish the company's project portfolio from the stage of business decision through final implementation. Among its activities, the CPO is responsible for the following: involvement in business decisions that result in new projects; strategic business planning; establishing priorities and negotiating resources for projects; supervising the implementation of strategic projects; assuming responsibility for the project management system at the company level; development of sensitization and project management capacities throughout the organization; periodic project evaluations, including the decision to discontinue them; managing the high level stakeholders; and facilitation and mentoring.

Verzuh (1999) also presents a classification of five different types of PMO:

- Center for Excellence;
- Project Support Office;
- Project Management Office;
- Program Management Office;
- Accountable Project Office.

The main purpose of a center of excellence is to maintain standards for project management and to promote their use in the organization. Despite the team frequently being called upon to lend consultation, it does not have a direct role in decision-making about the project. Instead, its authority within the organization derives almost exclusively from its knowledge of project management abilities. This means that, in addition to their knowledge, team members also have to be capable agents of change, persuasively offering advice to members of the organization at all levels.

In addition to maintaining and promoting project management standards and practices, the *project support office* (PSO) actively support a number of projects by, for example, creating and updating the project plan or its budget. Made up of planning analysts, the PSO is responsible for maintaining exact control while having responsibility for decisions about profit and loss. These planning analysts often become project managers. This means that contributing more project managers to the organization's pool of talent is another contribution of the PSO.

A *project management office* (PMO) can offer support in creating schedules and budgets in the same way as a PSO. The main difference is that the PMO will provide project managers for all the organization's projects. Thus the PMO becomes a long-term base for those who want to make a career in project management. Due to being made up of many project managers, the PMO is able to reinforce project management standards. Despite PMOs being responsible for managing the salaries and professional growth of their project managers, they are not responsible for the success or failure of the project. This responsibility lies with the organization to which the project manager is allocated. On the other hand, if a company develops a series of failed projects, the PMO will also be held responsible, since it is the source of the company's knowledge of project management.

Programs are a series of related projects. The main difference is that programs are so long that they develop some operational routines inside themselves. The role of the *program management office is* to provide knowledge in project management for the entire program, through the union of all projects together. The large *program management office* will have teams that carry out various project management functions such as scheduling, budgeting, and risk management. Like the PSO, the *program management office* is not directly responsible for meeting schedules and budgets; its role is mostly putting good management practices and projects into use and then supporting them. Differently than the PSO, the *program management office* participates in project decision-making. In contrast to the other form of *project office*, the *program management office* has a use life, i.e. it will be dismounted after the project is finished.

The *accountable project office* is the oldest, but in some cases, the most radical model of *project office*. Despite its being commonly referred to simply as the project office it is called the *accountable project office to* distinguish it from the other forms presented. It is called this because it has total responsibility for scheduling and for the quality and cost goals of the projects delegated to it. Like the project management office, it is a long-term sector for project managers, providing them with a career model and administrative management. It is made up of project managers and project support personnel.

It is worth stressing that, even though the PMO models appear to be evolutionary, they can have a stronger adherence to a specific type of organization depending on the role of project management in the type of corporate strategy.

It would be a mistake to think of the various *project* office forms as a progression that all companies should follow. This would suggest that a center for excellence is only the beginning and that the natural and proper evolution would always be in the direction of an *accountable project office* with responsibility for managing all project. This is an error common to all systems of thought with large projection, to think that if something is good, more is necessarily better. Instead, the project office should reflect the organizational structure and the allocation of projects inside the organization. The mere existence of a *project office*, no matter what type, represents a commitment on the part of the organization to improve project management. The most successful *project offices* specialize in both project management and evangelism, that is, they fight for their values (Verzuh, 1999).

Maturity Models

Capability Maturity Model (CMM)

The implementation of formal efficiency procedures is quite new in IT projects. There are different approaches regarding the best practices in the IT project management (Carvalho et al., 2003; Laurindo et al., 2003).

Humphrey (1989) identifies maturity levels in the IT project development process, based on the managerial behavior found in companies. The fundamental concepts of the maturity process derive from the belief that the development management process is evolutionary. Paulk et al. (1995) identify the distinguishing characteristics between immature and mature organizations, as shown in Table 4.2.

Table 4.2. Immature organization×mature organization (Paulk et al., 1995)

Immature organization	Mature organization
• *Ad hoc*; improvised process by practitioners and managers.	• Coherent with action plans; the work is effectively achieved.
• Not rigorously followed and not controlled.	• Processes are documented and continuously improved.
• Highly dependent on personal knowledge.	
• Little understanding of progress and quality.	• Perceptible top and middle management commitment.
• Compromising product functionality and quality to meet schedule.	• Well-controlled assessment of the process.
• High risk when new technology is applied.	• Product and process measures are used.
• High maintenance costs and unpredictable quality.	• Disciplined use of technology.

The CMM (Humphrey, 1989; Paulk et al., 1995; Pessôa and Spinola, 1997) was developed by SEI — the Software Engineering Institute, of Carnegie Mellon University, and presents five maturity levels, each corresponding to a set of structural requirements for key process areas. (Figure 4.2)

Although each project is unique, it could be organized in a process to be applied in other projects. IT projects managers used to apply a "methodology," i.e. they establish the steps to be followed in order to develop a system. Another singular characteristic is the dynamic technologies breakthrough that demands continuous improvements in the development methods and management of changing process, as described in CMM model, at level 5, the highest level of maturity.

The CMM second level has a consistent project management structure and the goal of this level is to deliver projects on time. To perform this, the model have several points that must be achieved, like effort and size estimation, strong process control (such as periodic meetings between technical people and managers), and several measures to show project status more clearly.

CMM is not an adequate reference for the assessment of internal methodologies, since it was not conceived to perform this kind of analysis. ISO 15504 (1998) proposed the standard project SPICE as a more appropriated model to evaluate maturity level of specific processes. While CMM level of maturity specifies a set of processes that have to be performed, ISO 15504 establishes maturity levels for each individual process: level 0-incomplete; level 1-performed; level 2-managed; level 3-established; level 4-predictable; level 5-optimizing. This is a different approach of CMM, since an organization does not perform a maturity level, but has a maturity profile: a maturity level is measured for each specific process. This new approach is a very useful to the organization

Figure 4.2. Maturity levels (adapted from Paulk et al., 1995)

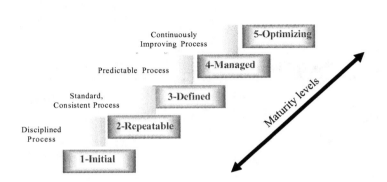

perspective because one can easily measure strong and weak points of their process and plan improvement activities. Furthermore, from the companie's point of view, it is easier to understand staged levels as the performed processes are already predefined.

The SPICE approach defined in standard ISO 15504 (1998) had originally influenced *CMM for Systems Engineering,* published in 1995, and more recently influenced CMM I (CMM-I1; CMM-I2), just published in 2002. CMM-I, the integration model, was enhanced in two dimensions: *scope dimension* and *evaluation dimension.*

In the scope dimension, this new model incorporated other published models and covers all project activities, not only software, as the original software CMM did, but also other engineering fields. In the evaluation dimension, CMM-Il incorporated both approaches: the traditional (called staged CMM) and the maturity profile (called continuous CMM). Figure 4.3 shows the continuous CMM-I representation to be compatible with ISO/IEC 15504 standard.

CMM-I (and software CMM) considers that maturity level is an organizational characteristic and it is independent of the professionals involved. Nowadays, there is a strong tendency towards the adoption of CMM-I models, which were sponsored by Department of Defense (DoD), meanwhile, ISO standards are less used.

Figure 4.3. Continuous maturity process representation in CMM-I (adapted from CMM-I1, 2002)

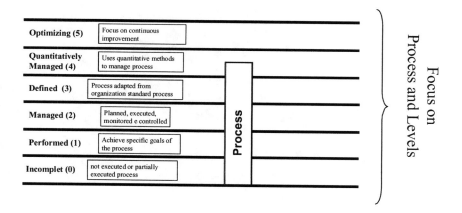

Project Management Maturity Model (PMMM)

Project Management plays an important role in the competitive scenario, and achieved in the 1990s the status of methodology. The model proposed by Project Management Institute - PMI (2000), called Project Management Body of Knowledge (PMBoK), provides a framework to manage project efficiency, balancing scope expectations and the available resources in nine key areas (Rabechini & Carvalho, 1999).

Nevertheless, the PMBoK framework cannot provide a standard benchmark for project management capability as CMM to software engineering capabilities. In order to extend the Capability Maturity Model (CMM) to project management, Kerzner (2000, 2001) proposes a Project Management Maturity Model (PMMM).

The PMMM differs in many aspects from the CMM, but this framework also introduces benchmarking instruments for measuring an organization's progress along the maturity model, detailing five levels of development for achieving maturity, as shown in Figure 4.4 (Carvalho et al., 2003).

It is important to highlight the differences in terminology between the CMM and PMMM, (compare Figures 4.3 and 4.4) which could lead to misunderstanding when both models are being implemented in the IT domain of the same organization.

Figure 4.4. Project Management Maturity Model (adapted from Kerzner, 2001)

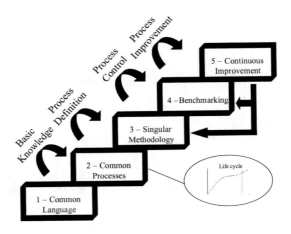

PMMM addresses the key knowledge areas across the project management process, in compliance with PMBoK, and integrates them with the Project Management Office — PMO in the strategic level.

Kerzner (2000) identifies a life cycle in PMMM level 2, common processes, which could be broken into five phases, as shown in Figure 4.5. It is important to note that some simultaneity among the phases can occur.

The embryonic phase means that the organization starts to recognize the benefits of project management — PM, usually by lower and middle levels of management. The two next phases are achieved when the PM concepts are

Table 4.3. Life cycle phase characteristics (Kezner, 2001)

Phase	Characteristics
embryonic	• recognizing the need for PM; • recognizing PM's potential benefits; • applications of PM to the business; • recognizing the changes necessary to implement PM.
executive management acceptance	• visible executive support; • executive understanding of PM; • project sponsorship; • willingness to change the way the company does business.
line management acceptance	• visible line management support; • line management commitment to PM; • line management education; • release of functional employees for PM training programs.
growth	• development of company PM life cycles; • development of a PM methodology; • a commitment to effective planning; • minimization of scope; • selection of PM software to support methodology.
maturity	• development of a management cost/schedule control system; • integration of schedule and cost control; • development of an educational curriculum to support PM.

Figure 4.5. Life cycle phases (adapted from Kerzner, 2001)

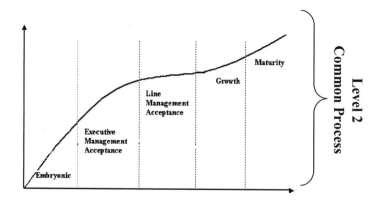

accepted and have visible support and commitment by executive and line management.

Kerzner (2001) emphasizes the growth phase as the most critical, because it is the beginning of the creation of the PM process, and warns that different methodologies for each project should be avoided.

The last life cycle phase — maturity — is difficult to achieve due to several factors such as organizational resistance to project cost control and horizontal accounting.

The main characteristics of these life cycle phases emphasized by Kerzner (2001) are described in Table 4.3.

Organizational Project Management Maturity Model OPM3

More recently, the *Project Management Institute*, (PMI, 2003), concluded the formulation of a maturity model called the OPM3, *Organizational Project Management Maturity Model*.

According to Schlichter et al. (2003), the PMI began to develop the OPM3 in 1998, using a team of volunteers. In 1999, in order to study existing maturity models, the team applied a questionnaire to more than 30,000 professionals. Formulating the model involved more than 700 volunteers until the beta version of the OPM3 production was released in mid-2004, when the first complete round of testing was completed at the end of the year.

According to the PMI (2003[a]), the meaning of the OPM3, or organization project management maturity model, can be defined as follows. *Organizational* increases the work domain, leaving the context of the project itself, which is a matter for PMBoK. The use of the word *maturity* implies that the capacities should grow during this period with that aim of producing repeated success in project management. *Maturity* can be understood as total development or in perfect condition. *Maturity* also demonstrates understanding or gives visibility to how success occurs and ways of correcting or preventing common problems. The model implies change, a progression, or steps in a process.

The following points show the strategic context of the OPM3 model (PMI, 2001b):

- Project management in an organization is not simply project management methodology; this is PMBoK;

- Its strategic domain includes more than systems for delivering multiple projects of project management;

- The model should join both activities that align projects to strategic priorities and to the infrastructure that prepares the project environment;

- The model should strengthen the link between organizational strategy and execution making project results equal organizational success;

- The model should include capacities that differentiate organizations that can repeatedly translate organizational strategy and supply it with successful project results;

Figure 4.6. The OPM3 (adapted from PMI, 2003)

Figure 4.7. Results of an evaluation using the OPM3 model (adapted from PMI, 2003)

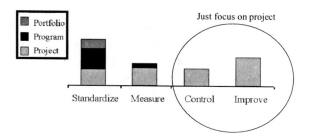

- Organizational routines can make projects responsive to strategic priorities, including the prioritization of projects, managing the project portfolio, and managing the organizational environment.

The OPM3 model starts with the concept of project's life cycle, already existing in PMBoK, as following: *initiating processes, planning processes, executing processes, controlling processes,* and *closing processes.* Besides, the model classifies improvement stages: *standardize, measure, control,* and *continuously improve.* Finally, this maturity model considers three constructs: *project, program,* and *portfolio.* Figure 4.6 shows the relation among life-cycle processes, improvement stages, and constructs.

After completing a company assessment, the results are displayed as shown in Figure 4.7.

In spite of different approaches regarding the best practices in the project management, there is a general consensus about the importance of the following widely used efficiency models: the CMM (Humphrey, 1989; Paulk et al., 1995), the Project Management Maturity Model – PMMM (Kerzner, 2000; 2001); and the Project Management Body of Knowledge — PMBoK (PMI, 2000). All of them are empirical and were developed based on the best practices used in real projects. Although they have different approaches in their conception, they are rather more complementary than conflictive. These models consider that maturity level is an organizational characteristic and it is independent of the professionals involved.

Case Study: Strategy and Decisions in Perspective

Case – In Search of Excellence in Project Management

A company belongs to the electric-electronic segment, which produces and installs a great variety of electric and electronic equipments, with the great majority delivered to customers through specific projects adapted to the necessities of each one. The products innovation tax is extremely high and the products actually sold were developed maximal three years ago. Besides, the company sells customized solutions to their customers, demanding high delivered competence in the services. This approach reflects in the principal company's resource, the labor force and their coordinated work together with the customers.

Project management for this company is a crucial issue, because 50% of its gross sales come from projects. It totalizes almost €32 billion in one fiscal year in the whole world.

This company established project management office (PMO) responsible for the elaboration of templates for project management main topics: contract management, project control, personnel management, qualification's program, PM-tools, knowledge management, process for transference and implementation, project assessment, claim management, risk management, project procurement, and small projects. Furthermore, the PMO functions encompass the implementation of a project management-training program, the identification of the capabilities to be developed and career. Finally, the PMO should have the control of the program implementation status in the departments and also of the hugest and most important projects.

The main objectives of the project management program of the analyzed company are: to have a systematic best practice sharing and standards in project management, to have sufficient number of qualified project managers, to uniform project culture throughout the company, and to achieve sustained profitability.

The actual status of this program achieves 17 different business units, participating in their implementation in the Mercosul region. There was a job for creation of a single project management methodology for the company in the whole Mercosul, with the aim to equalize the various methodologies existents as well the knowledge and to clearly define all process steps.

The nonmonetary benefits for the company are clear for the 17 areas. Some of them are:

- Better control in projects, such as cost and claims controls;
- Clear analysis of the project management maturity of the company;
- Better communication inside the company;
- The integration of different areas in a common objective;
- New projects obtained from the better methodology in project management.

The investment in the program also seems to have a very high economical return to the company. In the fiscal year of 2003/2004 it is calculated that the program will cost R$500,000.00 or US$167,000.00 and will provide an economy of R$10,000,000.00 or US$ 3,300,000.00 in the Mercosul region. Until December 2003, R$1,000,000.00 or US$330,000.00 was already obtained. It shows a return of 20 times the amount invested by the company!

Figure 4.8. Maturity evaluation

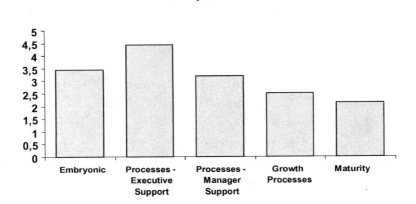

Figure 4.9. Detailed evaluation of project management life cycle

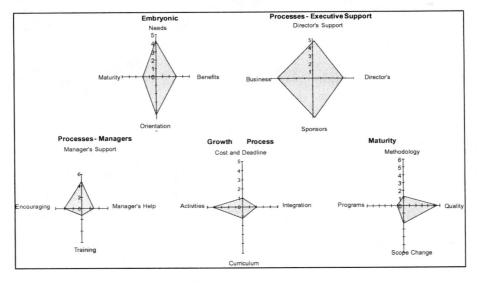

Furthermore, a new project was obtained because of the project management methodology of the analyzed company. This new project is with a client that the company has never made business. The value of this new project is R$14,000,000.00 or US$4,700,000.00. Thus, project management also improved the sales of the company!

Source: Adapted from Patah and Carvalho (2004).

Case – Project Management Maturity evaluation

An information technology company, which has approximately 500 employees, is 30% located in distant geographical points. The company works with infrastructure projects and system development in different market segments, distributed like this: telecommunication (30%), manufacture (20%), retail (25%), and finance and government (25%).

The data-rising evaluation pointed to some lacks in maturity levels. Figure 4.8 represents the perception of the personal about the company maturity in project management.

In order to detail each phase analysis, four parameters was chosen. The performance diagnosis of each variable is shown in Figure 4.9.

Source: Adapted from Rabechini Jr., Gelamo, and Carvalho (2005).

Questions for Discussion and Reflection

1. Discuss the models for structure and analyze which is the most recommended for the following types of organizations: a Software House, a soccer club, and a vehicle assembly plant.

2. For the same kinds of organizations in question 1, which would be the most appropriate types of PMO? Have all these organization invested in structuring a PMO?

3. For the same above organizations, which would be more prone to adopt a maturity model? Is there a better recommendation for what kind of model for each organization?

4. What is the difference between a CMM and the PMMM?

5. Considering the case in the section titled In Search of Excellence in Project Management, answer the following questions:

    - Classify the PMO of this company according to Dinsmore (1998).
    - Did the changes in the patterns of growth in this industry affect the intensity of the forces of competition? Which ones?

6. Considering the case in the section titled Project Management Maturity Evaluation, answer the following questions:

    - Make a project management maturity diagnosis of this company (see Figures 4.8 and 4.9).
    - Which maturity model was applied to make this evaluation?

References

Carvalho, M.M., Laurindo, F.J.B., & Pessôa, M.S.P. (2003). Information technology project management to achieve efficiency in Brazilian Companies. In S. Kamel, (Ed.). *Managing globally with information technology* (pp. 260-271). Hershey, PA: IRM Press.

CMM-I-1 (2002). Capability maturity model integration: version 1.1 for systems engineering and software engineering: continuous representation. CMU/SEI/SW, V1.1. CMU/SEI (2002-TR01). Retrieved from www.sei.cmu.edu 02-02-2002

CMM-I-2 (2002). Capability maturity model integration: version 1.1 for systems engineering and software engineering: staged representation. CMU/SEI/SW, V1.1. CMU/SEI (2002-TR02). Retrieved from www.sei.cmu.edu 02-02-2002

Daí, X. C. (2001). *The role of the project management office in achieving project success*. Doctoral thesis. Washington, DC: The George Washington University.

Dinsmore, P. C. (1998) *Winning business with enterprise project management*. New York: Amacom.

Fleury, A.C.C., & Fleury, M.T.L. (2000). *Estratégias empresariais e formação de competências: Um quebra-cabeça caleidoscópico da indústria brasileira* (2A ed.). São Paulo: Ed. Atlas.

Frame, J.D. (1999). *Project management competence: Building key skills for individuals, teams, and organizations.* San Francisco: Jossey-Bass Publishers.

Handy, C. (1995). *A era do paradoxo* (p. 229). Rio de Janeiro: Makron Books.

Humphrey, W. S. (1989). *Managing the software process.* Reading, MA: Addison-Wesley (SEI series in software engineering).

ISO 10006 (1997). *Quality management: Guidelines to quality in project management.* International Standard Organization. s.l.p., ISO.

ISO 12207 (1995). *Information technology: Software life cycle processes — ISO.* International Standard Organization. ISO/IEC, 12207:1995.

ISO 9000-3 (2001, May). *Software engineering-guidelines for the application of ISO 9001:2000 to software.* International Standard Organization. (working draft WD4 ISO/IEC JTC-1 /SC7/WG18 N48).

ISO/IEC/TR15505-2, SPICE (1998). *Technical report information technology: software process assessment — Part 2: A reference model for processes and process capability.* International Standard Organization. First edition 1998.

Kerzner, H. (2000). *Applied project management best practices on implementation.* New York: John Wiley & Sons.

Kerzner, H. (2001). *Strategic planning for project management: Using a project management maturity model.* New York: John Wiley & Sons.

Laurindo, F.J.B., Carvalho, M.M., & Shimizu, T. (2003). Information technology strategy alignment: Brazilian cases. In K. Kangas (Ed.), *Business strategies for information technology management* (pp. 186-199). Hershey, PA: IRM Press.

Maximiano, A.C.A. (1997). *Administração de projetos.* São Paulo: Atlas.

Meredith, J. R., & Mantel Jr, S. J. (2000). *Project Management: A managerial approach.* New York: John Wiley & Sons.

Mintzberg, H., & Heyden, L. V. (1999, September/October). *Organigraphs: Drawing how companies really work.* Harvard Business Review, (sine loco), 87-94.

Patah, L.A. & Carvalho, M. M. (2002a). *Estruturas de gerenciamento de projetos e competências em equipes de projetos.* In ENEGEP XXII, 2002, Curitiba, pp. 1-8. Porto Alegre: ABEPRO.

Patah, L.A. & Carvalho, M. M. (2002b). *O processo de escolha de estruturas de gerenciamento de projetos em empresas.* In: Simpósio de Engenharia de Produção, 9, 2002, Bauru. SIMPEP IX, pp. 1-11. Bauru: UNESP.

Patah, L. A. & Carvalho, M. M. (2004). *Strategic performance measurement in project management.* In EUROMA2004 — EUROPEAN OPERATIONS MANAGEMENT ASSOCIATION. Fontainebleau. Proceedings of EurOMA2004 — *Operations Management as a Change Agent*, v. 1, pp. 771-780. Fontainebleau: INSEAD.

Patah, L.A., Carvalho, M. M., & Laurindo, F. J. B. (2003). *O PMO como tradutor das estratégias corporativas: Um estudo de caso no setor de telecomunicações.* Working Paper, PRO-POLI-USP.

Paulk, M.C., Weber, C.V., Curtis, B., & Chrissis, M.B. (1995). *The capability maturity model: Guidelines for improving the software process / CMU / SEI.* Reading, MA: Addison-Wesley.

Pessôa, M.S.P., Spinola, M.M., & Volpe, R. L. D. (1997). Uma *experiência na implantação do modelo CMM.* In Simpósio Brasileiro De Engenharia De Software, 11, WQS'97 — Workshop Qualidade De Software, Fortaleza, 14/10/1997. Anais. Fortaleza, UFC, 49-57.

PMI (2000). *Project management institute — A guide to the project management body of knowledge (PMBoK).* MD: Project Management Institute Inc.

PMI (2003). *Project management institute — Organizational project management maturity model (OPM3).* MD: Project Management Institute Inc.

Rabechini, R. Jr., & Carvalho, M. M. (1999). *O ambiente de inovação e a gerência de projetos.* In Encontro Nacional de Engenharia de Producão, 19. Rio de Janeiro.

Rabechini, R. Jr., & Carvalho, M. M. (2003). Perfil das competências em equipes de projetos. *RAE Eletrônica, Fgv, São Paulo, 2*(1),1-18.

Rabechini, R. Jr. & Carvalho, M.M. (1999). *Concepção de um programa de gerência de projetos em instituição de pesquisa. Revista Valenciana Dèstudis Autonòmics.* Espanha: Valência.

Rabechini, R. Jr., Carvalho, M. M., & Laurindo, F. J. B. (2002). Fatores críticos para implementação de gerenciamento por projetos: Caso de uma organização de pesquisa. *Revista Produção, São Paulo, 2*(2), 28-41.

Rabechini, R. Jr., Gelamo, R.P., & Carvalho, M. M. (2005). *Organizing project management maturity in a system integrating company.* In IRMA 2005 — Information Resources Management Association International Conference, 2005, San Diego.

Rollins, S. (2003). *The value of a PMO.* Retrieved from http://www.pmousa.com/cfm/ligs_hm_pg_content_page.cfm?var=411. em 09/2003

Sabbag, P. Y. (1999, October). The nature of projects: A tool for improving management. *Proceedings of the 20th Annual Project Management Institute Seminars and Symposium,* Pennsylvania.

Schlichter, J., Friedrich, R., & Haeck, B. (2003). *The history of OPM3.* In PMI's Global Congress Europe. Den Haag, The Netherlands. Retrieved September 22, 2003, from http://www.pmforum.org/library/papers/TheHistoryofOPM3.htm

Tuman, G. J. (1983). Development and implementation of effective project management information and control systems. In D.I. Cleland & W.R. King (Eds.), *Project management handbook.* New York: Van Nostrand Reinhold.

Verzuh (1999). *MBA compacto gestão de projetos.* Rio de Janeiro: Campus, 2000.

Chapter V

Alignment Of Organizational Strategy With Information Technology Strategy

Introduction

Digital computers came into being after the Second World War. After a period of use solely in scientific and military areas, business perceived that this technological innovation could be very useful. The large, expensive equipment was very limited in terms of the information it could process and store, in addition to the restricted number of users who could access them simultaneously or from remote locations. Both the training and vision of professionals in the area of what was then called "data processing" was eminently technical. Thus, the early applications were developed to resolve well-structured problems, i.e., those whose stages and sequences were well-defined, such as payroll, stock control, and accounts due and received.

Technology evolved and by the end of the 1970s, there were a number of alternative uses for computers and basic applications had been installed in the large companies. At that point, specialists began discussing a way to use

Information Technology (IT), a term that came into use in the 1980s, better to make businesses more competitive. From that time on, many theories, models, and techniques have been studied and developed so that information technology can be used in tune with business strategies and operations.

IT progressively came to play an important role in the strategy of the leading companies in competitive markets.

Presently there are great expectations that IT applications will make possible new strategy alternatives for business and new opportunities for companies; as in the case of e-commerce and e-business (Porter, 2001; Evans & Wurster, 1999). However, there is also an extensive debate about the real gains derived from investments in IT. Focusing solely on the efficiency of IT applications will not provide a response to such questions. To evaluate the impact of IT on business strategy and operations, a focus on its effectiveness is needed. One must examine the results of IT applications in relation to the objectives, goals, and needs of an organization. Effectiveness should be maintained in the long run, and for this to happen, the concept of Strategic Alignment between IT and the business is fundamental.

The efficacious use of IT and the integration of IT strategy and business strategy extends beyond the concept of IT as a tool for productivity, which is often a factor critical to success. Today, the route to such success is no longer related just to the hardware and software employed, or even to development methodologies, but with the alignment of IT with the companies' strategies, characteristics and organizational structure.

In the words of Rockart et al. (1996):

> *"In sum, the load on IT organizations is heavier than ever before, and the management of IT is more complex."*

Therefore, this approach is the subject of the present chapter, which aims at elucidating the main points that transform IT into a real tool for the competitiveness of organizations' business strategies.

Conceptualizing Information Technology

What is *Information Technology,* after all?

The concept of *Information Technology* is more inclusive than those of data processing, information systems, software engineering, information science, or the set of hardware and software programs, since it also involves human, administrative and organizational dimensions (Keen, 1993).

Some authors, such as Alter (1992), distinguish between *Information Technology* and *Information Systems*, restricting the former to technical aspects, while the latter correspond to issues related to the flow of work and the people and information involved. Other authors, however, use the term information technology to include both aspects, and such is the view of Henderson and Venkatraman (1993).

According to Porter and Millar (1985), IT should be understood in a broad way "to include all information that is created and utilized by business, and thus as the broad spectrum of technologies which are increasingly convergent and interconnected, that process this information. In addition to computers, therefore, data recognition equipment, technologies for communication, industrial automation and other hardware and services are involved". Thus, in this chapter, the more inclusive term Information Technology (IT), which includes information systems, the use of hardware and software, telecommunications, automation, and multimedia resources utilized by organizations to provide data and knowledge will be used (Luftman et al., 1993; Weil, 1992).

The "Productivity Paradox"

In recent years, both the expectations around and the debate about the role of IT have grown in academic publications, those devoted to executive and business people and publications for the general public. On the one hand, there have been questions about the results derived from investments in IT. On the other, there is a kind of "enchantment" with IT applications making it possible to activate mechanisms in the so-called "globalized economy", and especially those known as e-commerce and e-business (Porter, 2001; Tapscott, 2001; Evans & Wurster, 1999; Frontini, 1999).

IT evolved from its traditional orientation toward administrative support to a strategic role within organizations. The vision of IT as a strategic competitive weapon has been discussed and emphasized, since IT not only sustains existing business operations, but also allows new business strategies to become viable.

Despite this, according to many authors (among them Henderson & Venkatraman, 1993), when the aggregated global economy is considered, a big doubt hovers around the existence of proof of significant gains in productivity due to the utilization of IT. This is what many refer to as the "IT productivity paradox" or the computer paradox (Landauer and Solow *apud* Willcocks & Lester, 1997; Brynjolfsson, 1993; Strassman, 1990). This debate also often comes up in the business world.

Recently the ideas of Carr (2003) have had a heavy and controversial repercussion. He defends the hypothesis that IT in itself has no strategic value, since its dissemination is so extensive that it is not possible to seek differentiation through it, and that what makes a resource truly strategic, is not it ubiquity, but its scarceness. Thus, since the basic functions of IT are available and accessible to all, their power and omnipresence have begun to transform them from potentially strategic resources into "commoditized" productions elements.

Nevertheless some hypotheses have been advance to explain the paradox involving investments in IT (Brynjolfsson, 1993):

- **Errors in productivity measures.** The productivity of IT use is usually measured poorly, and this is true for "inputs" (investments) as well as the "outputs" (benefits). The greater problems of appropriate measurement reside in the latter and there are special difficulties in the services sector and the work of white-collar professionals. IT characteristics related to quality, variety, customer service, speed, and response are particularly hard to measure.

- **Lag time between IT investments and benefits.** The benefits deriving from the use of IT can take years to appear. This is due to the need to accumulate experience in order to fully enjoy the potential of IT.

- **Redistribution.** IT can be a factor in productivity gains for an isolated company, but not for the overall set of companies in an industry. Under these circumstances, profits and participation in the market can be redistributed, but the size of this market cannot be altered. This could lead IT to modify the minimum requirements for participation in this market.

- **Bad IT management.** There are deficiencies in IT effectiveness evaluation practices and reasons on the order of internal company policies that can lead to a lack of gains with the use of IT.

One example of the problems in measuring IT productivity is the implantation of automatic bank tellers. When ATMs (automatic teller machines) were installed, people often stopped using checks. If there were a measure of productivity in the bank related to the number of check processed, a drop in revenues would be detected! The gains in client convenience resulting from the service, however, are hard to measure. In addition, it is just as hard, or even more so, to measure how much the bank profits with the increased customer satisfaction derived from this convenience.

It is emphasized that this debate about the return on IT investment is also taking place on the inside of companies.

According to Henderson and Venkatraman (1993), this lack of ability on the part of companies to obtain considerable return on their investment in IT is due (although not completely) to a lack of coordination and alignment of the strategies for business and for IT. This adjustment between business strategy, IT, and the internal structures of the company, with a view to it positioning and activity in the market is not an isolated event or one that is easy to obtain, but a dynamic process and one that continues over time.

Thus it can be stated that no application of IT, considered in isolation, for as sophisticated as it might be, can maintain a competitive advantage. This can only be obtained by the ability of the company to strategically exploit IT in a continuous way.

The Efficiency and Effectiveness of Information Technology Applications

The concepts of efficiency and effectiveness are very useful to an understanding of the role of IT in organizations (Laurindo, Carvalho & Shimizu, 2003; Maggiolini, 1981).

Usually, efficiency means making good use of things, while effectiveness means doing the right things. Efficiency is related to the use of resources, while effectiveness is related to meeting goals, objectives, and requirement. Efficiency is related to aspects internal to IT activity and the adequate use of resources, while effectiveness compares the results of IT applications with the results of the company's business and possible impacts on its operations and structure. To be efficacious in IT means using it to leverage the company's business, making it more competitive (Figure 5.1).

Critical Success Factors (CSF)

One of the first attempts to link the use of IT to companies' objectives and strategies arose at the end of the 1970s, and was proposed by Rockart (1979): the Critical Success Factor (CSF) method which is still widely used today to plan and prioritize IT applications. Rockart was seeking to resolve the problem of formulating managerial information systems.

According to this method, managerial information systems and those that produce performance indicators for a company should be based on the executive's own definitions of the information needs. The focus of the proposed approach is in the CSF, which "are a limited number of areas in which results, if satisfactory, guarantee the organization's successful competitive performance."

Figure 5.1. Efficiency and effectiveness of an information system (adapted from Maggiolini, 1981)

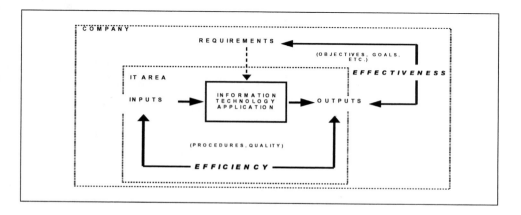

For Rockart, the main origins of CSF are: the structure of the industry, the competitive strategy, the positioning of the company within the industry, its geographic location, the environment, and circumstantial factors.

Basically, the CSF method includes an analysis of the industry in which the company is inserted, as well as its strategy, methods, and competitors. This analysis is followed by two or three interview sessions with the executives, aimed at identifying the CSF, indicating their relationship to the company's business objectives, and defining their respective qualitative or quantitative indicators. Finally, the information systems to control the CSF are defined, along with their indicators.

For Rockart, this process can be useful for each level of the company and should be repeated periodically, since the CSF change over time and can be different from one individual to another.

Despite its being conceived originally to design information systems and especially managerial and executive information systems, the CSF method had an important impact on managerial practices and strategic planning. Beyond its utilization in planning information systems and in administering IT projects, it has been used in the strategic planning of business and in the implementation of strategies, in managing changes and as a competitive analysis technique (Pollalis & Frieze, 1993). This method takes an approach based in directives, through focusing on the essential issues of companies. Further, the continuous measurement of CSF allows companies to identify strengths and weaknesses in their main departments, processes, and functions (Rockart, 1979; Sullivan, 1985; Rockart & Crescenzi, 1984; Martin, 1982).

Even though it is not a complete methodology since it leaves gaps with regard to transnational information systems, there is agreement that it is very useful in developing managerial information systems. It allows a vision of the means and alternatives for improving the functions and areas of crucial importance to the company, and makes the connection between information systems and the company's business clearer.

A proposal similar to Rockart's CSF model was developed by Broadbent and Weil (1997), who proposed a model called "*Management by Maxim*" which analyzes and defines the main principles which should guide the business and IT of each company. With this, it is possible to define the infrastructure and IT services that would combine with the company's competitive and strategic positioning.

The *Balanced Scorecard,* developed by Kaplan and Norton (1992), is, in a certain fashion, a more systematic extension of the CSF idea. It is a method for measuring and directing company activities in accordance with its strategy. The method uses four sets of interconnected measurements, each of which focuses on a perspective: the financial, that of the client, that of innovation and learning, and the perspective internal to the business. Each of these perspectives has its own set of goals and measures.

Even though the *Balanced Scorecard* is not an especially focused method for IT planning, it has direct implications for the definition of information systems with potential strategic impact. Willcocks and Lester (1997), among others, suggest using the *Balanced Scorecard* in the strategic planning of IT, especially in the phases of development and implementation.

The Strategic Role of IT Applications

McFarlan's (1984) strategic *Grid* allows us to visualize how IT is related to strategy and to business operations in a company. This model analyzes the present and future impact of IT applications on the business, defining four "quadrants" (Figure 5.2), each of which represents a situation for the company: "Support", "Factory", "Transition", and "Strategy" (see also Fernades & Kugler, 1990).

Figure 5.2. "Strategic Grid": Strategic impact of IT applications (adapted from McFarlan, 1984)

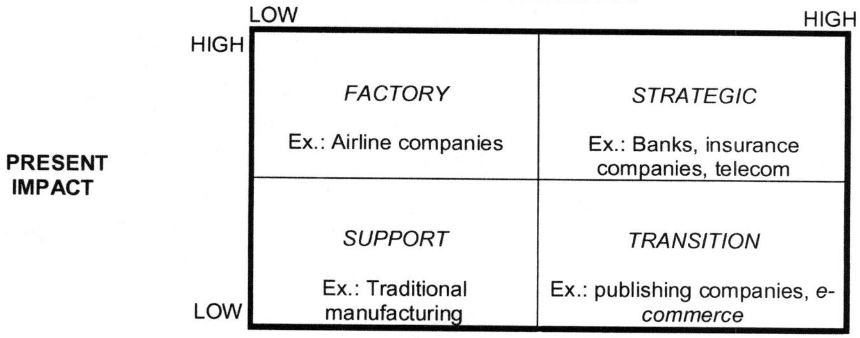

"Support": IT has little influence on present and future company strategies. There is no need for a highlighted positioning for the IT area in the company hierarchy. Usually this is what happens in a traditional manufacturing company.

"Factory": the existing IT applications contribute decisively to the company's success, but new applications with strategic impact are not contemplated. The IT department should be situated at a high level of hierarchy. The classic example is the case of airline companies, which depend on their ticket reservation systems, but new developments just update these applications.

"Transition": IT moves from a more discrete position (in the "support" quadrant) to one of greater visibility in the company strategy. The IT area tends toward a position of greater importance in the company's hierarchy. The example usually cited in the literature is electronic publishing. Today, e-commerce displays the same profile. From occupying a role in operational support in commercial enterprises, it has become an agent for

business transformation. "Strategic": IT has great influence on the general strategy of companies. Present as well as future applications are strategic and affect the company's business. In this case, it is important that IT be positioned at a high level of hierarchy. IT has a strategic role in banks for instance.

To evaluate the strategic impact of IT, McFarlan (1984) proposed an analysis of five basic questions about IT applications, related to the forces of competition forces (Porter, 1979):

- Can IT establish entry barriers for market competitors?
- Can IT influence the change of suppliers as well as alter bargaining power?
- Can IT change the basis of competition (based on cost, differentiation, or focus)?
- Can IT alter bargaining power in relationships with buyers?
- Can IT generate new products?

These questions serve to guide executives in their search for new competitive advantages through IT, whether it is in their internal organization or in their relationship with other companies or their customers. These questions can be used to orient the strategic use of IT, aiming at the creation of new inter-relationship among companies, such as forming partnership or cooperative networks.

In this way, the strategic importance of IT can vary from one industry to another and also among companies in the same industry.

IT has played an important role in the strategy of the leading companies in competitive markets. Two matters are basic to an understanding of the role of IT: obtaining advantages over competitors all along the value chain (Porter & Millar, 1985), and the creation and reinforcement of essential competencies (Duhan et al., 2001).

The concern with regard to the value chain is in understanding how IT can increase competitive advantages by cost reduction, constructing entry barriers, and strengthening the company's relations with suppliers and consumers. With regard to essential competencies, the focus of concern is on resources. Thus, competitive advantages are born of the ability to accumulate capacities and resources that are rare, valuable and hard to imitate.

Porter and Miller (1985) highlight the concepts of the *value chain* (activities inside the company linked by connections and which have one physical component and another of information processing) and *value systems* (the set of value chains of an industry from the suppliers to the final consumer).

Figure 5.3. IT applications along the value chain (adapted from Porter & Millar, 1985)

Support Activities	Firm Infrastructure	Planning Models, BSC					
	Human Resources Management	Automated Personnel Scheduling E-training					
	Technology Development	CAD (computer aided design) CAM (computer aided manufacturing) CRM (consumer relationship management)					
	Procurement	E-procurement					
		Warehouse Systems	MRP MRPII ERP	Automated Transports Control Routing	Tele-marketing Automated Points of Sales	Call Center	
		Inbound Logistics	Operations	Outbound Logistics	Marketing & Sales	Services	
		Primary Activities					**Margin**

IT permeates the chains of value, changing the way of executing activities of value and also the nature of the connections among them. In doing so, IT can affect competition in three possible ways:

- by changing the structure of the sector since it has the ability to influence each of the five forces of competition (Porter, 1979);
- by creating new competitive advantages, reducing costs, increasing differentiation, and altering the scope of competition scope;
- by generating completely new business.

In Figure 5.3 there are examples of IT applications according to the nine generic middle activities and the generic end activities presented along the value chain. The impact on the value system will be studied in the chapter on the New Economy.

The potential that IT has to make these changes varies according to the characteristics of the process (value chain) and the product, with reference to information needs. The "Information intensity matrix" considers the value chain and analyzes "how much" information is contained in the process and the product (see Figure 5.4). In companies whose products and processes contain a lot of information, the information system will be very important (Porter & Miller, 1985).

In their original article, Porter and Millar, (1985) did not cite an example for "high information content in the product" or "low information intensity in the process", a position which is corroborated by Doyle (1991). However, for

Figure 5.4. Information intensity matrix (adapted from Porter & Millar, 1985)

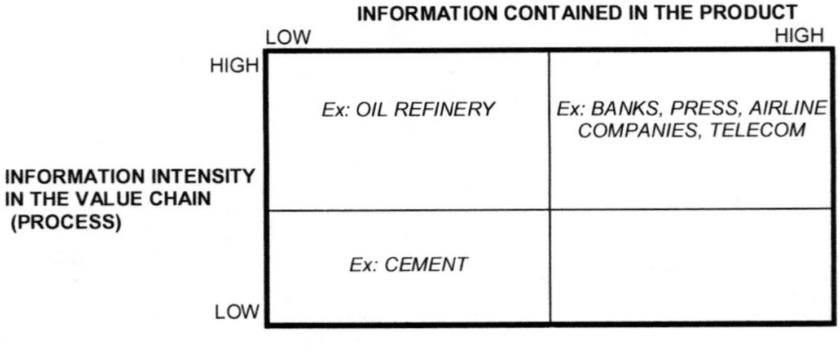

INFORMATION CONTAINED IN THE PRODUCT

	LOW	HIGH
HIGH	Ex: OIL REFINERY	Ex: BANKS, PRESS, AIRLINE COMPANIES, TELECOM
LOW	Ex: CEMENT	

INFORMATION INTENSITY IN THE VALUE CHAIN (PROCESS)

Ward (1988), this would be the case of educational and law firms; for Duhan et al. (2001), consulting firms would also fit in this same quadrant.

Further, according Dunah et. al. (2001), an analysis of the value chain would be impaired in the case of knowledge based companies (such as consulting firms) where it is hard to identify the value that is aggregated to each activity. In these situations, the authors propose that using the essential competencies of Prahalad and Hamel (1990) would be more appropriate to plan the strategic use of information systems.

Strategic Alignment

Henderson and Venkatraman (1993) proposed a model that emphasizes and analyzes the strategic importance of the role performed by IT inside companies. The proposed model is based on factors inside and outside the company. IT impacts on the company's business and how these affect its organization and IT strategy are analyzed, along with what is available in the market in terms of new technologies. This proposal is called the "Strategic Alignment Model."

Henderson and Venkatraman also propose that I addition to the widely recognized need for an adjustment between the company's strategy and its internal structure, it should analogously have made adjustments between the external IT strategy (positioning in the IT market) and the internal structure of its information systems (their organization and administration).

Therefore, according to this model, in order to plan IT, the external factors (strategy) and internal factors (infrastructure) that should be considered are: *negotiating strategy, IT strategy, organizational infrastructure and processes, and the infrastructure of information systems and processes.*

Another premise of the *Model for Strategic Alignment* is that an efficacious administration of IT requires a balance among the decisions in all four factors listed above. The model highlights two types of integration between the domains of business and IT: the strategic and operational.

This model's novelty is that it considers that IT strategy can change a company's business strategy, when usually the business strategy is considered as the starting point for IT planning. Planning has to a continuous process, since external factors are constantly changing. If the company does not accompany these changes, it can be seriously impaired in the sharp competition for markets.

This is particularly true when a new technology is adopted by almost all companies in a sector of activity and thus it is no longer an element of competitive advantage for the user and becomes a factor of disadvantage for the nonuser.

The Perspectives for Strategic Alignment

Henderson and Venkatraman (1993), and Luftman et al. (1993) point to four main perspectives on strategic alignment, taking as their start point either the negotiating strategy or IT strategy as the driver of this process:

1. **Executing the strategy**

   Business Strategy → Business Structure → IT Structure

   This is the most widely disseminated and best understood perspective since it corresponds to the classical model of a hierarchical vision of strategic administration. As an example, we cite the case of the publisher McGraw Hill whose strategy for publishing books on order for American universities required support from an IT application.

2. **Technological transformation**

   Business Strategy → IT Strategy → IT Structure

   From this perspective, note that the IT structure is not limited by the structure of the organization of business. The negotiating strategy requires new IT strategies (including new competencies) to be implemented. This

Table 5.1. Characteristics of the strategic alignment perspectives (adapted from Henderson & Venkatraman, 1993)

PERSPECTIVE	DRIVER	ROLE OF UPPER MANAGEMENT	ROLE OF IT MANAGMENT	PERFORMANCE CRITERIA
1 EXECUTING THE STRATEGY	NEGOTIATING STRATEGY	FORMULATING STRATEGIES	IMPLANTING STRATEGIES	COSTS / SERVICE CENTERS
2 TECHNOLOGICAL TRANSFORMATION	BUSINESS STRATEGY	PROVIDER OF VISION OF TECHNOLOGY	ARQUITECT OF TECNOLOGY	TECHOLOGICAL LEADERSHIP
3 POTENTIAL FOR COMPETITIVENSS	IT STRATEGY	BUSINESS VISIONARY	CATALYST	BUSINESS LEADERSHIP
4 LEVEL OF SERVICES	IT STRATEGY	PRIORITIZOR	EXECUTVIE LEADERSHIP	CUSTOMER SATISFACTION

perspective can be illustrated by the case of a traditional bookstore (such as Siciliano, Saraiva, or Cultura) which, when setting up a computerized "megastore" or an internet site, needs a new IT strategy, since formerly this resource had not been used so intensely.

3. **Competitive potential**

   IT strategy → Business Strategy → Business Structure

   The choice of business strategy derives from the new IT strategy adopted. The typical example of this perspective is companies that are born as pure players on the Internet (like Amazon.com). There was an IT strategy (to dominate the Internet) and it made the business strategy that made use of this IT strategy viable.

4. **Services level**

   IT Strategy → IT Structure → Business Structure

   This perspective aims at serving a world class clientele in Information System services. It can be exemplified by companies that outsource IT services such as Kodak and British Petroleum.

Table 5.1 shows the role of company management and the role of IT as well as the respective basic criteria to evaluate performance for each of these perspectives. Note that the role of the managers changes, which results in different abilities. Figure 5.5 shows a schematic for the flow of the alignment process from each of the four perspectives.

Figure 5.5. Perspectives on strategic alignment (adapted from Henderson & Venkatraman, 1993)

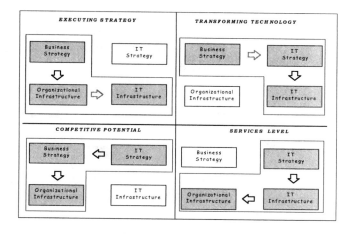

Luftman (1996) also proposed that in some situations there could be a *merger* of two perspectives. In these cases, two perspectives are identified as occurring simultaneously; they have the same starting and arrival points, but run different routes.

Some research has suggested factors, which, when present along with good performance, work as *enablers* of strategic alignment. Luftman (2001) listed five of these factors: support of senior executives for IT, involvement of IT in the development of strategy, understanding IT in the company's business, partnership between business and IT, well-prioritized design of IT and, IT exercising leadership. On the other hand, the absence or poor performance of these factors is considered *inhibitors* of strategic alignment.

Prairie (1996), in turn, studied the critical points for the use of IT that lead to leveraging business:

- existence of a defined strategy;
- development of customer-centered measurements;
- fitting IT processes and capabilities to business objectives and the insertion of business goals in IT processes and capabilities;
- finally, IT should be a matter of interest to all, not just to technicians.

Even though the strategic alignment model was conceived for analyzing IT strategy in organizations, its concepts can be very useful for the strategic planning of relationships among companies, which are relationship among companies enabled or potentialized by IT.

As a complement, Weill and Ross (2002) highlight the importance of having decisions about the use of IT involve the business people in the company, and not just the IT team, so that business-strategy issues be contemplated. An exclusively technical focus does not allow decision-making that leads to the use of IT as a factor for competitive advantage.

Integrated Management Systems and Strategic Alignment

Companies have often adopted solutions that encompass the entire range of the company's information systems: these are the Integrated Management Systems, or as they are generally known, ERP (Enterprise Resource Planning). The intensity of resources needed to implement these systems has raised doubts from the financial point of view about the return on these investments, as well as their real strategic impact.

ERP systems were born of the evolution of companies' information needs.

Initially, the appearance of MRP (*Materials Requirements Planning*), in the 1970s, allowed for the equation of problems to calculate production materials for the mix of products whose structures contained a large number of components. MRP systems evolved to MRPII (*Manufacturing Resources Planning*), that had wider coverage, allowing for the inclusion of planning of other aspects, such as *Capacity Requirements Planning* (CRP) to allow management of other resources (equipment, labor, etc.) in addition to materials. The next step was to include various other aspects, in addition to the industrial module (MRPII), such as accounting, finance, commercialization, human resources, and engineering, among others. This new generation of systems was named "ERP Systems," generically called Business Management Systems (Laurindo & Mesquita, 2000). The next evolution consisted of integrating IT into the various stages of the supply chain, at first via EDI and presently via, B2B (business-to-business) e-commerce (Laurindo et al., 2002). This subject will be dealt with in the chapter on the New Economy.

In its basic concept, ERP is an applications system that serves as the "backbone" for the entire company. It integrates management and business processes, providing a global view of the organization (Laurindo & Pessoa, 2001). It has the enormous benefit of providing the opportunity to have a single database, a single application and a unified interface throughout the company (Bingi et al., 1999). When systems are not integrated, information necessary for operations can be repeated within several systems, a fact that creates problems of lost, outdated and conflicting information. In large organizations, this is a very sensitive problem.

Integrating information systems has the built in advantage of broader inclusion of the different business functions, which increased the company's overall performance. It also implicitly holds out the expectation that the ready-made system (although there can be customization) will be less expensive than an equally efficient and integrated system developed internally by a systems architect.

When the company is transnational with affiliates spread over various countries on different continents, this advantage can be even more significant. There are also great advantages when, due to the nature of its business, a company has a centralizing bias, whether strategic or cultural. In this case, in addition to operational gains, there is the perspective of organizational gain from the homogenization of operational practices and management forms.

On the other hand, in implanting an ERP, the company is implicitly acquiring a generic solution that has the best management practices built in from the point of view of software providers. In many cases, this means a more efficient way of working, but there are times when the company can lose important differentiating techniques that make it more competitive than its rivals. Therefore, one needs to analyze whether the business practices included in the ERP "package" coincide with the practices most appropriate to the particularities of the business of the client company.

In the case of Apple Computer, for example, the differentiation of its product is so great and so clear that any homogenization of services resulting from implanting an ERP would not mean a loss of competitiveness in relation to competitors. However, for the majority of companies that produce microcomputers this is not the scenario, since their differentiation lies much more in services and price than in the product itself. In these cases, implanting an ERP implies the risk of a loss of differentiation (Davenport, 1998). Gains in efficiency are obscured by the loss of effectiveness.

Thus the integration of information systems, which permits a more efficient flow of processes, does not necessarily result in the desired strategic alignment.

Routes to a Strategic Role for IT

The Debate about IT Strategic Planning

There are authors who contest the need for strategic planning of IT due to the intense rate of technological change and the patterns of competition in globalized markets (a matter which will be discussed in the chapter on the New Economy). Some authors, like Ciborra (1998), state the strategic success of IT applications might be achieved through a tentative approach, rather than structured methods of strategic IT planning. These authors argue that frequently the drivers of strategic IT applications are efficiency issues, instead of a result of a strategic IT plan.

Some well-known cases of successful information systems, with clear and recognized strategic impact, do not show evidence of prior planning, which seems to corroborate with this line of thinking as studied by Eardley et al. (1996).

These authors developed a study in which they analyze eight "classics" of strategic systems, whose histories of development, implantation and operation have been sufficiently well documented. The systems studied were the following:

- American Airlines: Sabre (booking)
- United Airlines: Apollo (booking)
- American Hospital: Asap (Stock and order control)
- Federal Express: Cosmos (Routing/allocation)
- McKesson: Economost (Stock and order control for pharmacies)
- Citicorp: GTN (Negócio Global - *Global Trading*, global investment management)
- Merrill Lynch: CMA (Integrated Management of Investment Accounts)
- Philadelphia National Bank: MAC (Networks of shared Automatic Teller Machines)

To verify why the systems are called strategic, the authors looked for these systems' impact on each of Porter's (1979) forces of competition, as shown in Table 5.2.

Table 5.2. The Impact of "classic" cases of strategic information systems on Porter's forces of competition (adapted from Eardley et al., 1996)

COMPANY	SYSTEM	FORCES OF COMPETITION				
		COMPETI-TION AMONG RIVALS	CUSTOMER MOBILITY	SUPPLIER BARGAINING POWER	SUBSTITUTE PRODUCTS /SERVICES	NEW MARKET ENTRIES
AMERICAN AIRLINES	SABRE	CHANGE OF BASE	INCENTIVE		VALUE ADDED	
UNITED AIRLINES	APOLLO		COSTS OF CHANGE			
AMERICAN HOSPITAL	ASAP	CHANGE OF BASE	COSTS OF CHANGE			ERECTING BARRIERS
FEDERAL EXPRESS	COSMOS	CHANGE OF BASE			VALUE ADDED	DEMOLISHING BARRIERS
McKESSON	ECONOMOST	CHANGE OF BASE	COSTS OF CHANGE			
CITICORP	GTN		COSTS OF CHANGE			
MERRIL LYNCH	CMA	CHANGE OF BASE	BREADTH OF SERVICES			ERECTING BARRIERS
PHILADELPHIA NATIONAL BANK	MAC	CHANGE OF BASE				DEMOLISHING BARRIERS

In addition to finding no evidence that the strategic impact of these systems had been previously planned (even though reinforced and exploited intensely after realizing their strategic impact), another significant conclusion was that several of these systems did not pass through the filter of a financial analysis with the data available at the time they were developed.

Classifying Models that Analyze IT and Strategy

Over the years, many authors have tried to contribute to the understanding and construction of a process to transform IT into a real strategic tool.

Reviewing the various publications produced since the end of the 1970s, generally the various models analyzed which deal with the role of IT in organizations can be classified into four groups (Laurindo et al., 2001):

- **Diagnostic models:** provide instruments and criteria to diagnose the role of IT in organizations;
- **Prescriptive models:** are those that indicate benchmark standards to be followed, or which report the best practices related to the strategic use of IT;
- **Models dedicated to action:** indicate procedures for IT planning and for the selection of IT applications to be developed in a way that will have positive impact on the organizations' performance;
- **Integrative models:** are those that group various elements from the above approaches to form a broader structure of analysis.

Table 5.3 presents some examples of different models of each of the groups above.

The Issue of Efficiency and Effectiveness: What the Company Should Do

Throughout this chapter the importance of focusing on the effectiveness of IT utilization has been emphasized, since frequently analysis is done only from the point of view of efficiency. However, this does not mean that being efficient is not positive; it means that one needs to be efficient in certain areas. In other

Table 5.3. Examples of models for analyzing the strategic role of IT (adapted from Laurindo et al., 2001)

MODEL	IDEA / HIGHLIGHTS
FOCUS ON DIAGNOSIS	
MAHMOOD (1993),	Relationship between the use of IT and financial indicators showing a positive relationship/
BYRD & MARSHALL (1997)	Relationship between the use of IT and financial indicators showing inconclusive results.
NOLAN (1979)	Model of stages of information from the companies.
DONOVAN (1988)	Model of decentralized IT stages
MCFARLAN (1984)	Strategic Grid: the strategic role of present and future IT applications for different types of companies.
PORTER & MILLAR (1985)	Information Intensity matrix for products and processes
HENDERSON & VENKATRAMAN (1993)	Alignment between IT and business strategies and infrastructure. Alignment Perspective (what drives the alignment)
EARDLEY *et al.* (1996)	Studies of "classic" successes in IT strategic systems according to the Porter's forces of competition
LI & YE (1999)	IT and company performance according to the environmental, strategic and administrative context based on IT investments.
FOCUS ON PRESCRIPTION	
LUFTMAN (1996)	Discussion of factors which enable and inhibit alignment according to the view of an IT business executive
PRAIRIE (1996)	Benchmarking of strategic alignment, using the research base of large companies with successful IT use
ROCKART *et al.* (1996)	"Imperatives" for IT organization, according to the present scenario of globalized competition
SMITHSON & HIRSCHEIM (1998)	Classification of IT evaluation model; history of IT evaluation
MCFARLAN (1990)	Analysis of the Information Decade (1990s) focusing on IT trends, characteristics of strategic systems and reasons for failures in IT design.
FOCUS ON ACTION	
ROCKART (1979)	Critical Success Factors Model relating factors to information systems which support them or to their measurement
ROSS *et al.* (1996)	Competitiveness in the long term based on three IT "assets": IT staff, a reusable technology base and partnership between the IT and business administrations.
FARBEY *et al.* (1995)	"Scale" of benefits evaluation: classification of IT applications into eight groups with their respective evaluation methods.
INTEGRATIVE MODELS	
WILLCOCKS & LESTER (1997)	Discussion of the factors to be considered in IT analysis, explaining the origin of the productivity "paradox". Model for evaluating "system life cycles", using various other models
LAURINDO (2002)	Model for analyzing the role of IT in organizations, utilizing diverse models in an integrated fashion.

Figure 5.6. Efficiency vs. effectiveness in IT applications (adapted from Laurindo, 2002)

words, once effectiveness is achieved, increased efficiency can result in important gains.

Figure 5.6 contains a proposed diagram for viewing the situations related to efficiency and effectiveness in the use of IT.

When companies demonstrate low efficiency and high effectiveness, they are in "CHAOS" in a critical situation. The first move to get out of this situation should be to aim at increased effectiveness, and to align the IT strategy with the business strategy.

If the company has low effectiveness, but high efficiency in the use of IT, it means that it should redirect its efforts, and change the focus of its activities, in order to use its good capacity where it can add value to the company's competitiveness.

In the case of a company with high effectiveness, but low efficiency in IT utilization, it is necessary to work to improve its processes, with a view to exploiting to the maximum the focus that is already on the right things, and which can contribute to the success of the company's strategy.

Finally, a company that is efficient and efficacious in the use of IT will arrive in "Eden", the ideal situation that should be the goal for all.

Seeking the Most Important Points in IT's Strategic Role

Surveying various means of analyzing the strategic role of IT inside the organizations points to the growing complexity of the issue, in response to the increased strategic opportunities opened up by IT. Today, business and IT strategies are often confused, especially with companies active on the Internet.

Even though a large number of articles are devoted to analyzing the relationship between IT and company strategy, this theme remains a fertile field for more research, due to the dynamism of IT potentialities and to the new strategies for the market.

However, it is possible to list some points that allow for diverse approaches and which therefore merit emphasis in IT use in alignment with business strategy:

- **The need to have a clear strategic vision for both business and IT, to view IT as a competitive advantage for the business, and that it be dedicated to the market and to the IT user.**

Having a clear strategic vision for business and for IT is the starting point for making a significant impact on the organization's performance. IT needs to be seen as a means for the company to obtain competitive advantages in the market. It needs to act in concert with the company's operations and strategy. Technological advances in themselves are not justified without this vision.

- **Competitive advantage resulting from IT management and its strategic alignment with the business and not from specific applications of IT.**

  Various authors (Henderson & Venkatraman, 1993; Luftman et al., 1993; Rockart et al., 1996; Willcocks & Lester, 1997; Luftman, 1996; Avison et al., 1998) argue that it is not enough to have an IT strategy, it has to be aligned with the business strategy of the company. Further, there is a notion that this alignment should be developed and maintained over time in a dynamic process. It is not possible to maintain a competitive advantage with a specific IT application since it is increasingly easy to copy this application and an increasing number of companies use common software, such as, for example, ERP systems (Laurindo et al., 2002). Only an advantage based on IT management aligned with the business permits companies to maintain an advantage for a longer time.

- **The importance of considering all the technical (including monitoring the evolution of what is available in the IT market) as well as the organizational aspects.**

  As Henderson and Venkatraman (1993) stress, it is necessary for organizations to pay attention to what is newly available in the IT market and that there exist integration between its strategies and structures, both of IT and the business.

- **Seeking effectiveness and not just efficiency.**

  Even though it is recognized that there is a need for efficiency and high technical capacity in IT operations, it is consensus that a company will only be able to obtain competitive advantages by procuring effectiveness in the use of IT as well. The search for IT effectiveness means analyzing its impact on the results the company obtains, as well as considering gains in productivity and the competitiveness of the business as measures of IT effectiveness.

- **The need for a close and intense relationship between the executives of the IT and business areas.**

One of the most cited manners for obtaining strategic IT applications is the existence of a good relationship between executives from the IT and business areas. This means that there exist structures and procedures aimed at strengthening and ensuring the continuity of this good relationship. In companies where IT has or is beginning to have a strategic role for the business, the closeness of IT and business executives in the hierarchy takes on greater importance (Li & Ye, 1999; Prairie, 1996; Rockart et al., 1996; McFarlan, 1990; Willcocks & Lester, 1997; Earl & Feeny, 1994) In addition there should be the realization that it is not a matter just for technicians, but is an issue to be considered throughout the organization, and especially by those who formulate and decide business strategy. In turn, the IT executives should develop abilities in addition to technology management; they also need to have a clear vision of the business.

- **Variable evaluation criteria according to the application.**

  Given the many different strategies for business and IT, as well as the different importance of IT in each organization, IT should be evaluated based on several criteria (encompassing the technical, organizational, and strategic aspects) and adapted to each company. Thus adopting a single standard for evaluating the effectiveness of IT is not viable.

- **Dynamic and flexible management of IT (as a continuous process) and of its evaluation.**

  IT management (its strategy and planning) must be a continuous process, not restricted to the "moment of planning", but monitoring IT throughout its life cycle. IT management should also be flexible enough to monitor outside changes in terms of opportunities for business strategies and the availability of IT.

- **The issue of the "productivity paradox."**

  The debate about whether productivity gains do result from IT still hovers in the air; therefore, analyses to explain or deny it are becoming progressively broader.

  Productivity indicators (measures) for IT cannot be based solely on technical and efficiency aspects; they must be connected to business productivity measures that truly represent what is significant for the company's progress.

Trends in the Strategic Role of IT

Researches had been developed in order to find the enablers of Strategic Alignment. Luftman (2001) listed five of them: senior executive support for IT, IT involved in strategy development, IT understands the business, business-IT partnership, well-prioritized IT projects, and IT demonstrates leadership. The absence or poor performance of these same factors is considered an inhibitor of Strategic Alignment.

Some authors, like Ciborra (1998), state the strategic success of IT applications might be achieved through a tentative approach, rather than structured methods of strategic IT planning. These authors argue that frequently the drivers of strategic IT applications are efficiency issues, instead of a result of a strategic IT plan. Some important and well-known successful information systems, with clear strategic impacts, do not present evidences of being previously planned, what seems to be in agreement with this kind of thinking (Eardley et al., 1996).

What does the future hold for the role of IT in the strategy of organizations? At present there are a series of applications that have captivated the attention of many and have opened up new possibilities, just as there are new concerns. Terms such as Knowledge Management and CRM (*Customer Relationship Management*), have been much used and are strongly associated to IT. In fact, without IT these concepts have difficulty becoming resources effectively used in companies.

Despite the failure of many virtual enterprises (the so-called "dot.coms"), e-business and e-commerce applications appear to have reached a new level of maturity, especially B2B (business-to-business — the connection between companies via internet).

There are various success stories and large companies are increasingly investing in this success. According to Porter (2001), the Internet is the IT tool that, up to the present, has shown the greatest potential of being a factor in obtaining strategic advantages. This matter is explored in the chapter on the New Economy.

Within this scenario, an appropriate analysis and evaluation of IT effectiveness can take on a fundamental role, enabling it to really become a powerful tool for competitiveness.

Case Studies: Strategy and Decisions in Perspective

Case – IT is Worth its Weight in Results

According to the 2003 reports from the Federal Reserve, the US central bank, software sales in the United States rose just 6% in 2002, after a drop of 3% in 2001. For the Gartner Group, which researches the IT sector, a 4.9% increase in demand for products and services for this sector was predicted for 2003, but the majority of expenditures in new projects will only take place if a return on these investments can be demonstrated.

In this analysis of investments in IT, these studies shows that companies use financial indicators such as the ROI (return on investment) and TCO (total cost of ownership). In a simplified way, the ROI measures financial returns on investments undertaken, while the TCO lists the direct and indirect costs of a product or service. However, calculating these indicators for IT projects is not an easy task.

Meanwhile, a study of large companies in Brazil by the Grupo IT Mídia, indicated that 59% of the executives declared their intention to increase investment in IT in 2003. But 46% of the amounts that will be applied include the intention to realize immediate returns.

For example, Ásia Shipping, which is in the business of marine freight transportation, invested R$250 thousand between 2001 and 2002 to modernize its IT infrastructure, and significantly reduced its costs. Among the IT applications were rapid connections via Internet of its offices in São Paulo, Santos (SP), Paranaguá (PR), and Vitória (ES) and the ability of clients to monitor their shipments.

Another example is the adoption by Siemen's Brazilian affiliate of a single standard operational system to facilitate technical support involved an investment of R$3 million, which was paid off in one year of operation.

Meanwhile, Industil, a paint manufacturing industry in the eastern region of the city of São Paulo, invested R$35 thousand to install rapid Internet and e-mail accounts for its employees and a new network, and experienced large cost reductions with improvements in the security of data critical to the company and the elimination of paper correspondence.

Portal Agência Estado, February 17, 2003

Case – Between Trucks and Refrigerators, Computers

Casas Bahia, the major retail outlet for household appliances in Brazil, is known for selling at low prices to a low-income public and for not being on the Internet; the site only provides general information such as store addresses and contains nothing of electronic commerce.

However, within its culture of divestment and pragmatism, IT has guaranteed its place in the company and the results have been very positive. And both the space and the results are appreciable. One indication is the fact that Casas Bahia is one of the three largest among IBM's retail and consumer goods clients.

An integrated management system allows the company managers to accompany daily sales by type of product and daily invoicing by store. Until now, the lack of the Internet has been premeditated and is due to the fact that its low-income clients do not have Internet access.

However, since credit service is the key to its operations since sales on credit make up 90% of the total, Casas Bahia has invested in a complex and sophisticated system of business intelligence which can analyze the company's database to find patterns not evident at first glance. This is a new and expensive technology that incorporates elements of artificial intelligence.

In this way, clients with a higher probability for payment default (about 6% of annual billing of 3.6 billion reais in 2001) can be identified.

Significant investments (around 7 million reais) were made in modernizing the data network. With this, all the stores and warehouses became linked to an intranet that transmits both voice and data traffic six times quicker.

Thanks to this network, management can monitor all the company's operations from its headquarters in São Caetano do Sul, in the ABC region of São Paulo.

Another critical point where IT has made an important contribution is to logistics. In 1995, an enormous investment was made in a gigantic 170 thousand square meter distribution center in Jundiaí, São Paulo where more than 1.2 million items from eight states arrived, destined to 24,000 different addresses. The IT logistical system is integrated into the purchasing and sales system and product entry and exit is controlled by bar code. The extension of integration from sales to delivery is contemplated. Once the sale is concluded, this system allows merchandise to be located in the warehouse and cleared, and the truck route to deliver the product is elaborated automatically. Thus the client can be informed of the exact delivery date at the time of purchase.

The company's IT team is comprised of approximately 100 people and performs all operations internally, from developing the payroll system to providing support to computers in the stores. The policy of not outsourcing is characteristic of the company. Note that all the logistics are also internally operated. The company has, for example, a team of 1,000 drivers.

Adapted from Revista Exame, 03/06/2002 and Portal Exame, 03/04/2002.

Case – IT is Highlighted in Four Different Situations

The following four situations in companies active in Brazil demonstrate different possibilities for using IT and its impact on strategies: CTBC Telecom, Bunge Fertilizer, Siemens and Michelin.

CTBC Telecom

At the end of 2000, CTBC Telecom, a telephone operator which serves the states of Minas Gerais, São Paulo, Mato Grosso do Sul and Goiás, included the improvement of the indices of customer satisfaction in its strategy. Its importance was emphasized by tying the annual bonuses to it. Feeling a lack of good IT application support that would collaborate to this end, it decided to invest in a CRM project at the end of 2000. In its first phase, the project cost 24 million reais, but the results were promising.

Before CRM, when clients asked for information, they had to wait while an attendant looked up the necessary information in eight different databases (main records, service orders, billing, directory assistance, etc.) After the implantation of the initial phase, five of these systems were merged; there was a 30% average reduction in response time and customer satisfaction surveys showed signs of improvement. All the annual bonuses were paid.

Bunge Fertilizantes

Bunge Fertilizers, which belongs to the Bunge group (discussed earlier in this book), billed one billion dollars in 2001. The company was the result of a merger of five fertilizer manufacturers, only one of which had an ERP system. There was a need to integrate all their IT systems, so that there would be adequate, precise, and rapid information about all 63 units of the company available to headquarters in São Paulo. This was crucial for the success of its business plan.

According to a company executive, the director of technology and strategic planning, "technology was a result of a company necessity."

Siemens

At Siemens of Brazil, there are only nine people on the IT team, which includes business analysts, technical experts, and process analysts to care for the design and definition of business needs. This was possible due to a company decision to heavily outsource its IT services, for which Siemens Business Service was created. This latter is a separate organization that is responsible for the German conglomerate's infrastructure worldwide, which made it possible for IT costs to fall from 3% to 2% of billing.

According to International Data Corporation (IDC), a market research company, in 2001 Brazilian companies paid 663 million dollars to outsourcing companies to operate their IT areas, in addition to more than 95 million to rent the use of applications. CPAM, of São Paulo, one of the largest Brazilian IT firms, billed 473 million *reais* in 2001, 21% over what it had billed in 2000. Two-thirds was for service delivery, and one-third was for the commercialization of equipment and programs.

However, there are not just positive aspects to the outsourcing of IT (such as cost reduction). Among other risks, there is the possibility that service providers go bankrupt and leave their clients without coverage.

Michelin

Michelin of Brazil, a tire manufacturer, successfully implanted its integrated CRM, a customer relations system that involves several of the company's departments. The project, which was undertaken in February 2001 with an investment of 800 thousand dollars and an expected return on investment timeline of two years, is continuing on schedule within the time and cost guidelines. The system will be expanded to other countries in Latin America, which could generate an economy of scale for use of the technology and expand the integration of information.

These good project results are due in large part to the way the implantation team was put together and led; it has professionals from the areas of business, IT, and marketing

Initially in 1999, the decision to implant a CRM was due to the need to improve the service provided by the company's call center, which served the company's distributors and sales personnel in the field, who phoned in with questions, requests for information, and to place orders for merchandise.

With the installation of a factory in São Paulo and the resulting increase in the number of distributors (from 80 in 1995 to 200 in 1999), the call center could not handle the job. Thus CRM computerized the service.

But the CRM allowed the company to go beyond resolving this operational problem. This IT application lent support for developing new initiatives including new strategies in the areas of e-business and sales.

Beginning in 2000, each salesperson was given a laptop with access to company information available in an intranet. With this, the need for integration among data received by the call center and the sales forces was perceived, due to the redundancy of answering the same questions from sales personnel. The new integrated system eliminated this problem, in addition to providing automatic answers to requests and questions and this improved the company's image.

Later, a network with information about the company was implanted which was accessible even by employees. Orders no longer needed to be written down by sales personnel, who could then act as consultants.

The integration of this system permitted the company to visualize other areas that synchronize with data collected by the call center and the Internet, among these are the areas of logistics and the billing and marketing departments. With its reformulated information system, the internal areas could assume a performance commitment to one another, which led to a tangible improvement in the quality of customer service.

Revista Exame, Feb. 13/2002, edition 760   São Paulo, 14/2 (Portal EXAME)

Questions for Reflection and Discussion

Considering the case in the section titled IT is Worth it's Weight in Results, answer the following questions:

1.   What are the tangible possible benefits of being listed in each of the three categories cited? What strategic impact could this have?

2. What intangible benefits could be related to each of these cases and what strategic benefits could arise?

Considering the case in the section titled Between Trust and Refrigerators, Computers, answer the following questions:

3. Analyze the forces of competition in the sector of retail store sales and the generic sales strategy of Casas Bahia.

4. Discuss the potential that Information Technology has to alter the forces of competition in this sector and place them in the Strategic Grid.

5. Analyze the information needs in the product and the process (value chain) and position the sector on the Information Intensity Matrix.

6. Analyze the role of Information Technology at Casas Bahia, placing it on the Strategic Grid and on the Information Intensity Matrix.

7. Discuss the solutions adopted by the company in light of the above analyses.

Considering the case in item IT is Highlighted in Four Different Situations, answer the following questions:

8. Discuss IT's potential for affecting industry strategies in the areas where the companies in the chart above are active. Repeat the analysis for each company.

9. Think of at least two critical success factors that fit each of these companies.

10. What is the positioning of these companies on McFarlan's Strategic Grid and on the Information Intensity Matrix?

11. Considering Henderson and Venkatraman's Strategic Alignment model, what are the perspectives for alignment to be adopted in each of these companies?

12. Among the five companies considered by the Portal Info Exame as the "most connected" in Brazil in 2001, four are banks (Itaú, Bradesco, Banco Santos, and the Caixa Econômica Federal); the other company is Siemens. Discuss this fact, taking as a basis the models of IT analysis cited in the above questions.

References

Alter, S. (1992). *Information systems: A management perspective*. MA: Addison-Wesley Publishing.

Avison, D., Eardley A., & Powell, P. (1998). Suggestions for capturing corporate vision in strategic information systems. *Omega, International Journal of Management Science, 26*(4), 443-459.

Bingi, P., Sharma, M.K., & Godla, J. K. (1999). Critical issues affecting an ERP implementation. *Information Systems Management, 16*(5), 7-14.

Broadbent, M., & Weil, P. (1997) Management by maxim: How business and IT managers can create IT infrastructures. *Sloan Management Review, 38*(3), 77-92.

Brynjolfsson, E. (1993). The productivity paradox of information technology. *Communications of the ACM, 36*(12), 67-77.

Brynjolfsson, E., & Hitt, L. M. (1998). Beyond the productivity paradox. *Communications of the ACM, 41*(8), 49-55.

Byrd, T.A., & Marshall, T.T. (1997). Relating information technology investment to organizational performance: A causal model analysis. *Omega, International Journal of Management Science, 25*(1), 43-56.

Carr, N.G. (2003). IT doesn't matter. *Harvard Business Review, 81*(5), 41-49.

Ciborra, C. U. (1998). Crisis and foundations: an inquiry into the nature and limits of models and methods in the information systems discipline. *Journal of Strategic Information Systems, 7*(1), 5-16.

Donovan, J.J. (1988). Beyond chief information officer to network manager. *Harvard Business Review, 66*(5), 134-140.

Doyle, J.R. (1991). Problems with strategic information systems frameworks. *European Journal of Information Systems, 1*(4), 273-280.

Duhan, S., Levy, M., & Powell, P. (2001). Information ystems strategies in knowledge-based SME's: The role of core competencies. *European Journal of Information Systems, 10*(1), 25-40.

Eardley A., Lewis, T., Avison, D., & Powell, P. (1996). The linkage between IT and business competitive systems: A reappraisal of some 'classic' cases using a competitive analysis framework. *International Journal of Technology Management, 11*(3/4), 395-411.

Earl, M.J., & Feeny, D.F. (1994). Is your CIO adding value? *Sloan Management Review, 35*(3), 11-20.

Evans, P.B., & Wurster, T.S. (1999). Getting real about virtual commerce. *Harvard Business Review, 77*(6), 84-94.

Farbey, B., Land, F.F., & Targett, D. (1995). A taxonomy of information systems applications: the benefits evaluation ladder. *European Journal of Information Systems, 4*(1), 41-50.

Fernandes, A.A., & Kugler, J.L.C. (1990). *Gerência de projetos de sistemas: Uma abordagem prática.* 2a. Edição. LTC — Livros Técnicos e Científicos Ed.

Frontini, M.A. (1999). *A decision making model for investing in electronic business.* Dissertation for obtaining the degree of Master of Science in Management of technology. Massachusetts Institute of Technology.

Henderson, J.C., & Venkatraman, N. (1993). Strategic alignment: Leveraging information technology for transforming organizations. *IBM Systems Journal, 32*(1), 4-16.

Kaplan, R.S., & Norton, D.P. (1992). The balanced scorecard — Measures that drive performance. *Harvard Business Review, 70*(1), 71-79.

Keen, P.G.W. (1993.) Information technology and management theory: The Fusion Map. *IBM Systems Journal, 32*(1), 17-38.

Laurindo, F.J.B., Carvalho, M.M., Pessôa, M.S.P., & Shimizu, T. (2002). Selecionando uma aplicação de tecnologia da informação com enfoque na eficácia: um Estudo de caso de um sistema para PCP. *Revista G&P: Gestão e Produção, 9*(3), 377-396.

Laurindo, F. J. B., Carvalho, M. M., & Shimizu, T. (2003). Information technology strategy alignment: Brazilian cases. In K. Kangas (Ed.), *Business strategies for information technology management* (pp. 186-199). Hershey, PA: IRM Press.

Laurindo, F.J.B., & Mesquita, M.A. (2000). Material requirements planning : 25 anos de história, uma revisão do passado e prospecção do futuro. *Revista Gestão & Produção, 7*(3), 320-337.

Laurindo, F.J.B., & Pessôa, M.S.P. (2001). Sistemas integrados de gestão. In J. Amato Neto (Ed.) *Manufatura Classe Mundial*, São Paulo, Editora Atlas.

Laurindo, F.J.B., Shimizu, T., Carvalho, M.M., & Rabechini, R. Jr. (2001). O papel da tecnologia da informação (TI) na estratégia das organizações. *Revista G&P: Gestão e Produção, 8*(2), 160-179.

Li, M., & Ye, L.R. (1999). Information technology and firm performance: Linking with environmental, strategic and managerial contexts. *Information & Management, 35*(1), 43-51.

Luftman, J.N., Lewis, P.R., & Oldach, S.H. (1993). Transforming the enterprise: The alignment of business and information technology strategies. *IBM Systems Journal, 32*(1), 198-221.

Luftman, J.N. (1996). Applying the strategic alignment model. In J.N. Luftman (Ed.), *Competing in the information age: Strategic alignment in practice* (pp. 43-69). New York. Oxford University Press.

Luftman, J.N. (2001). Business-IT alignment maturity. In R. Papp (Ed.), *Strategic information technology: Opportunities for competitive advantage* (pp. 105-134). Hershey, PA: Idea Group Publishing.

Maggiolini, P. (1981). *Costi e benefici di un sistema informativo.* Itália, Etas Libri.

Mahmood, M.A. (1993). Associating organizational strategic performance with information technology investment: an exploratory research. *European Journal of Information Systems, 2*(3), 185-200.

Martin, E.W. (1982). Critical success factors of chief MIS/DP executives, *MIS Quarterly, 6*(2), 1-19.

McFarlan, W.E. (1984). Information technology changes the way you compete. *Harvard Business Review, 62*(3), 98-103.

McFarlan, W.F. (1990). The 1990's: The information decade. *Business Quarterly, 55*(1), 73-79.

Nolan, R.L. (1979). Managing the crises in data processing. *Harvard Business Review, 57*(2), 115-126.

Pollalis, Y.A., & Frieze, I.H. (1993.) A new look at critical success factors in IT. *Information Strategy: The Executive's Journal, 10*(1), 24-34.

Porter, M.E. (1979) How competitive forces shape strategy. *Harvard Business Review, 57*(6), 137-145.

Porter, M.E. (1996). What is strategy? *Harvard Business Review, 74*(6), 61-78.

Porter, M.E. (2001). Strategy and the Internet. *Harvard Business Review, 79*(1), 63-78.

Porter, M.E., & Millar, V.E. (1985). How information gives you competitive advantage. *Harvard Business Review, 63*(4), 149-160.

Prahalad, C.K., & Hamel, G. (1990). The Core competence of the corporation. *Harvard Business Review, 68*(3), 79-91.

Prairie, P. (1996). Benchmarking IT strategic alignment. In J.N. Luftman (Ed.), *Competing in the information age: Strategic alignment in practice* (pp. 242-290). New York. Oxford University Press.

Rockart, J., & Crescenzi, A.D.(1984). Engaging top management in information technology. *Sloan Management Review, 25*(4), 3-16.

Rockart, J.F. (1979). Chief executives define their own data needs. *Harvard Business Review, 57*(2), 81-92.

Rockart, J.F., Earl, M.J., & Ross, J.W. (1996). Eight imperatives for the new IT organization. *Sloan Management Review, 38*(1), 43-55.

Ross, J.W., Beath, C.M., & Goodhue, D.L. (1996). Develop long-term competitiveness through IT assets. *Sloan Management Review, 38*(1), 31-42.

Smithson, S., & Hirscheim, R. (1998). Analysing information systems evaluation: another look at an old problem. *European Journal of Information Systems, 7*(3), 158-174.

Strassman, P. A. (1990). *The business value of computers*. New Canaan: The Information Economic Press.

Sullivan, C.H. (1985). Systems planning in information age. *Sloan Management Review, 26*(2), 3-12.

Tapscott, D. (2001). Rethinking strategy in a networked world. *Strategy + Business, 24*, 1-8.

Ward, J.M. (1988). Information systems & technology application portfolio management: An assessment of matrix based analyses. *Journal of Information Technology, 3*(3), 205-215.

Weil, P. (1992). The relationship between investment in information technology and firm performance: A study of the valve manufacturing sector. *Information Systems Research, 3*(4), 307-333.

Weil, P., & Ross, J.W. (2002). Six IT decisions your IT people shouldn't make. *Harvard Business Review, 80*(10), 84-91.

Willcocks, L.P., & Lester, S. (1997). In search of information technology productivity: Assessment issues. *Journal of the Operational Research Society, 48*(11), 1082-1094.

Chapter VI

Performance Measurement Systems

Introduction

Up to now, this book has shown readers the important components in formulating a successful strategy and good decision-making processes.

Now imagine the challenge of implementing a strategy formulated in a company such as Microsoft, with subsidiaries in many countries and a legion of collaborators! How can one ensure that the strategy not be lost in the implementation?

This chapter intends to touch on issues related to the strategic alignment of the organization to effectively implement the outlined strategy, as well as the elements, which are important to developing performance measurement systems to monitor and measure the results obtained from the strategy in process.

Building a Rapid Strategic Process

Have you asked yourself what is the reigning strategy in the organization where you work? Do you know that your daily activities contribute (or not) to the organization reaching it strategic objectives?

Unfortunately, often the response to these questions is "no". This happens because the process of formulating and implementing strategy is very slow and it is carried out in isolation by the highest levels of administration, so that it is lost in the day-to-day operations of the organization.

Mintzberg (1994) stresses that planning cannot be dissociated from action, and requires the involvement of the entire organization, while also warning of three fallacies of strategic planning: prediction is possible; *detachment,* i.e., the separation of the strategist from the objects of strategy; and the strategic planning process can be *formalized.*

These three fallacies help to dissociate strategic planning from strategic thinking. They lead to bureaucratic decision-making processes. What should be a support tool to facilitate human thinking could become a straight jacket, an arbitrary formalization.

Mintzberg and Waters (1985) give more emphasis to an organization's actions than its systematized plans and goals. These plans are created by top management or consultants and are called *intentional strategies.*

However, there is another pattern of strategic action that occurs in the absence of intentions called *emergent strategies.* Theses strategies result from threats and opportunities, which are in the course of everyday work life and demand responses from those managers who have the task of executing the organization's strategy.

Any process that does not take into account *intentional* as well as *emerging* strategies will dissociate strategy from action, resulting in a lack of alignment.

Formulating and Implementing Strategy in Turbulent Environments

Various authors emphasize the need for change in the process of formulating and implementing strategy in the face of ever more rapid changes in the competitive environment (Christensen, 1997; Eisenhardt & Browns, 2000; Eisenhardt & Sull, 2001).

Eisenhardt and Browns (2000) researched top management teams at a dozen companies in the Silicon Valley, trying to identify the strategic decision-making process, especially in turbulent markets. At a second stage of research, another 12 companies were studied, six leaders and six followers from different European, Asian, and North American origins.

In both research phases, the differences between the strategic decision-making processes used by the more efficient and less efficient companies were clear. Successful strategies are the result of decision-making processes in which executives develop collective intuition, stimulate constructive conflict, maintain the pace of decisions and avoid petty politicking, making rapid, high quality, and widely supported decisions. The trade-offs between speed and quality of the decisions were not verified however.

Eisenhardt and Browns (2000) identified four basic subprocesses for creating strategy:

- Creation of a collective understanding (intuition), which strengthens the ability of top management to identify opportunities and threats earlier and more accurately.
- Stimulation of rapid conflicts to improve the quality of strategic thinking without losing time.
- Maintenance of a disciplined pace in the decision-making process, which leads to concluding it on time.
- Discouragement of corporate petty politicking, since it creates non-productive conflicts and wastes time.

In an earlier work, Eisenhardt and Sull (2001) identified a new way of leading the strategic process that they called *simple rules*. Of course it is important to write the correct rules, avoiding creating heavy guideline manuals in order to keep from paralyzing the organization. In the companies studied, the number of rules varied from two to seven.

These rules should be followed religiously, as if they were the organization's *Ten Commandments*, and any temptation to change them frequently should be avoided.

The strategic process of simple rules, appropriate for turbulent markets, has broad categories of rules as the following: *how-to, frontier, priority, time,* and *exit*.

Strategic Performance
Measurement and Monitoring

According to Carvalho and Laurindo (2003), the relevance of alignment between business strategy and its operational performance has been increasingly studied. Different approaches can be found in the academic and practitioner's bibliography, emphasizing the importance of linking effectiveness to goals, objectives and requirements of organizations, in order to manage operational performance continuously (Tonchia, 2000; Kaplan & Norton, 1992, 1993, 1996, 2000; Rockart, 1979; Broadbent & Weill, 1997).

An effective performance measurement system (PMS) has the following constituent parts: "(1) individual measures that quantify the efficiency and effectiveness of actions; (2) a set of measures that combine to assess the performance of an organization as a whole; and (3) a supporting infrastructure that enables data to be acquired, collated, sorted, analyzed, interpreted and disseminated" (Kennery & Neely, 2000). With regard to this second part of PMS, currently popular methods, such as the Balanced Scorecard (BSC) (Kaplan & Norton, 1992), the Performance Pyramid (Kerseens-van Drongelen, 2000) and the Performance Prism (Kennerly & Neely, 2000), can be found. Among them, BSC became the most widely used method.

The BSC was developed by Kaplan and Norton (1992) with the aim of learning about all the complexity existing in organizational performance evaluation (Epstein & Manzoni, 1997). Traditional methods of measurement always prioritize a financial-accounting measure that does not measure intangible assets, which are fundamental in the competitive environment. Intangible assets such as client relations, the ability and knowledge of the work force, information technology, and a corporate culture that encourages innovation and continuous improvement, despite having become a source of competitive advantage, were not contemplated by traditional tools since intangible assets depend on the organization's context and its strategy.

The BSC sums up, therefore, in a single document — the strategic map — the organization's performance from four perspectives, involving, besides the traditional *financial perspective, the client perspective, the learning and growth perspective,* and the *perspective of internal processes,* forming a balanced set of performance indicators for a company.

This balanced set of indicators, the balanced scorecard, results in a clear map of the vision and strategies of an organization, converting them into action. The

BSC provides feedback from internal as well as external processes with the aim of continuously seeking better strategic performance and better results (Kaplan & Norton, 1992). With the BSC, the perspectives of all the stakeholders are contemplated, providing the strategic alignment of the organization and its business units, promoting a vision of the business which is both synthetic and far-reaching.

Kaplan and Norton (1992) make an analogy of the BSC to the map used by a general to lead troops in foreign territory. This map is necessary to have detailed local knowledge and to communicate war strategy to the officers and the rest of the troops.

The BSC helps to overcome the lack of ability that traditional strategic management systems have in connecting long-term strategy with short-term activities (Kaplan & Norton, 1996).

Figure 6.1 illustrates the BSC model. Observe that each perspective should have its own cast of performance indicators, which should reflect the singular needs of each organization in the search for its vision.

The BSC translates vision and strategy into learning, abilities, and systems that employees need to develop (their *learning* and *growth*) to innovate and build the correct and efficient strategic capacities (*internal processes*) that will deliver specific value to the market (*clients*) that can increase value (*financial*) to the shareholder (Epstein and Manzoni, 1997). This comprehension of the way one intends to reach the desired performance level for each of the perspectives, with the strategy at the center, is one of the main advantages of this model. It is stressed that the perception of trade-offs among the measures and the creation of a network of performance indicators constitutes an important tool to promote and commit the entire organization to the strategy at all levels (Epstein & Manzoni, 1997).

Figure 6.1. Four perspectives (adapted from Kaplan & Norton, 1996a)

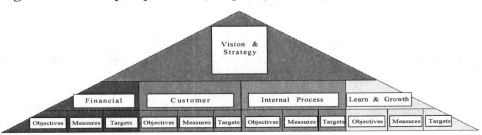

Following is a presentation of the four perspectives of the BSC, as well as the main requirements for installing this model.

Financial Perspective

The strategic map begins with financial strategy to increase value to the shareholder. As remarked earlier, Kaplan and Norton (1992) did not discard the traditional financial side, but emphasized the search for balance with the other perspectives.

The objectives and financial measures need to perform a double function: to define the financial performance expected of the strategy and to serve as the main goal for the objectives and measures of all the other BSC perspectives.

The *financial perspective* defines the long-term goals of the business unit, not limiting it to profitability objectives. However, within this perspective, companies generally work with three financial themes: *revenue growth and mix, cost reduction/productivity gains,* and *utilization of assets/strategic investment*. The theme of *revenue growth* and mix is concentrated on developing new sources of revenue and profitability, such as franchises or increasing value to clients. Franchises provide new sources of revenue deriving from new markets, new products or new clients, requiring, however, greater changes and longer execution times. Immediately increasing value to clients, by means of broadening the relationship with clients and a change in the mix of existing products and services with offers of greater added value, can generate results in the midterm. The issue of *costs reduction/ productivity gains* seeks the efficient execution of operational activities, reducing direct and indirect costs of products and services, sharing common resources with other units of the business and increasing efficiency, with the current client base. The issue of *utilization of assets and strategic investment* intends to reduce the levels of capital investment required to support a given volume and mix in the business unit.

Kaplan and Norton (1996) stress however, that there is a range of possible financial objectives that should be considered, which vary depending on the stage of the business; there are three stages in which the business unit can be located — *rapid growth, maintenance,* and *harvesting*. The business units that are at the stage of rapid growth are those in the initial stages of their life cycle. At this stage, the business needs to make significant investments to develop and expand its productive capacity, new products and services, systems, infrastructure, distribution networks, and client relations. Business at the maintenance stage aims to ensure its market share and perhaps increase it, focusing on investments in bottlenecks and expanded capacity as well as continuous improvement. Finally, business at the harvesting stage has reached the phase of maturity in its life cycle, making only the investments necessary to maintain equipment and capacity, prioritizing short-term investments with short periods of return with the main objective to maximize the corporate cash flow. The *portfolio* models can help in comprehending these stages. It is possible to suggest some financial objectives that translate the specifics of each of these stages as presented in Table 6.1.

Kaplan and Norton (2000) summarize two basic strategies for this perspective: revenue growth and productivity. The strategy for revenue growth is concentrated on developing new sources of revenue and profitability, by means of creating franchises and or increasing value to clients. Franchises are sources of revenue deriving from new markets, new products and new clients, which cause greater changes and involving longer timeframes for their execution. To increase value to clients means expanding existing client relations, obtaining results in the midterm. Finally, the *strategy for productivity*, seeks to efficiently carry out operational activities in support of present clients with a focus on reducing costs and/or increasing efficiency in addition to better utilizing assets.

Table 6.1. Financial measures and business strategies (adapted from Kaplan & Norton, 1996b)

	Revenue & Mix	Cost & Productivity	Asset Utilization
Growth	− Sales growth rate by segment − % revenue from new product/ service and customers	− Revenue/employee	− Investment (% of sales) − R&D (% of sales)
Sustain	− Share of targeted customers − Cross-selling − % revenues from new applications − Customer and product line profitability	Cost x competitors Cost reduction rates Indirect expenses (% of sales)	− Working capital ratios (cash-t0-cash cycle) − ROCE by key asset categories − Asset utilization rates
Harvest	− Customer and product line profitability − % unprofitable customers	− Unit cost/ unit − Unit cost/transaction	− Payback − Throughput

Client Perspective

The client perspective should provide a clear vision of the market and client segments and the performance of the business unit in these segments. An unsatisfactory performance from this perspective is an indicator of future decline, even if the financial perspective shows favorable results, although often the financial scenario reveals itself to be favorable. But to translate the processes into financial success, companies should put satisfying their clients in first place.

In this perspective, there are a series of generic measures such as *client satisfaction, client retention, conquering new clients, client profitability, and market share in the target segments* that could be useful.

Although the value proposition can vary from the industrial to another sector and even within market segments inside an industry, the measures shown are key elements to comprehending what value is for the key segment. Kaplan and Norton (1996) observe, nevertheless, common sets of attributes, which organize the values proposed in all industries where they applied the BSC, which were: *product/service characteristics, relationship with clients, and image and reputation.*

Based on the value proposition, the business unit is able to formulate measures from the *client perspective* that translate into market strategy in such as way as to reap financial returns from the financial perspective.

Internal Processes Perspective

The *perspective of internal processes* allows identification of critical processes in which the business unit should do better. These processes should enable the business to deliver the value proposal of the target segment and satisfy shareholders' expectations.

Measurements should focus on the internal processes that will have a greater impact on customer satisfaction and in meeting financial goals, as Figure 6.2 illustrates.

Managing processes in the BSC context should not be tied to existing processes; it is frequently necessary to map new ones. Kaplan and Norton (1992) identify four levels of process of interest for this perspective: building business by innovating in products and services and by entering new markets

Figure 6.2. Model of the generic value chain (Kaplan & Norton, 1996b)

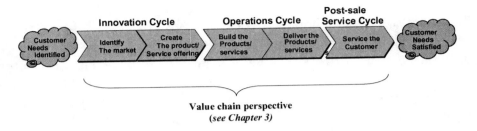

The financial benefits which come from improving processes usually take place in stages: control and improvement of existing processes (short term), increased revenue by improving relations with clients (midterm), and the process of innovation (long-term). A complete strategy should have a return from all three areas.

and client segments; deepening the relationship with existing clients; obtaining operational excellence through management of supply, cost, quality, and cycle time; utilization of assets and management capacity. Figure 6.2 shows the internal processes in a generic value chain.

Learning and Growth Perspective

The *learning and growth perspective* identifies the infrastructure, which the organization needs to build to create learning and growth in the long-term. These are required to meet the objectives from other perspectives. Thus,

Figure 6.3. Customer perspective (adapted from Carvalho & Laurindo, 2003; Kaplan & Norton, 1996b)

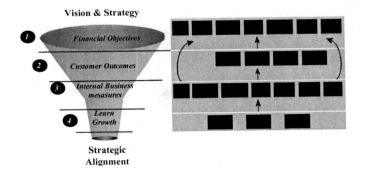

investing in this perspective is a critical factor for the survival and development of the organization in the long-term.

According to Kaplan and Norton (2000), all strategic maps should define the core competencies, technologies, and the organizational culture needed to support the organization's strategy.

There are three basic points to define measures for learning and growth: personal, systems, and procedures (Kaplan & Norton, 1996). These objectives enable the company to align its human resources, information, and technology to its strategy.

In order to guarantee the alignment among the four perspectives, each perspective should be integrated in with other perspectives as shown in Figure 6.3.

Implementing the BSC

Implementing the BSC is a long process, since it does not consist only of defining perspectives and their extension into objectives, indicators, and goals. Involvement, knowledge of internal processes, and a good system of information are needed. Imagine a company that does not have its processes mapped out! It would have to incorporate management by processes, which always is a complex task.

Figure 6.4. Managing strategy: four processes (adapted from Kaplan & Norton, 1996a)

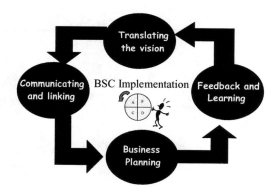

Kaplan and Norton (1996) identify four management processes, which in combination with the four perspectives, contribute to connecting long-term strategic objectives to short-term actions. It could be used also the concept of P-D-C-C cycle (*plan, do, check* and *action*) to BSC implementation. Figure 6.4 illustrates the BSC implementation process.

The *process of translating the vision* helps to build consensus around the company's vision and strategy. One should avoid vague statements such as "best in its class", expressing this instead along with performance goals and measurements.

The *process of communication and connection* allows the BSC to be communicated to all levels, thus linking departmental to individual objectives, creating a cascading process. One should avoid letting individual incentives prioritize the short-term goals; they should be aligned to the organizational strategy.

The *business planning process* allows for the integration of the financial and business planes. Since most organizations implement a number of change programs simultaneously, each with its gurus and consultants and all competing for the time and resources of the principal executives, the BSC can be a form of integrating them around long-term strategies.

The *feedback and learning process* gives an organization the capacity for strategic learning. With the BSC, and organization can monitor its short term results in the four perspectives, permitting modifications to strategies in progress, thus reflecting organizational learning.

These four processes reflect an iterative sequence of actions. To arrive at a stable management system, according to the example presented by Kaplan and Norton (1996), can require about thirty months, and an organization can need to go through these four processes two or three times.

Difficulties in Implementing the BSC

Implementing the BSC is not an easy process, some organizations have invested considerable financial and human effort in this process without attaining the hoped for results (Kaplan & Norton, 2000; Kaplan, 1999; Mercer, 1999; Schneiderman 1999).

Kaplan (1999) identified six critical aspects in the process of implementing the BSC that can lead to failure:

- Top level management was not involved and the BSC was delegated to middle management, which does not have a clear vision of the organization's strategy overall.

- A top-level executive attempted to construct the BSC alone; generally this is someone from finance or planning.

- Responsibilities for the BS are not shared by the lower levels of the organization — divisions, business units and individual departments.

- Treating the BSC at a single event and not as a continuous process in which the objectives, indicators and goals can be revised based on organizational learning.

- Confusing the BSC with a project, delegating its implementation to an outside consultant, spending for the computerization of all the data and creating a standard reporting interface.

- Introducing the BSC just for compensation, adding non-financial measures to the incentive programs.

Mercer (1999) did a study of 214 companies and discovered that 88% consider that the results of the BSC are more effective when linked to compensation systems. One the other hand, they found that developing a system of compensation appropriate to the BSC is not easy.

Another curious point has to do with developing measurements for the BSC. Some organizations use too few measures in their BSC (one or two per perspective) and never achieve a balance between the desired results and the performance drivers of these results. Others include so many measurements that they spend little time on those that have an effective impact on strategy. Finally, the organization cannot identify the correct drivers, i.e., those that do, in fact, translate into strategy. But these errors can be easily corrected if it is realized that the BSC is a continuing process and that measurements can be redefined.

Table 6.2. Benefits and success factors of the BSC

Benefits	Success Factors
• Summarize the indicators for the four perspectives in an easy to visualize document • Encourage the administrators to share a clear strategy for what they are trying to accomplish	• Risk of not articulating a clear strategy. • Need for constant, face to face discussion to meet goals. • Risk of not achieving balance among the four perspectives. • Need to develop a compensation system for employees.

An article by Epstein and Manzoni does a critical analysis of the process of implanting the Balanced Scorecard and *Tableau de Bord* methodologies, of American and French origin, respectively. Table 6.2 shows the benefits and success factors in applying these tools.

For Hauser and Katz (1998) in their provocatively titled article, "Metrics: You are what you measure!" metrics feed a process of action and reaction, and if they are not well defined, can have critical consequences for organizations. According to these authors, metrics, independently of the way they are used, affect actions and decisions within an organization, which in turn affects the results obtained.

Hauser and Katz (1998) allege that good measures are hard to implement and require a lot of work, warning of *seven pitfalls* that should be avoided:

1.   **Delaying rewards:** avoid tying goals and benefits just to the long term;

2.   employing **risky rewards** that affect the selection/rejection of projects in function of unclear metrics, which permit choosing the lesser risk compromising the probability of results in the long term;

3.   use of **metrics that are hard to control**, which are difficult to correlate with day-to-day activities;

4.   **losing sight of the goal** such that metrics distort the real objectives of the organization because they are not in line with the real needs of clients and the business of the company;

5.   choice of **metrics that are precisely wrong**, i.e., metrics that are calibrated with great precision, but lose their focus since they are not clear to managers and employees;

6.   **Assuming your managers and employees have no options**, i.e., the entire cost and effort of implementation, control, and search for the desired results through a system of metrics that does not reflect the value added to employees and managers;

7.   **thinking narrowly**, i.e., it should be a system of creative measurements – breaking paradigms.

On the other hand, the authors recommend seven steps to obtain a good system of metrics, as follows:

1. **Start by listening to the voice of customer** (VOC) in order to determine which results should be procured and consequently what goals should be implemented.

2. **Understand the job** (voice of employee — VOE), i.e., what generates value for the employee beyond financial bonuses, ponder these values and understand the processes and activities of the business.

3. **Understand the interrelationships** among the metrics, aiming to assure harmony in the use of various metrics, avoiding conflicting goals between departments that hinder the search for an overall result for the organization.

4. **Understand the linkages** among different measurements, identifying client needs, seeking to understand how they can be reached through internal processes, and establish a link between these processes and the expected results.

5. **Try to test the correlations and test manager and employee reaction,** i.e., test correlation among metrics and results, obtaining information from managers and employees during implementation and utilizing pilot projects, research and communication.

6. **Involve managers and employees**, i.e. involve people who will use and suffer the pressures of the measurement system while developing it; this will guarantee that participation lead to legitimacy, commitment, and better understanding.

7. **Seek new paradigms**, utilizing steps one to six creatively, not limiting the organization.

Case Study: Strategy and Decisions in Perspective

Case – Implementing the BSC at Unibanco Bank

Unibanco, the third largest private financial institution in Brazil, has been disseminating the Balanced Scorecard (BSC) among its 28,000 employees since December of 1999.

The system was baptized the management panel (PDG), involving the four business units of the bank- retail, wholesale, insurance, and asset management —which had to define their strategy and refine it into more specific objectives.

At the end of 2000, *Unibanco's* plan was defined, aligning the BSC of each business unit with the corporate plan. The executives opted to explain the methodology to the 28,000 employees and created a symbol for the PDG. Several events were promoted where Pedro Moreira Salles, shareholder and president, and the executives from the business units spoke to the managers about the mechanisms of BSC functioning. Other resources used for dissemination were an explanatory video with Salles' participation, favors that alluded to the use of the tool, as well as a broad dissemination of the theme in the internal newsletter and the intranet.

Even though BSC is used simultaneously in the four business units, the pace of implementation is different for each.

In the wholesale unit, the process of disseminating the BSC needed to be revised. According to Maria Luisa Mendes, director of the wholesale bank, "We perceived that the BSC was being discussed only at monthly meetings of the executive council". To reverse this picture and to involve other executives, it was permitted that they also have access to the software programs for monitoring the progress of BSC activities in the wholesale unit. The unit also needed to review some of its performance indicators.

For example, the wholesale bank did image research which measured the success of a strategic goal, *"to be seen by client companies as a solid, credible institution,"* comparing itself to 16 other banks. According to Cristiano Cagne, planning manager for the wholesale unit, "We analyzed our position in relation to banks with little representation in the market or with activities different than ours." The study was not abolished, but the number of banks was reduced, and the bank compared itself only to rival institutions such as Bradesco, Itaú, ABN, and BankBoston.

On the other hand, one of Unibanco's business units, AIG Insurance and Pension funds, had already begun to harvest the fruits of adopting the BSC. Success in implanting the BSC in this unit can be associated to the good development of its strategic map and to incorporating it into the unit's everyday life. The first BSC was in 2000, when executives decided that the system was to be used to help the unit arrive among the three largest insurance companies in the country in a period of three years, in terms of measures of liquid profit, client satisfaction, and market participation. Of these goals, it has already reached second place in the item client satisfaction, and expects to reach third place in liquid profit this year, and should be in fourth place in market participation, making it a nearly complete victory.

Unibanco AIG carried out its action plans and met the objectives defined by the strategic map. Among them is maintaining the combined index below 100%, meaning reducing the chances of casualties by clients and operating expenses, and thus profiting more with revenue from annuities. Presently Unibanco AIG's combined index is 99.8%, against the 107% market average.

Another objective described in the strategic map, which is to increase sales of the more profitable products such as life insurance and private retirement plans, was also achieved. The sale of private retirement plans and insurance such as life, home, and freight, which had an average 800,000 *reais* (November 2000), recorded premiums at the prize-winning level of 22 million *reais* (in December 2002). One of those responsible was the Rally of incentive program, focused on brokers. This goal of increasing revenue by widening market participation for more lucrative products is balanced by other objectives linked to increased productivity, with respect for the budget from the financial perspective.

Every Monday, the main executives of the unit check the progress of the BSC. Three executives directing the BSC in the unit advise José Rudge, president of Unibanco AIG. He calls Irany Strumiello, the project manager, the "control panel. Irany tells me what actions are in process and when it is necessary to turn on the red light." Ana Paula Hubert, quality manager, is a kind of guardian of BSC methodology, clearing up conceptual doubts and defining better indicators. Finally, Valeria Luchesi, human resources supervisor, defines compensation for employees when goals are met.

For the period 2003-2006, *Unibanco Insurance* is already working with a new balanced scorecard.

Source: Adapted from Herzog (2003).

Questions for Discussion and Reflection

1. What is the *Balanced Scorecard?*
2. What are the perspectives of this model? Give examples of measures for each of the perspectives.
3. What are the main difficulties in implementing the BSC?

4. What are the main difficulties in directing the strategic process?

5. Considering the case in the section titled Implementing the BSC at Unibanco Bank, answer the following questions:

- What was the process for introducing the management panel (PDG)?
- What differentiates the implementation in the business units of *Unibanco*, AIG and the wholesale units?
- Identify the main components of AIG's BSC, and compare it with the model presented in the chapter.

References

Broadbent, M., & Weil, P. (1997, Spring). Management by maxim: How business and IT managers can create IT infrastructures. *Sloan Management Review, 38*(3), 77-92.

Carvalho, M.M., & Laurindo, F.J.B. (2003). Linking strategy with a network of performance indicators: A Brazilian research centre. *International Journal of Business Performance Management*, 5(4), 285-301.

Christensen & Christensen, C.M. (1997, November/December). Making strategy: learning by doing. *Harvard Business Review*, 141-156.

Eisenhardt, K.M. (1999, Spring). Strategy as strategic decision making. *Sloan management Review*, 65-72.

Eisenhardt, K.M., & Brown, S.L. (2000, May/June). Patching restitching business portfolios in dynamic markets. *Harvard Business Review*, 72-82.

Eisenhardt, K.M., & Sull, D.N. (2001, January). Strategy as simple rules. *Harvard Business Review*, 107-116.

Epstein, M., & Manzoni, J.F. (1998). Implementing corporate strategy: From tableaux de bord to balanced scorecards. *European Management Journal, 16*(2), 190-203.

Hauser, J., & Katz, G. (1998, October). Metrics: You are what you measure! *European Management Journal, 16*(5), 517-528.

Herzog, A. (2003). Pensar, planejar... e fazer. *Revista Exame.*

Kaplan, R. S. (1999). *Can bad things happen to good scorecards?* Part II of Implementation Pitfalls. Harvard Business School Press.

Kaplan, R. S. (1999). *Can bad things happen to good scorecards?* Harvard Business School Press.

Kaplan, R. S. (2000). *Communication and education to make strategy everyone's job.* Harvard Business School Press.

Kaplan, R. S. (2001). *Using strategic themes to achieve organizational alignment.* Harvard Business School Press.

Kaplan, R.S., & Norton, D.P. (1992, January/Februrary). The balanced scorecard: Measures that drive performance. *Harvard Business Review, 70*(1), 71-79.

Kennerly, M., & Neely, A. (2000). Performance measurement framework — A review. In A. Neely (Ed.), *Performance measurement: Past, present and future.* Centre for Business Performance, Cranfield School of Management, Cranfield University, Bedfordshire, UK.

Kerseens-van Drongelen, I.C. (2000). Systematic design of performance measurement systems In A. Neely (Ed.), *Performance measurement: Past, present and future.* Centre for Business Performance, Cranfield School of Management, Cranfield University, Bedfordshire, UK.

Mercer & Mercer, W. M. *Balanced scorecards determine employees rewards.* News Release, April 5.

Mintzberg, H. (1994, January/February). The fall and rise of strategic planning. *Harvard Business Review,* 107-114.

Mintzberg, H., & Waters, J. (1985). Of strategies, deliberate and emergent. *Strategic Management Journal,* 6.

Rockart, J.F. (1979, March/April). Chief executives define their own data needs. *Harvard Business Review, 57*(2), 81-92.

Schneiderman, A. (1999). Why balanced scorecards fail. *Journal of strategic performance measurement.* January.

Tonchia, S. (2000). Linking performance measurement system to strategic and organizational choices. *International Journal of Business Performance, 2*(1,2,3), 15-29.

Chapter VII

Strategies For The New Economy And Dynamic Competitive Environment

Introduction

The so-called "New Economy" has expanded market competition to a world scale — no longer is it local or regional. Thus, decisions which are made or events that occur in one part of the planet can have repercussions for the rest of the world. In addition, the interrelationships between companies can involve actors who are very far away from each other.

Information Technology (IT) is seen as the factor that has made this worldwide integration possible, along with the creation of new business strategies, new organizational structures, and new modes of relationship among companies and between business and consumers (Laurindo et al., 2003; Laurindo et al., 2001).

The Internet is the IT application with highest visibility, since it provides the infrastructure for developing strategic IT applications, of which *e-business* and *e-commerce* are the most outstanding (Evans & Wuster, 1997; Frontini, 1999).

This has given rise to virtual organizations, the companies whose activities are exclusively on the Internet, while simultaneously, traditional businesses have become active on the web. New forms of association and relationships in business have also come into being. IT makes a new form of integration viable: virtual integration, which has become a strong alternative to vertical integration, which is losing its potential as a source of competitive advantage, according to Venkatraman and Henderson (1998).

After the initial period during which many innovative initiatives appeared and then disappeared, the need for a well-defined strategy became clear. Early interest in business to consumer (B2C) shifted to an interest in business-to-business (B2B), where large companies explored the features of this new and powerful tool.

In Porter's (2001) opinion, while the Internet is the best IT platform developed to date to reinforce a distinctive strategy, businesses have committed many errors in utilizing it, because they lack a strategic vision. Further, he argues that the founding principles of traditional strategy are necessary to the success of companies that use the Internet. He does not believe in a "New Economy" or the revolutionary nature of the Internet. In turn, other authors such as Tapscott (2001) see in the Internet an agent that ruptures economic activities, to the point that strategy must be revised totally.

With this scenario in mind, it is important to understand these concepts and paths for strategy in the midst of this turbulent environment and in virtual space, so that the entire potential of the Interest can yield new organizational forms, both intra and extra-company.

Seeking to Understand the New Economy

What is usually called the New Economy is strongly connected to two other terms: globalization and virtuality.

The term "globalization" has been widely disseminated and gained both fans and enemies. Since the 1970s, countries have become more interdependent due to the flow of goods, services, and capital. An orientation toward the external market has become strongly correlated with development in several countries. This process has been underscored with the distribution of production activities to different countries, involving international investment and outsourcing and promoting a functional integration of the world economy.

Thus a new global capitalism has come into being. Both activities and the organization of these activities have been internationalized, yet there is a perception that gains from globalization have not been distributed in an egalitarian manne (Gereffi et al., 2001).

As these same authors stress, the phenomenon of internationalization itself is not new, since in a certain sense it has been going on since the 18th century, with the founding of the colonial empires, which sought new sources for raw materials and new consumers markets for their manufactured products. Even in the ancient Roman Empire a similar situation could be observed. Globalization implies a functional integration among activities dispersed throughout several countries. This lends great importance to an examination of the chains of value as a way to understand the means to promote this integration.

Three major groups of factors are determinants for globalized competition: technologies, institutions, and organizational innovations (Gereffi, 2001).

The so-called "New Economy" is related to this new globalized reality, with an emphasis on the issue of technology, in which the Internet has become the agent that makes it possible to give a new configuration to activities (Tapscott, 2001). According to Gereffi (2001), many call this new situation the "digital economy", the "economy of innovation", "network economy" or "electronic economy" (*e-economy*). Thus, the New Economy is frequently viewed as the economy of the Internet, of *e-business*, where organizational relationships take on new forms and new dimensions where the virtual aspect stands out.

It is worth discussing what "virtual" means, since this term comes up so often when talking about the New Economy and the Internet. According to Chandrashekar and Schary (1999), virtuality can take on three different meanings in the context of business and the supply chain (see Chapter III).

Firstly, it can mean all the computer communications which have replaced human participation. This includes IT applications such as CAD/CAM or PCP systems, which permit better processing of orders, quicker production, automated requisitions and office administration.

The second meaning is related to the idea of a "supra-organization", in which each partner has a specific role. Even before IT resources existed, there were "supra-organizations", for example, construction firms, travel agencies, and clothing manufacturers. However, the use of IT allowed the pre-existing "supra-organizations" to operate more efficiently.

Finally, the third meaning has to do with the development of organizations united fundamentally through IT networks, where establishing networks still requires personal contact, but once the network has been set up, future transactions are all electronic.

The turbulent environment of the New Economy will be discussed in this chapter, based on these two concepts: globalization and virtuality linked to the use of the Internet, which are new variables to be used in building a successful strategy.

The Electronic Markets

For a long time, vertical integration (including in the same organization, assembly activities and the flow of the value chain) was seen as an important means of reducing costs with a significant strategic impacts.

But, by expanding the range of possibilities, the use of IT modified the importance of verticalization.

As we saw in Chapter V, Information Technology (IT) has played a primary roll in the strategy of the leading companies in competitive markets, changing competitiveness throughout the chains and systems of value (Porter, 2001; Porter & Millar, 1985, among others). Special mention is given to applications based in the Internet, such as *e-commerce* and/or *e-business*. Still, the idea of commercializing goods and services via IT predates the commercial dissemination of the Internet.

Malone et al. (1989) conjectured that IT might cause a break in the patterns of commerce and distribution, as well as producing a new form of connection among suppliers and their clients. Since it reduced the cost of transactions (including the cost of negotiations, of celebrating contracts, and of locating the best suppliers) companies started to purchase goods and service that formerly would have been advantageous to produce internally. As a result, vertical integration became the least interesting option in many cases and the business networks that carried our different stages in the value chain could form partnerships of aggregated value and play a more important role within the structure of industries.

At first there were IT connections between a company and a supplier or a business and buyer. When IT applications became able to allow access to various alternatives for buyers and sellers, the electronic market came into being. Manufacturing enterprises, according to Malone et al., were in a privileged position to establish the electronic market, since they are both buyers and sellers. These authors also believe that companies with a strong market position could require that their information needs be supplied in the format that they used. When an isolated company did not have sufficient power to create an electronic market, it could associate with others, as in the case cited by Malone et al. of an electronic market created by an association of cotton producers in the United States. In this way, even small companies could associate and thus confront the larger participants in the established electronic markets.

The existence of electronic markets could be a threat as well as an opportunity for the traditional intermediaries, since they represented new opportunities for relating and for seeking information for companies and made locating businesses with better performance and better price conditions easier.

According to Rayport and Sviokla (1995), there are differences between the real market (*marketplace*) and the virtual market (*marketspace*). To be successful in the *marketspace,* five principles should be followed:

- The law of digital assets, which are not consumed upon being used and therefore can be used indefinitely;
- New economies of scale, allowing small companies to achieve low unit costs in markets dominated by large companies;
- New economies of scope, permitting the creation of new digital assets, providing value in various different markets;
- Compression of the cost of transaction, which is lower in the virtual value chain than in the physical value chain;
- Balance between supply and demand, as a result of combining the four above principles, shifting one's view from the supply to the demand side.

These principles, and especially the economies of scope and of scale, point to opportunities for new forms of both intra and interbusiness organization that can occur.

The Internet as a New Strategic Agent

As seen above, the appearance and dissemination of the commercial use of the Internet made the virtual market a reality, and new forms of cooperation and relationship among businesses became viable. But it is not enough just to use the Internet: the way the Internet is used should aim at obtaining greater efficacy in the results (Laurindo & Lamounier, 2000).

To understand better the "virtual market" that some call *Cyber Space*, Anghern (1997) developed a model called ICDT (*Information, Communication, Distribution, and Transaction*) Four ways of acting on the internet can be visualized using the model (Figure 7.1).

First is the *virtual information space* by which the company becomes visible to consumers throughout the world, 24 hours a day. It can collect valuable information about visitors, but the risk is that it is easy for customers to comparison shop.

The next space is the *virtual communication space* where the key word is interaction. It allows one to get beyond physical limitations to create different forms of communication among companies and clients: e-mail, discussion forums, virtual meetings, etc.

In the *virtual distribution space*, businesses can dispense with intermediaries to reach their customers, gain time, and reduce costs. They can lend varied types of services; collect important information, which would be difficult or costly to obtain by other means (such as opinions of books by readers throughout the world); and make it available to clients.

Figure 7.1. Virtual space according to the ICDT model (adapted from Anghern, 1997)

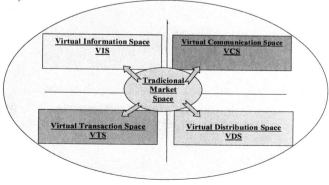

Finally, there is *e-commerce*, both B2C (*business to consumer*) and B2B (*business-to-business*) in the *virtual transaction space.*

Note that in addition to B2B (the link between companies) and B2C (the link between business and customers), we can speak of C2B (the link from customer to company) and C2C (the link among customers). These last two cases can include portals for auctions. Another connection that became possible with the Internet was the interaction of government with the private sector, especially with suppliers, which is called B2G (business-to-government).

There are many strategies available to compete in *Cyber Space,* depending on whether they are for B2B or B2C, or among "pure players" (businesses that were born on the Internet and are only active there) or traditional businesses also active on the Web. It should be stressed that when Angherns analysis was done, the general idea was that barriers to entry in virtual space would be much reduced.

Evans and Wurster (1999) posit three important variables for understanding competition in the virtual market of the Web, which they call "navigational advantage" — reach, wealth, and affiliation.

Reach is related to access and to the connection. This means knowing how many consumers can be accessed and how many products can be offered to them. Usually, the reach is the most perceptible difference between *e-commerce* and traditional commerce, since the Web allows one to reach a much greater number of customers, both individuals and businesses.

Wealth is related to the depth and level of detail of the information provided to consumers. Usually, businesses have had problems in using this dimension of the virtual market adequately. Problems can be overcome if businesses strengthen connections with their customers and if they use a more strategic vision.

Affiliation is a new dimension of competition on the Web and is related to which interests the virtual business represents: a company, a group of companies, consumers, an independent agent, etc.

These authors also explain the different strategies for different kinds of business acting on the Internet. For a "pure player" type, for example, competing for reach is a critical factor in success. For a company that provides a virtual service as an alternative to a traditional service, the wealth variable has important significance. The affiliation variable is relevant Evans and Wurster (1999) for a portal that intermediates among companies.

The Internet also permits that networks inside businesses be created using the same standard electronic communication protocol and the same interface with the users: these are called intranets which can be very wide-ranging as in the case of geographically disperse companies, such as the multinationals.

The Appearance of
Virtual Organizations

The concept of virtual organizations precedes the use of the Internet. Chandrashekar and Schary (1999) highlight the earlier idea of "imaginary organizations", based on trust, synergy among partners, contracts, and a central concept of business and of IT. Civil engineering companies, travel agencies, and software developers were able to operate without long-term relationships and networks among businesses could be created or deactivated in real time.

IT made a new form of integration possible: *virtual integration*, which arrived as a strong alternative to vertical integration, which then began to lose its potential as a source of competitive advantage. This fact, alongside greater opportunity to interact with clients, the leveling of knowledge and the importance of a solid IT platform, constituted the bases of the strategy of virtual organizations according to Venkatraman and Henderson (1998).

For these authors, *virtual organization* can be a strategic approach aimed at creating and distributing intellectual assets, at the same time that it permits the search for physical tangible benefits, creating a complex network of relationships. Virtual organization comprises the three vectors cited above (interaction with consumers, shaping IT assets and leveling of knowledge) and three stages: the level of the tasks, the level of organization and the level of inter- organizational networks.

These three stages were usually approached independently, as for example, isolated applications of EDI (Electronic Data Interchange) and the integration of CAD/CAM between purchasers and suppliers. With the dissemination of integrated ERP (Enterprise Resource Planning) and, more importantly, the adoption of the standardized Internet protocols, it was possible to have a common technological platform which facilitated the existence of virtual organizations.

Prior to the Internet, the concept of virtual organizations had existed, but there were several barriers to their becoming a reality according to Upton and McAffe (1996).

According to these authors, within the concept of a virtual organization, a single factory could be replaced by a network of countless manufacturers, each of them doing what they knew best how to do. There are sectors where these networks can be identified, such as within the textile and automobile industries. In many cases, however, the virtual organization cannot be made concrete. Upton and McAffe posit three requirements for a virtual factory: that it be capable of incorporating partners at any *stage* of relationship, that it be able to include partners at all *levels* of sophistication in IT, and that it be capable of providing all the required *functionalities*. Further, according to these authors, only IT applications based in the Internet can encompass the entire spectrum defined by the three above requirements.

Chesbrough and Teece (1996) allege that virtual business has advantages over traditional, vertically integrated business with regard to participation in a market where one can freely seek out purchasers and vendors of goods and services. On the other hand, as benefits increase, the risks, mostly related to growing problems with coordination, are greater,

Within this perspective of virtual integration via IT application, it is necessary to clarify the role of ERP, EDI, and the Internet.

While EDI and the Internet have made commercial transactions among businesses possible via electronic means, one must distinguish one from the other. EDI permitted an interconnection of businesses via IT, using telephone connections, private networks and dedicated information systems which must be dedicated and installed at each new company that is connected. This was therefore a case by case connection of defined and previously contracted partners. Because it is based in dedicated telecommunications applications and infrastructure, it presented a good level of security, even though its cost was high.

The Internet, in turn, is based on an open protocol, which was conceived to be tolerant of errors due to the use of redundant paths, with the idea of being a public network (anyone can access it) of worldwide scope. It permits continued growth and the adherence of new participants without high cost. The level of security is lower, but the entry and operation are much lower and its coverage is much greater.

The coverage of integration resulting from IT applications, involving the use of ERP, EDI, and the Internet can be seen in Figure 7.2. ERP includes information from the environment of a company (or sometimes a corporation). EDI allows for the exchange of information with some purchasers and providers who have specific contracts signed for this purpose. Finally, the Internet allows for the extension of the integration of the chains of production, including those of worldwide coverage (Chandrashekar & Schary, 1999; Gereffi, 2001).

In addition, it should be highlighted that there is interaction among these kinds of IT applications. Experience with EDI created bases for the B2B, while the growing use of ERP systems that while integrating the various areas of the organizations and standardizing information processing, facilitated business integration in the local as well as the worldwide environment (Laurindo & Pessôa, 2001).

However, it must be stressed that it is not just in buying and selling transactions that the Internet can have an important impact on businesses, since the range of IT applications via the Internet involving many business relations is growing every day.

Hameri and Nihtilä (1997) emphasize Internet use in new product development. They cite the case of a large project involving hundreds of people and many companies and research institutes in which the Internet played a crucial role. Thanks to its use, project participants in different places had access to all the relevant information: engineering plans, three-dimensional models, lists of parameters, results of prototype tests, and other technical engineering informa-

Figure 7.2. Integration of information via IT applications (adapted from Chandrashekar & Schary (1999)

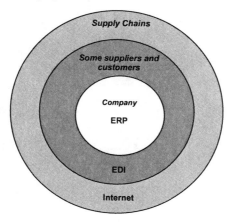

tion. All the project team members could also access information on the project structure, timetable, and minutes from meetings, and could participate in discussion groups. They note that the Internet was used primarily to share information, rather than in an attempt to reinforce collaboration among the different groups. Internet use also emphasized the importance of milestones to coordinate the different teams' participation in the project, which can be seen in the increase of sharing files on dates close to the milestones.

Virtual Chains of Production

The concept of virtual organization can be extended to the entire supply or value chains (or value systems in the terminology of Porter & Millar, 1985), also having the use of IT and especially the Internet as a basis.

Chandrashekar and Schary (1999) underscore that the very notion of chains (originally in the text they treated supply chains, but this can be extended to chains of value or chains of production in general) contains a virtual component, since it involves different organizations. For them, virtual chains involve systems of production and distribution that utilize formal physical structures among different organizations, with the virtual component deriving from flexibility in the formation of networks using rapid real-time communication via IT. Members are often just temporary and frequently enter the chain for specific projects, without being known to all network participants.

These same authors list the characteristics of a virtual chain:

- operation in real-time in response to consumer orders;
- organization in terms of dominant tasks, instead of general competencies of a functional or organizational nature;
- flexible responses to changes in requirements of the market or consumers;
- complementariness of competencies in an orientation by processes;
- direct targeting of the market.

They further point out that such virtual chains operate by means of interrelationships based on reciprocity among complementary businesses, combining partnership for aggregated value and cooperation to administer the flow of products. For them, the governance characteristic of this chain is one of the near autonomy of its members, which is configured more like a federation than a hierarchical organization. The virtual chain combines a structure based in IT with temporary organizations, usually organized by a dominant organizations (a broker) who involves the temporary partners in specific tasks or projects (a "meta-organization").

Virtual chains have a modular structure which can be defined as the capacity to create goods or complex processes based on small subsystems that can be independently designed but that function together as a whole (Baldwin & Clark, 1997).

As positive aspects characteristic of these virtual chains, Chandrashekar and Schary (1999) highlight the orientation toward consumers and products, the opportunity for this orientation to direct production and distribution of goods in several chains, the orientation toward specific tasks and rapid responses. Additionally, they emphasize the flexibility in choice of partners for production and distribution.

Nevertheless, they also point out some negative aspects, such as the focus on the short-term, which makes longer-term horizontal partnerships more difficult, and can generate problems of trust, given the transitory nature of these relationships.

The Internet and Virtual Chains

As seen in Chapter III, Gereffi (2001) identified the existence of three kinds of global chains of production according to the agent who exercises governance of the chain. Initially he identified the chains directed by the producer (producer-driven chains) and those directed by the buyer (buyer-driven chain), but

Table 7.1. Internet oriented chains (adapted from Gereffi, 2001)

Types of Industries	Main Leaders	Forms of Integrating the value chain	Institutional and Organizational Innovations
• Services (B2C): Retail *Online* Intermediation *Online* • Intermediaries (B2B) Autos (Covisint) Computers	• B2C Internet intermediaries (infomediaries) • B2B Some established producers	Virtual Integration and access	• Appearance of e-*commerce* • Mass customization • Non intermediation Direct Sales (without retailers) On line services (intermediation) • New navigators on the Internet

later added the chains of production directed by the Internet (internet-oriented chains) whose characteristics are listed in Table 7.1 and which will be discussed in the following.

The Internet is the basis of *e-commerce* and of *e-business* which for Gereffi are concepts that go beyond the technological aspect, since they make possible profound changes in the organization of business, in market structure, in governmental regulation, in human experience and finally in the competitive dynamics of global chains.

As seen previously, the two most important forms of electronic commerce are *business-to-consumer* — B2C or *business-to-business* — B2B.

B2C markets have to do with the transfer of goods and services to individual consumers, i.e., it is a retail model. B2B markets refer to procurement (research to acquire goods, prices and suppliers), logistical and the administrative processes among companies, therefore this is a model of supply chain. The volume of transactions on the B2B is much greater than on the B2C, corresponding to 80% of what is marketed via e-commerce, whose total was US$401 billion in 2000 (Gereffi, 2001).

According to this same author, the potential that the Internet has to transform the global chains (*producer-driven* as well as *buyer-driven*) is due to two factors:

- it permits the creation of economies of scales and at a level of efficiency that was not possible formerly;

- it makes possible radical change in the structure of business, exercising a "pull" instead of a "push" effect on production, replacing stock with

Table 7.2. Organizational chain of the Internet (adapted from Gereffi, 2001)

Internet Equipment Suppliers	PC Manufacturers component suppliers	Software for PCs and e-business	Web Browser (Navegators)	Internet Service Providers	Providers of Internet Content	Consumers
Cisco Systems Lucent Technology Nortel Networks Sum Microsystems	PCs: Dell, HP, IBM, Micro-processors: Intel, AMD Disk drives: Seagate, Quantum	Software Microsoft, Apple, Servers Unix, Linux E-business Oracle, Ariba, SAP	Microsoft/ Netscape/AOL	AOL/ Microsoft/ A&T	AOL/Microsoft / Yahoo/Lycos Google	Business B2B Covisint, E-steel Consumers B2C Amazon/Dell

information that make production possible, and expediting items only when there is a real demand by consumers.

This last aspect appears to be a long-term trend in many industries, since there are advantages in this model of producing against orders (build to order), allied with a focus on customer satisfaction, such as the case of Dell in Chapter I. The strategy of pushing in supply-chain management (SCM) is imbedded in concepts well disseminated in the business environment, such as mass customization, lean production, and lean retailing.

The organizational chain of the Internet involves service providers, producers of hardware and software, needed to make viable the grand worldwide network which interconnects millions of computers and thousands of servers, as shown in Table 7.2.

However, this new form of command of the global chains proposed by Gereffi (2001) is questioned by Humphrey et al. (2003), among others, who defend the position that while the Internet has had an important role in global commerce, it retains the preexisting governance structures.

Intermediation via Internet

While the Internet has made direct sales to consumers possible, thus eliminating the need for some kinds of intermediation, Gereffi stresses that one of the prime effects attributed to the Internet has been the appearance of new forms of electronic intermediation that have important impact on business strategies.

Upton nd McAffe (1996) stress that *information brokers* appeared with the Internet. They do the integrating that makes the existence of virtual factories possible. These intermediaries perform an important function in the electronic markets.

For Ehrens and Zapf (1999) these new intermediaries are the *"metamediaries"* who go beyond linking buyers and providers, and make services available to facilitate their transactions. Gereffi (2001) created another, similar term to name the players who carry out this role: *"infomediaries"*.

In the context of B2C, Gereffi understands infomediaries to be the companies that provide on-line access to consumers, while they collect valuable information about their consuming habits (which is the basis of the CRM systems that we will see soon). Normally, these infomediaries in the B2C represent the interests of consumers who are to attain the advantages of using the Internet. However, they are also associated with producers, vendors and traditional intermediaries. In B2C, there are dominant infomediaries, such as AOL, Yahoo! (in Brazil we have examples such as UOL) who control the portals that allow Internet access.

In turn, in the B2B ambit, large businesses make their presence known. Even though there are infomediaries independent of them, the biggest initiatives are related to the large companies. An important example exists in the automobile industry with the Covisint portal that unites acquisition of supplies for General Motors, Ford, Daimler/Chrysler, and Renault/Nissan.

In Ehren and Zapf's (1999) conception, metamediaries are agents independent of the buying and selling companies. Market characteristics which favor the appearance of metamediaries are: large scale markets, fragmented supply chains, nondifferentiation of products and vendors, high cost for procuring information, high cost for product comparison, and high cost for processing purchases. Although in situations where there is no dominant oligopoly, neither are the product brand names an important differentiating agent.

According to Kaplan and Sawhney (2000), a similar, better disseminated concept is that of "e-hubs", which are virtual markets among companies (B2B marketplaces). E-hubs can neutral, i.e., belong to "independent" companies, close to the concept of infomediaries or metamediaries (for example, a software provider) or biased, i.e., companies that participate in the transaction that occur. Rudberg et al. (2002) subdivide this last situation into two others: those where one or more large companies participating in the market own and administer the marketplace, or situations where there is a consortium among the market companies and the providers of the technology platform.

E-hubs can be vertical (serving a specific industry) or horizontal (serving several industries). Rudberg et al. (2002) includes a third category, with vertical as well as horizontal coverage to serve a specific segment, which they call mega-exchanges. For horizontal e-hubs, success is determined by standardization and cost reduction. In vertical e-hubs, companies usually seek competitive advantages as rapid responses to the uncertainties of dynamic markets.

E-hub clients purchase either operational products, which are not part of the final product, such as office supplies, or inputs for manufacturing, which are part of the final product or of the manufacturing process, such as raw materials or components.

E-hubs perform either systematic or spot operations to serve the different ways companies buy. Note that systematic purchases involve contracts negotiated

Figure 7.3. Structure of the electronic B2B markets (adapted from Rudberg et al., 2002)

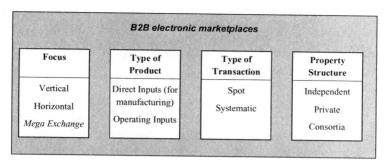

with qualified providers while in spot purchases, the buyers aim to satisfy their immediate needs at the lowest cost possible.

Thus, according to the forms cited above, the *B2B electronic marketplaces* will have structures like those designed in Figure 7.3 (Rudberg et al., 2002).

Kaplan and Sawhney (2000) identify four different types of *e-hubs* (and give respective examples), according to the type of product the client purchases — either operational or manufacturing — and by the kind of operation, whether systematic or spot (Figure 7.4):

- **MRO (maintenance, repair, and operating):** horizontal e-hubs that sell systematically. Examples: Ariba, W.W. Grainger, MRO.com, BizBuyer.com.

Figure 7.4. Classification of e-hubs (adapted from Kaplan & Sawhney, 2000)

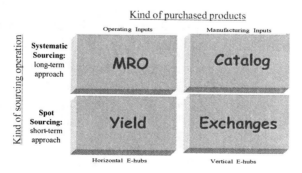

- **Yield manager:** horizontal e-hubs that perform spot selling. Examples: Employease, Adauctiuon.com, Capacity*Web*.com.

- **Exchanges:** vertical e-hubs that perform spot operations. Examples: e-Steel, PaperExchange.com, Altra Energy, IMX Exchange.

- **Catalog:** vertical e-hubs that sell systematically. Examples: Chemdex, SciQuest.com, PlasticsNet.com.

Kaplan and Sawhney also cite another *e-hub* format: the reverse aggregators where buyers in a specific horizontal or vertical market get together to make purchases, thus increasing their bargaining power and adding other correlated services.

Gereffi (2001) sees three kinds of impact the Internet has had on competition in the global chains:

- The Internet leading the creation of information intermediaries, which results in a whole gamut of strategic and organizational changes;

- The Internet inverting the logic of the producer or retailer in favor of the consumer, i.e., expanding the scope of the buyer-drive chains, as long as producers do not use the capacity of the Internet to facilitate mass customization;

- The impact of the Internet (B2B as well as B2c) being absorbed and integrated into the practices of the dominant players already existing in various industries, promoting the integration of business transactions involving producers, retailers, and consumers.

Note that, corroborating the third scenario envisioned by Gereffi (2001), more and more traditional (brick and mortar) businesses, leaders in producer-driven or buyer-driven chains are becoming active in e-business using the Internet as an additional channel. These are being called "click and mortar" companies, which ally the traditional to the virtual side.

Rudberg et al. (2002) see yet another consequence of Internet use: competition that takes place not just within the ambit of businesses, but among chains. Under these circumstances, companies participating in the same chain have adopted a more collaborative focus.

Revolution or Evolution:
That is the Question

One point that has generated controversy lies in determining whether the nature of *e-business* applications based on the Internet is evolutionary or revolutionary. Michael Porter (2001) and Don Tapscott (2001) are figures who are emblematic of this discussion. Both take the view that the Internet is a powerful technology, which greatly increases operational efficiency and opens up new business opportunities. Both also agree that it was used in an erroneous manner by many companies in the euphoria of the explosion of *e-commerce* and *e-business* during the second half of the 1990s. However, each sees different reasons for and consequences of what has occurred.

Porter defends the idea that the Internet is the most powerful IT tool that has yet existed to implement a distinctive strategy, but it should follow the traditional, consecrated principles of competitive strategy. On the other side, Tapscott counter-argues that there has not yet been time for the revolutionary impact of *e-business* to be perceived clearly and that traditional strategies cannot keep up with the pace of changes imposed by the dissemination of the Internet.

Both points of view are presented in the following.

The Internet Following the Principles of Strategy

For Porter (2001), the first market signals captured when *e-commerce* and *e-business* began to operate were illusory, because businesses were faced with a new, important, and promising technology. The reality of both earnings and costs was distorted by the concession of discount prices and investing according to the desire for results on the stock market.

Thus, in Porter's view, *e-business* competitors have disobeyed the precepts of good strategy in numerous ways:

First, in the rush to show short-term results, the "dot.com" enterprises promoted veritable indiscriminant "hunts" for clients, by granting unreal discounts, through incentives to channels and publicity, instead of seeking profit; in other words, seeking sales and not results. In the same line of conduct, they sought income from publicity and in rates for clicks per site, instead of concentrating on delivering value to clients in order to "deserve" a premium price.

There was also a lot of precipitation in offering just any product or service, instead of searching out the necessary trade-offs (see Chapter I), i.e., solutions of compromise between meeting the needs and anxieties of consumers and attaining a level of operational efficiency compatible with their activities.

The Internet, since it is available to everyone, can lead to competition based solely on lower prices, and can end up eroding the industry's profitability. To make the Internet a source of generating value, Porter warns us to look beyond the immediate market signs and focus on two fundamental factors for determining profitability:

- the industry structure, which determines the average profitability of the competitor in the industry;
- sustainable competitive advantage, which makes it possible for a company to profit more than the industry average.

Porter does not consider the generic classification of the New Economy of *business-to-consumer* (B2C) and *business-to-business* (B2B) to have importance in determining profit potential. Potential profitability can only be understood by analyzing each specific industry.

The impacts that the Internet can have on each of the five competitive forces of an industry are summarized in Table 7.3. Note that the effects in general lead to increased competition, which reduces the perspective for profits.

Porter likewise disputes that there are advantages in being the first mover on the Internet, since the cost of change is low and it is hard to create a trademark exclusively on the Internet.

Table 7.3. Effects of the Internet on the competitive forces of an industry (adapted from Porter, 2001)

Forces of Competition	Effect of the Internet
Existing competitors	Reduce differences, sharpen price wars, increased markets
New Entrants	Diminish entry barriers, attract new entrants
Replacement/substitute products	Make substitute products viable, increase market
Buyers	More power to consumers who consult prices on-line, reduce cost of changes, eliminate some intermediaries
Suppliers	Increase bargaining power since access to suppliers is easier, in counterpart; suppliers have access to more clients.

In addition, the Internet has caused other problems, such as the outsourcing of key activities and the indiscriminant formation of partnerships, which causes the loss of important proprietary advantages.

Nevertheless, Porter also detects positive aspects of the Internet. For him, the Internet is the largest IT platform developed to date to reinforce strategic distinctive positioning, due to its range of coverage and uniformization of the internal standards of an organization's information system.

As seen earlier, in Chapter I, for Porter, the creation of a sustainable competitive advantage can come from operational efficiency (doing the same things as the competitors, but in a better way) or from strategic positioning (doing different things than the competitors do). Given the broad dissemination of the Internet, the large gains that it can mean in terms of operational efficiency (flexibility, speed, etc.) can be copied easily. When all businesses are on the Internet, this will no longer be a source of advantage for gains in efficiency, and will become a qualifying criterion, no longer a winner of orders, according to the classification proposed by Slack (1993).

On the other hand, Porter recognizes that the Internet has opened a new wide range of opportunities for sustainable strategic positioning, such as new product features or services or even different logistical arrangements.

Contrary to what many believe, Porter does not think that the Internet is revolutionary for the majority of established industries and companies. While it has created some new industries (such as on-line auctions and electronic markets), Porter understands that its main effect have been to reshape preexisting industries, that experienced restrictions due to the high cost of communications, of collecting information and of transactions.

For this author, more solid competitive advantages derive from more traditional sources, such as differentiated products, proprietary content, and distinctive physical activities. Rarely has the Internet annulled sources of competitive advantage: usually it makes them more valuable, especially the creation of distinctive positions.

According to Porter, to obtain competitive advantage via the Internet, a radically new approach to business is not necessary, but one can use the principles of good strategy. This explains the reason that many traditional companies have obtained good results using the Internet as one more channel, rather than a separate business (moving from brick and mortar to click and mortar). The best way of using its potential is to integrate physical and virtual activities, such as for example, creating a good postsales service team to service clients who have made purchases via *e-commerce*.

Within the approach, which proposes the use of traditional tools of structural analysis for an industry, Porter seen no need for the distinction between B2B and B2C. Further: he sees no "New Economy," but rather an old economy with access to a new and powerful technology. There is thus no rupture, since "in our anxiety to see how the Internet is different, we failed to see how the Internet is the same".

Thus, according to this line of thinking, the route to efficacious use of the Internet is the necessary employment of a strategic vision for its use in order to make new forms of organization and relationships among companies viable.

Internet Revolutionizing Strategy

Tapscott's (2001) view is directly contrary to Porter's (2001), since he understands the Internet and the New Economy to be revolutionary.

Firstly, he highlights the grand role of the Internet in forming networks that have made partnerships for outsourcing and processing a reality that has led to the success of numerous companies. Among these cases, he cites the companies that rather than producing have taken on a role as integrators, such as Boeing, IBM, and Mercedes Benz. He also points to the growth of contract manufacturing (such as the well-known Celstica Flextornics and Soletron) as signs of the correctness of this strategy. He also contests the idea that this eliminates competitive advantage as well as the claim that verticalization would be a better alternative.

Tapscott believes that the Internet is much more than a simple natural evolution of IT applications. It represents a qualitatively new resource for universal communication. The public nature of the Internet, allied to its growing reach and functionality, has produced a scenario that is revolutionizing the corporate structure of the industrial era and forging new paths for competitive strategy. This new structure, allying technology to this new way of doing business, Tapscott has called the *business web* or *b-web*. He defines this as any system composed of suppliers, distributors, service providers, infrastructure, and clients who use the Internet for business communications and transactions.

He also emphasizes that it is not just pure-player companies that are making gains with this. On the contrary, the greatest beneficiaries are the traditional companies, which are more and more undertaking partnerships to develop their businesses.

For this author, it is important to perceive that the Internet is still undergoing evolution and that much of its potential has yet to be explored. It is growing and learning from the use of the technology. In this way, the Internet will be the infrastructure of the economy of the 21st century just as the electricity, railroads, highways, and other transportation systems served this purpose at the beginning of the 20th century.

However, the Internet has already produced unquestionable gains by reducing the costs of transactions, facilitating searches, coordinating and contracting among companies, different from the traditional model of the industrial era, which included the emphasis on verticalization. Tapscott understands the term *business model* to mean a company's central architecture, especially as it develops and deploys all relevant resources (not just those within the limits of the corporation) to create differentiated values for the clients.

Tapscott lists six reasons for the existence of a New Economy:

1. **New Infrastructure for the Creation of Wealth.** Networks, especially the Internet, are becoming the basis for economic activity and progress, in the same way that railroads, highways, electricity, and telephones are for the vertically-integrated corporations.

2. **New Models for Business.** The companies of the New Economy should not be understood to be those of the Internet or the "dot.coms", but companies that use the Internet infrastructure to create efficacious models for business based in the *b-web*.

3. **New Sources of Value.** In today's economy, value is created by the brain, not muscle,s and the majority of work is focused on knowledge.

4. **The New Proprietors of Wealth.** Powerful investors own the majority of industrial capital goods. At the beginning of the 21st century, 60% of Americans owned shares of stock and the largest shareholders are the workers' pension funds. In addition, economic growth will be located in small businesses.

5. **New Institutions and Educational Models.** Private companies, and not public institutions, will meet the growing demand for educational services. The pedagogical model is changing with the increase in interactivity and learning focused on the student. Universities will become places on the communication network and not just places where people go to study.

6. **New Forms of Governance.** The bureaucracy of the industrial era grew simultaneously with the vertically-integrated corporations and imitated

their structure. New governmental structures based on the Internet permit cooperation between public and private organizations to deliver services to citizens. This is called *e-government*. One can imagine similar changes in democratic procedures (as, for example, in the electoral process) and in the relationship between citizen and state.

Orthodox strategic thinking does not allow the exploration of these new opportunities, which Tapscott calls "innovation in the business model", or the search for new tools, including strategic concepts and methods for analysis to understand and explore business architectures such as the *b-webs*. In these circumstances companies can greatly benefit from resources they do not own, because of the network environment. They can thus concentrate on their essential competencies, searching both inside and outside, via the Internet, for better components of operational activities and projects, to obtain the best solutions at lower cost.

Porter's idea that the Internet neutralizes sources of competitive advantage is contested by Tapscott, who argues that companies have different efficacies in implementing its use.

Tapscott does recognize, however, that the second half of the 1990s was a bad time for strategy, since it was believed that everything done on the Internet would be profitable, which did not turn out to be true. He also recognizes that rivalry among competitors was sharpened, the barriers to admissions diminished and that bargaining power of buyers and suppliers increased. But this does not justify denying that the Internet significantly changed the economy. There will be a need for strategy, but it will be a strategy consonant with the new times.

Final Considerations and Perspectives

The discussion of the turbulent environment of the New Economy goes further than the role of IT in organizations. As the reader has been able to observe, the heralds of the New Economy have a strategic approach devoted to the dynamism of the process of formulating and implementing strategies.

In their articles *"Making strategy: Learning by doing"* and *"Strategy as simple rules"*, by Christensen (1997) and Eisenhardt and Sull (2001) respectively, the authors make clear the need for integration between the formulation and implementation of strategy, to form a continuous process, with constant feedback to avoid strategy becoming precociously obsolete due to the rapid rate of change in the environment.

But it is important that the reader not understand these recommendations as a negation of the structured process of analysis and the formulation of strategy, but as a warning about the need for a more agile process, one which is strongly connected to daily operations.

One concept that can help to comprehend the need for organizations to respond to change and to maintain their competitiveness is resilience, i.e. the ability to absorb the competitive environment and respond with efficacy to this turbulence (Starr et al., 2002).

In this way, the holistic-strategic model developed over the course of this book is ready for the New Economy, concerning itself with the issue of the dynamism of the strategic processes, with the interconnectedness of business, the speed of the IT revolution and the changes that the economy and the society are undergoing at the start of this century.

However, all the strategic concepts and support techniques are, explicitly or implicitly, included in the model and they should not be neglected due to a priority on immediate responses. In sum, exchanging consistently developed analyses via checklists and ad hoc scripts is unnecessarily risky.

Therefore, with a good implementation process, guided by continuous monitoring of the environmental changes and making use of IT and virtual resources, one can use the enduring consecrated models in an agile, quick, and integrated manner.

Case Studies: Strategy and Decisions in Perspective

Case – Uniting the New and Old Economy and Profiting from It: Magazine Luiza

Magazine Luiza, one of the four largest department store chains in Brazil (billing of R$588 million in 2201) was founded in 1957, in França, a city in the state of São Paulo. It had 127 stores in 2002, located in 105 cities in five states: São Paulo, Minas Gerais, Paraná, Mato Grosso do Sul and Pará.

In 1992, (before commercial use of the Internet!) this company launched the pioneering concept of "Virtual Stores", which are establishments without products in stock or on display, where the client makes purchases with the aid of multimedia terminals and trained salespeople. In 2002, 34 of their total stores were virtual, billing R$48 million in 2001. Beginning in 2002, their virtual and conventional sales departments were unified (they were already working in an integrated fashion) and the virtual area disseminated its experiences to the rest of the company.

While the majority of businesses that began to work via the Internet had serious problems and reduced investments in this area, Magazine Luiza enjoyed success with its initiative.

What was the difference that meant success where so many others failed in Brazil?

As other retail stores separated their virtual from their conventional operations and worked to adapt themselves to the virtual world, Magazine Luiza did the opposite: its virtual operations were always integrated with its conventional ones and followed the traditional retail precepts. Backed up by the strength of its brand name, it used the Internet to expand its chain to cities where there were still no physical stores, but demand for products existed. To do so, it adopted a creative solution: its virtual stores are small establishments (at 15% of the cost of conventional stores) which neither display merchandise nor maintain stock. To consult the product catalog (electronics, household appliances, furniture and bath, table and bedroom accessories) eight computer terminals are used to make purchases, always in the company of a salesperson. Prior to the existence of the Internet with its graphic resources, products were presented to customers through the use of video. Products were delivered to clients within 24 hours.

Hence, instead of betting on just the construction of a user-friendly and well-planned site, the company also invested in human contact to leverage sales. Service by trained salespeople was the key to its operations. They talked with the client, explaining the methods of payment and showing the daily specials. Further, the stores promoted courses on the use of the products it sold to consumers, as well as the use of electronic commerce.

With its acquired experience, the company began to sell at a distance via its Internet site, even reaching customers in the capital of São Paulo.

Internet assisted sales (both local and remote) also allowed Magazine Luiza to collect a considerable amount of information on customer habits. Using these data based, it could advantageously target its marketing campaigns. For example, it could offer a flat surface television screen to those who had already purchased a DVD. In this way, CRM is one more important application of IT to support its strategy.

All this required a significant IT infrastructure, which had to include a new integrated management system and an intranet connecting all its stores.

Adapted from news on the portals of *Exame* and *Agência Estado* and from the company's site.

Case – Intermediation Using Portals

Some existing initiatives illustrate the idea of electronic intermediation.

CVRD

The Companhia Vale do Rio Doce (CVRD) is developing a portal together with 13 other large mining companies, which will market minerals such as iron, copper, or aluminum. To do so, it has created a separate company, Velepontocom, which will be devoted to electronic commerce and CVRD's strategy on the Internet. It aims to reach a larger number of buyers, principally the small and medium-sized companies, which in traditional commerce would have difficulty in negotiating directly with the large mining companies. Small providers will also be beneficiaries of the initiative. The logistical area of the CVRC will tend to grow with the portal, since it will be able to provide services to an increasing range of clients. However, the contracts in this market tend to be of a long-term nature and require a lot of negotiation, which will still demand direct contact. This portal can be considered an example of an *e-hub* of the catalog type (Guimarães, 2001).

NetCana, an initiative involving smaller companies, has set itself up in the sugar cane production sector, by developing the NetCana portal. The main idea was to eliminate intermediaries and reduces the cost of purchasing items unrelated to the focus of the business, such as office supplies, spare parts, fertilizers, sacks or agricultural equipment. Initially it will include the producing refineries in the state of São Paulo, as well as their potential suppliers of operational items.

The refineries' bargaining power will be considerably greater compared to purchasing individually. For the suppliers, it represents an opportunity to be accessed by a much greater number of buyers. This is a case of reverse aggregation (Sordili, 2001).

Adapted from news in the *Exame* Portal.

Case – EMBRAER, Virtually Flying

Embraer, symbol of the successful Brazilian company in the high technology, globalized market, is an important example of the strategic use of IT in the perspective of networks which integrate and propel business.

To achieve this level of performance, the company followed the vision of serving clients' needs and desires by developing products at low cost and within the time frame demanded by the market it knew well.

IT was allied to the company's overall strategy and made Embraer an international example in terms of product development, within the characteristic model of the New Economy: creating networks of clients and suppliers who participated together in projects, sharing information and taking on risks.

By adopting this concept, the development time for Embraer's new family of commercial airplanes fell from five to 3.2 years.

This enormous project involved 2,500 people (1,000 from Embraer and 1,500 from partners) from sixteen companies in eight countries (Brazil, France, the USA, Germany, Belgium, Japan, Switzerland, and Spain) connected through an extranet (private network among companies created by Embraer following the Internet standards).

Through this network, projects participants could access a collaborative portal where information on the project was exchanged, including design files (with CAD tools), which are usually very large and would have to be transferred by mailing diskettes or CDs.

The digital model, one of the main tools available in the portal, is a large three-dimensional file which represents the airplane at its exact stage of development and can be updated on line with each change made by the teams. Thus it is guaranteed that all those involved are working on the same version of the same project, without delays or duplication of information.

Tests are done at a Center of Virtual Reality using three-dimensional images on a screen which is almost two and a half meters high. With special glasses and helmets, the engineers can examine and develop the digital model in real size, which is quicker and less cumbersome than having to wait for the construction of a physical model.

Thus, the use of IT aligned with a strategy, taking advantage of virtual chains has been decisive in gaining competitive advantages.

Revista Exame, June 13, 2001 (Edition 742)

Questions for Reflection and Discussion

Considering the case in the section titled Uniting the New and Old Economy and Profiting from it: Magazine Luiza, answer the following questions:

1. How did the company use virtual space in its strategy?
2. How did the company travel through virtual space in its strategy?
3. How did it employ the strategic alignment of IT (see Chapter V) to propel both its conventional and virtual business strategy?

Considering the case in the section titled Intermediation using Portals, answer the following questions:

4. Discuss the properties of each of these three portals.
5. What impact can each of these portals have on the industries where they are active?

Considering the case in the section titled EMBRAER, Virtually Flying, answer the following questions:

6. Analyze Embraer's strategy in terms of its organizational concepts and virtual chains.
7. Which vision better accounts for Embraer's success on the internet: evolution (Porter) or revolution (Tapscott)? Which better explains the case of Magazine Luiza?

8. Compare the case of Embraer with the portals discussed in this chapter (CVRD and NetCana). Identify the main points of difference and similarity.

References

Anghern, A. (1997). Design matures internet business strategies: The ICDT model. *European Management Journal, 15*(4), 360-368.

Chandrashekar, A., & Schary, P.B. (1999). Toward the virtual supply chain: the convergence of IT and organization. *International Journal of Logisitics Management, 10*(2), 27-39.

Chesbrough, H.W., & Teece, D.J. (1996). When is virtual virtuous? *Harvard Business Review, 74*(1),65-73.

Christensen, C.M. (1997). Making strategy: Learning by doing. *Harvard Business Review, 75*(6), 141-156.

Ehrens,S., & Zpf, P. (1999). *The internet business to business report.* Bear Stearns Equity Research Technology. Retrieved from http://www.bearstearns.com

Eisenhardt, K.M., & Sull, D.N. (2001). Strategy as simple rules. *Harvard Business Review, 79*(1), 107-116.

Evans, P.B., & Wurster, T.S. (1997). Strategy and the new economics of information. *Harvard Business Review, 75*(5), 71-82.

Evans, P.B., & Wurster, T.S. (1999). Getting real about virtual commerce. *Harvard Business Review, 77*(6), 84-94.

Frontini, M.A. (1999). *A decision making model for investing in electronic business.* Dissertation for obtaining the degree of Master of Science in Management of technology. Massachusetts Institute of Technology.

Gereffi,G. (2001). Beyond the producer-driven/buyer-driven dichotomy: The evolution of global value chains in the internet era. *IDS Bulletin, 32*(3), 30-40.

Gereffi, G., Humprhey, J., Kaplinsky, R., & Sturgeon, T.J. (2001). Introduction: Globalisation, value chains and development. *IDS Bulletin, 32*(3), 1-8.

Guimarães, C. (2001). Vale tudo. "Negócios Exame", 5. In *Revista "Exame"*, 733.

Hameri, A.P., & NihtiläJ. (1997). Distributed new product development project based on internet and worldwide Web: A Case study. *Journal of Product Innovation Management, 14,* 77-87.

Humphrey, J, Mansell, R., Paré, D., & Schmitz, H. (2003). The reality of e-commerce with developing countries. *Research Report, LSE & IDS.*

Kaplan, S., & Sawhney, M. (2000). E-hubs: The new B2B marketplaces. *Harvard Business Review, 78*(3), 97-103.

Laurindo, F.J.B., Carvalho, M.M., & Pessôa, M.S.P. (2001). Information technology projects management: Brazilian cases. *POMS 2001, Proceedings of the Conference of the Production and Operations Management Society* (pp. 304-312).

Laurindo, F.J.B., Carvalho, M.M., Pessôa, M.S.P., & Shimizu, T. (2002). Selecionando uma aplicação de tecnologia da informação com enfoque na eficácia: Um Estudo de Caso de um Sistema para PCP. *Revista G&P: Gestão e Produção, 9*(3), 377-396.

Laurindo, F. J. B., Carvalho, M. M., & Shimizu, T. (2003). Information technology strategy alignment: Brazilian cases. In K. Kangas (Ed.), *Business strategies for information technology management* (pp. 186-199). Hershey, PA: IRM Press.

Laurindo, F.J.B., & Lamounier, A.E.B. (2000). Mapping the cyber space: Strategies and implications. *Proceedings of the VI International Conference on Industrial Engineering and Operations Management* (pp. 278-283).

Laurindo, F.J.B., & Pessôa, M.S.P. (2001). Sistemas integrados de gestão. In J. Amato Neto (Ed.), *Manufatura classe mundial*. São Paulo, Editora Atlas.

Malone, T.W., Yates, J., & Benjamin, R.I. (1989, May/June). The logic of electronic markets. *Harvard Business Review, 67*(3).

Porter, M.E. (1979). How competitive forces shape strategy. *Harvard Business Review, 57*(6), 137-145.

Porter, M.E. (2001). Strategy and the Internet. *Harvard Business Review, 79*(1), 63-78.

Porter, M.E., & Millar, V.E. (1985). How information gives you competitive advantage. *Harvard Business Review, 63*(4), 149-160.

Prahalad, C.K., & Hamel, G. (1990). The core competence of the corporation. *Harvard Business Review, 68*(3), 79-91.

Rayport, J.F., & Sviokla, J.J. (1995). Exploiting the virtual value chain. *Harvard Business Review, 73*(6), 75-85.

Rudberg, M., Klingenberg, & Kronhamn, K. (2002). Collaborative supply chain planning using electronic marketplaces. *Integrated Manufacturing Systems, 13*(8), 596-610.

Slack, N. (1993). *Vantagem competitiva em manufatura: Atingindo competitividade nas operações industriais.* São Paulo, Editora Atlas.

Sordili, A. (2001). Clica que a cana é doce. "Negócios Exame", 6. *Revista "Exame", 735.*

Tapscott, D. (2001). Rethinking strategy in a networked world. Strategy+ Business, 24, 1-8.

Upton, D.M., & Mcaffe, A. (1996). The real virtual factory. *Harvard Business Review, 74*(4), 123-133.

Venkatraman, N., & Henderson, J. C. (1998). Real strategies for virtual organizing. *Sloan management Review, 40*(1), 33-48.

Chapter VIII

An Overview Of The Decision-Making Process In Organizations

Introduction: Situations and Facts that Affect Organizations

Organizations frequently find themselves faced with serious decision-making problems. An individual can analyze the problem and choose the better alternative in an entirely informal manner. In an organization, the problems are much broader and more complex, involving risk and uncertainty. They require the opinion and participation of many people at different levels of hierarchy. The decision-making process in a business or organization should be structured and resolved in a formal, detailed, consistent, and transparent manner.

Political events such as the end of the Soviet Empire and the consequent fall of the Berlin Wall, the Petroleum War, the invasion of Iraq, conflicts in various countries, terrorism, etc., immediately affect the destiny and behavior of nations or organizations. As everyone knows, Japan, which had been demolished by the Second World War, became a world economic power in just a few decades, thanks to massive economic aid from the West in the postwar period, social reconstruction, and the joint efforts of its government and people. Nevertheless, beginning in 1989, the year called the "turning point" of the Japanese economy, there were abrupt changes in politics and the economy that resulted in the fall of the Japanese economic index (Dow Nikkey) from 39,000 yen to 14,000 yen. The Japanese economy underwent a contraction that included the phenomenon known as the bursting of the "bubble", and the country's economy still has not fully recovered from its devastating effects. Countries and organizations constantly have to face problems due to changes in governmental regimes (communist, socialist or capitalist) and economic stability.

World financial crises provoked by financial speculators have made it clear that the practical and theoretical knowledge in economy or finance are only the starting background to confront the market of financial speculation. What has proved necessary has been the experience and level of expertise of someone familiar with the financial trading tables in order to make choices in dealing with the alternatives in day-to-day or moment-to-moment financial operations, and many other factors (see the Case Study - LTCM, presented at the end of this chapter).

Other problems such as the globalization of the world economy, the need to manage the environment, combat poverty, etc., affect an organization's choice of strategy.

Procedures for Analyzing a Strategic Decision-Making Situation

Problems of strategic decision-making can be structured and analyzed through methodologies and instruments provided by Operations Research and Management Science (Hillier & Liebermann, 1980; Cook & Russel, 1993), augmented by knowledge of organizational theory (Simon, 1958, 1997; Cyert & March, 1963; Bass, 1983), sociology, psychology, etc.

Simon (1997) stresses that the solution to any decision problems in the business, scientific, or artistic areas can be visualized in four stages: the perception of the need for a decision or an opportunity, the formulation of action alternatives, evaluation of the alternatives in terms of their respective contributions, and the choice of one or more activities to be carried out.

One can say that a strategic decision-making situation can be analyzed and resolved in the following phases: 1) Select: Select an appropriate strategy; 2)

Plan: Formulate a master plan; 3) Do: List the action alternatives; 4) Check or see: Evaluate the preliminary results and decide upon a control procedure, and 5) Action: Implement. These stages are based on the procedure known to Management Science as PDCA, or Plan, Do, Check, and Action.

A more detailed description of each phase follows (Kinoshita, 1996, Porter, 1980):

1. **Select phase:** A strategy can be selected according to the problem the organization faces, and it can be: a strategy in a situation of risk or uncertainty, a strategy in a situation of competition or conflict, a strategy of multiple objectives or goals, a strategy for economic analysis, a strategy for optimization, decision making in a complex situation, etc.

2. **Plan phase:** Planning should define "who" is the decision maker, e.g., the government, a school, a certain company; "what" is the purpose of the decision, e.g., to purchase real estate, sell new products, and "why" this decision-making process is necessary, e.g., to obtain more space, earn more revenue, etc. Then, through theoretical and empirical research, possible trade-offs of several alternatives are found, and then a master plan to proceed with the decision-making strategy can be developed.

3. **Do phase:** In a case of alternatives to construct a building or produce goods, one needs to define the requirements for functionality, security, quality, durability, form (beauty, harmony), the materials to be used (new materials), and the production process (how?) for this product or good. To choose a service or a technology, a similar procedure should be adopted. The new elements that have been incorporated should be measured in a quantitative or qualitative way to gauge the trade-offs of the master plan.

4. **Check phase:** In this phase the alternatives of the master plan, detailed to include the characteristics listed in phase three, should be tested for performance in aspects of quality, economic factors, efficiency, and security. The results obtained in this phase are taken into consideration to improve the decision-making master plan. Procedures that make restructuring possible from the systemic point of view, procedures for control and administration of the process, as well as a system to evaluate the results obtained should be incorporated in this phase.

5. **Action phase:** This is the phase of implementing procedures; the results obtained are evaluated and the original problem is restructured through

feedback from the learning acquired. The need to broaden the scope and the finality of the problem by incorporating new goals or functional characteristics can be considered at this stage, sending the problem back to the planning stage.

For example, how would one describe the five stages in detail in the following cases?

a.   XYZ company is studying the possibility of purchasing land to install a new branch office. What would the structured procedures be to determine the *alternatives* or *strategies* for this decision-making problem? What kind of land, where should it be located and how many pieces of real estate should be considered? What are the *criteria, goals,* or *objectives* for the choice of this land? Should the price of the land, payment conditions, estimates of final profit, the location, size, etc. be taken into consideration? What would other criteria or objectives be?

b.   Another common decision-making problem is about financial investment. Should one invest in real estate, the stock market, savings, dollars, or investment funds? What are the rates of return and under what economic conditions or perspectives would one investment be more advantageous than another? Does the company or investor want an indication for investment in the short, medium, or long-term? Would the investors like to learn to improve the composition of an investment portfolio? Or would they like to learn the advantages and disadvantages of the process of migrating from one investment to another?

Sensitivity Analysis

In addition to making the BEST DECISION at the time, the company might also like to know the other possible decision alternatives. The company could be content with a *good decision* within its possibilities or, the *second-best decision* might be more appropriate. A procedure known as sensitivity analysis, that analyzes the possibilities of decision around a chosen solution, is usually used. In general, the company or the decider would like to ask the following type of question (known as *what-if? question*) (Turban & Aronson, 1998; Mallach, 2000):

"What would happen to the chosen decision, if the panorama or conditions were different?"

Rationality Used in Decision Models

Simon (1958) posits two basic kinds of decisions in arguing that:

> *"...in social science, at one extreme we have the economists who attribute to economic man a preposterously omniscient rationality.* **Economic man** *has a complete and consistent system of preferences that allows him always to choose among the alternatives open to him; he is completely aware of what these alternatives are; there are no limits on the complexity of the computations he can perform in order to determine which alternatives are best; probability calculations are neither frightening nor mysterious to him....*

> *...it seems obvious enough that human behavior in organizations is, if not wholly rational, at least in good part intendedly so. Much behavior in organizations is, or seems to be, task oriented — and sometimes efficacious in attaining its goals....*

> *But, it seems equally apparent to one who observes behavior in organization, that there is none of the global omniscience that is attributed to economic man.*

> *While economic man maximizes — selects the best alternative from among all those available to him; his cousin, whom we shall call* **administrative man** *looks for a course of action that is satisfactory or 'good enough'. Examples of satisfactory criteria that are familiar enough to businessmen are ' share of market', 'adequate profit', 'fair price'.*

Administrative man recognizes that the world perceives is a drastically simplified model of the real world. He makes his choices using a simple picture of the situation that takes into account just a few of the factors that he regards as most relevant and crucial.

*We will then describe people as rational human beings, but with a less grandiose rationality than that proclaimed by the economic man. That is, we are admitting the existence of **Bounded Rationality**."*

To sum up Simon's thinking, we can say that:

a.   the **economic man:**

  (i)   works with the *real world* in all its complexity and confusion;
  (ii) adopts an "optimum standard" of reality, choosing the best existing alternative.

Nevertheless, it is not difficult to perceive that these complete or perfect models are hard to formulate and manipulate in practice, due to the difficulty of obtaining complete knowledge of the problem from this point of view and the related difficulties in computation. The economist model considers *all* the possible alternatives, the large majority of which are superfluous or of little importance with reference to the decision to be taken. Thus the process of decision making is almost always conducted by using the strategies and models professed by the administrative man.

b.   the **administrative man**

  (i)   works with a *drastically simplified model* of reality, since he or she perceives that most of the facts of this real world are not of great relevance to the specific situation and that the link between cause and effect should be simple.
  (ii) adopts a *"satisfactory or good enough standard"* of the world formed by a limited number of choice alternatives that satisfactorily

meet the problem, and is content to find satisfactory or adequate solutions.

What is a *drastically simplified model*? What do we understand by *satisfactory standard*? In the following sections we will try to define the characteristics of a decision-making model that can answer these questions

Behavior of People and Organizations

The behavior of a person or organization faced with a decision is guided by objectives and general goals. This comportment is of the rational kind because persons or organizations select alternatives that lead in the best way possible to achieve their objectives.

An organization is characterized by specialization, i.e., the execution of specific tasks is delegated to specific parts of the organization. This specialization can take the form of "vertical" delegation of responsibilities or tasks, or of the "horizontal" type when division of labor is the basic characteristic of the organization. More modern proposals from organizational theory have other names for organizational structures such as: "matrix" form of organization, organization by projects, or departmentalization. Thus, it is inevitable that there exists a "hierarchy of decisions", i.e., a decision made by someone in a certain position in the hierarchy prevails over decision made by subordinates. Thus, a decision made by a subordinate should be in accordance with decisions taken by his superior (Simon 1958, 1997).

Generally, a decision of society prevails over a decision made by an organization; a decision taken in a stockholders' meeting prevails over a decision taken by the president of an organization, and so on.

In practice, it is possible to find some organization, or part of it, that can be called an "anarchic organization," and is represented by the "garbage can model" proposed by Cohen et al. (1972). This model considers the decision-making process in such anarchic organizations as an enormous *garbage can* where problems to be resolved are tossed. Well-structured or top priority problems are resolved immediately and taken out of the garbage can. Other problems are taken out after a superficial examination or are taken out of the can because they are taking up space. Many problems which are ignored remain on the bottom of the garbage can, which requires periodic emptying of its contents.

Under the behavioral point of view, decision theory also classifies persons and organizations into three types:

- those that have a *preference for risk,*
- those that are *neutral toward risk,* and
- those that have an *aversion for risk.*

This variation in behavior allows for conservative decision making, or neutral toward risk or that which runs a greater risk in the attempt to attain the maximum possible profit.

The business model presented in this section specifies an alternative set of variables and relations in an attempt to obtain a modern representation of a company. This modern representation corresponds to a large-sized firm or company, manipulating multiple products and operating with uncertainties in a market ruled by imperfect information.

Rational Concepts Adopted

The following four concepts, which represent the essence of decision making theory in the companies, were developed to define the concept of rational decision-making process (Cyert & March, 1963). They are:

1. **Near resolution of conflict in the organization's objectives.** In considering the dimension of the objectives or goals, it is inevitable that each group inside the organization desires different objectives. Traditionally, these differences were specified by assigning monetary values which correspond to the objectives of each group. In the new conception, the organization's goals correspond to a series of restrictions imposed by independent levels of aspiration of the groups inside the organization. After listing and prioritizing all the requirements and limitations, including the nonessential, sporadic and nonoperational ones, only the essential objectives that will be operational are taken into consideration.

2. **Minimize uncertainty and risk.** All modern organizations constantly live under risk conditions caused by uncertainties of various kinds, and these uncertainties should be avoided or minimized through:

    (a) an emphasis on *immediate response and short term feedback*, avoiding uncertainties deriving from long-term strategies or events.

    (b) adopting *day-to-day decisions and planning* that do not depend on predicting the future and market uncertainties: for example, a decision about production levels is often made using predictions based on experience, even though there are data resulting from scientifically formulated predictions.

    (c) an environment of *negotiation* with the organizational divisions, with the customers, with the supplier, banks, etc. Negotiations minimize risks, although they do not necessarily maximize the gains.

3. **Search for solutions in the neighborhood of the main objective.** The search for solutions to a problem should be neither random nor exhaustive. The search for a solution within the organization should be guided around the main objective of the problem and the possible alternative solutions should be sought in the neighborhood of the current alternatives.

    If the search for a solution does not yield satisfactory results, the company usually seeks ever more complex solutions or looks to other areas distant from the original solution or in the last instance, seeks solutions for some "weak areas" of the company, for example, "training competent professionals" in order to improve quality and productivity or, "prioritizing research activity", taking on the risk of a no-return investment.

4. **Constant learning and adaptation of the organization.** An organization always shows adaptive behavior over time. It can be assumed that the organization will change its objective, refocus its attention and revise its problem-solving procedures based on its experiences.

    Organizational learning can take place in various ways, such as:

    (a) **adaptation of the rules and priorities** — the organization prefers some criteria, ignoring others, e.g., the concern with environmental factors obliges it to pay more attention to certain problems in the production process, and

(b)   **adaptation of the rules of problem solving** because the organization may experience either success or failure during the implementation of chosen alternatives.

The organization can feel that its decision-making methods should be changed (to an alternative method or a more complex one) to the extent that it senses incompatibilities between the desired objectives and the results obtained. For example, a local problem can become global, a problem with a single objective can become one of multiple objectives, a problem with uncertainty based on probability theory can be explained using new properties of the possibility theory. All these problems may require additional rules to include some problems of environmental conflict, legislation, etc.

Classification of Decision-Making Situations

The simplification suggested by Simon's *bounded rationality principle* can be considered as a starting point to analyze the complex decision-making problem found in organizations. Simon's principle helps us to start classifying and analyzing the decision making process in detail.

First, problems can be classified into three categories: *structured, semi-structured,* and *nonstructured problems* (Dyson, 1990; Turban & Aronson, 1998).

A problem is considered to be *structured* if its definition and the phases of operation required to arrive at the desired results are very clear and its repeated execution is always possible. As examples of structured problems, we mention the payroll problem, accounting procedures, and data processing operations in general.

Semi-structured problems are problems with well known operations, but that have some variable factors or criteria that can influence the results, that are common in forecasting problems and sales strategies.

In *nonstructured problems,* neither the scenarios nor the decision making-criteria are fixed or previously known.

In addition, a decision about any one of the three kinds of problems (structured, semi-structured, and nonstructured) can be differentiated by the *level of decision:*

- **strategic** (usually, a decision for two to five years),
- **tactical** (decision for a few months up to two years),
- **operational** (a few days or a few months), and
- **dispatching** (an "in loco" decision just for some hours).

In general, strategic decision problems are semi or nonstructured problems. An example of a non-structured problem with operational level of decision, mentioned by Turban, is the operation of choosing the cover for a weekly magazine (or the front page of a daily newspaper), where diverse alternatives are foreseen, but all can be replaced at the last minute if something important happens.

There are superimpositions among the types of problems and the levels of decision, but the responsibility for the decision belongs to distinct groups of deciders. For example, the problem of choosing the cover for a weekly magazine can be decided at the operational level by the staff of editors, or it can be decided by the dispatch kind of decision if the need for change occurs during the printing phase of the magazine. A nonstructured problem such as investing in R&D cannot be decided at the operational level, but only at the strategic level. Large-sized semi-structured or nonstructured problems can only be analyzed and resolved appropriately through the support of decision-making software.

Usually, a *strategic decision* is mainly concerned with outside problems, or with problems involving the entire company and its environment. *Tactical decisions* are concerned with the structuring of company resources to create alternatives for execution, aiming for the best results. *Operational decisions* aim at maximizing the efficiency of the process of converting resources, or maximizing income from current operations. While distinct, all of these decisions interact among themselves, and are interdependent and complementary. Saaty (1994) contends that many excellent deciders do not use theory to help them decide and asks the following question, "are good decisions accidental or are there logical principles that guide reasoning in the decision making process? Are these principles complete and consistent?"

In the decision-making process, there are several concerns about group or individual decisions. Strategic decisions tend to be taken by groups and the operational decisions by individuals.

Table 8.1 sums up the kinds of problems and levels of decision that can be adopted. The choice of a model depends on the purpose of the decision, time,

Table 8.1. Types of problems and level of decision (adapted from Turban & Aronson, 1998)

Decision level / Problem type		Operational	Tactical	Strategic
Structured	Characteristics	Well-defined Repeatable	Defined Process Varied Results	Well -defined objective Several alternatives
	Duration/ Frequency	Days / a month	Months / a year	One to five years
	Decider	Operations manager	Functional Manager	Board of Directors
	Examples	Accounting Payroll	Budget Analysis Short term forecast Low	Investments Logistics
	Complexity	None		Average
Semi Structured	Characteristics	Well-Defined Varied Routine	Layers of decision	New services Planning
	Duration/ Frequency	Days / Week	Months to a year	Years
	Decider	Operations Manager	Manager, Board of Directors	Board of Directors
	Examples	Production Scheduling Inventory Control Low	Prizes Budgets	New branch offices Merger Acquisitions High
	Complexity		Average	
Nonstructured	Characteristics	Routine subject to unforeseen	Non routine	New undertakings
	Duration/ Frequency	Days/by period	Case by case	Years
	Decider	Operations Manager	Manager / Director	Board of Directors Stockholders
	Examples	Magazine Cover Newspaper Lay-out	Hiring Firing Negotiations	New products R&D New technology
	Complexity	Average	High	Very High

cost limitations, and on the *complexity* of the problem. A problem can be considered to be complex when:

a.   the number of variables and/or objectives increases (these are the *multidimensional problems with multiple objectives)*;

b.   when the occurrence of the values of the variables and/or objectives is subject to *risks or uncertainty*; and

c.   when the values of the variable and objective are defined in an *imprecise or ambiguous way (they are fuzzy)*.

Figure 8.1. Classification of decision-making problems (adapted from Choo,1998; Kickert, 1978)

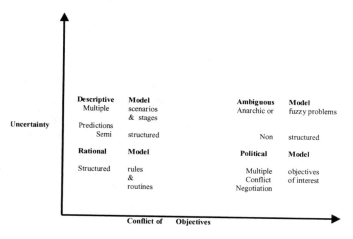

It is also possible to classify decision-making problems according to their *degree of uncertainty* (from absolute certainly to total lack of knowledge of the problem) and the level of *conflict of objectives* (involving complex, nonstructured and ambiguous problems) as shown in Figure 8.1.

According to this classification we may have four basic models of decision problems: *rational model, descriptive model, political model,* and *ambiguous model.* Examples of these models are presented in this chapter. Detailed analysis and discussion of each type of model will be given in the next chapters.

Example 8.1. Selecting a real estate

The XYZ Company analyzes three alternatives for buying land to build a new office, based on the criterion of estimated Net Profit, as follows:

Location	Cash Payment	Maintenance cost	Gross Annual Income (*)
A_1	$ 300 (**)	$ 80	$ 850
A_2	250	50	800
A_3	200	80	700

(*) Estimated. (**) in thousands of $.

Using the equation Net Profit = Gross Annual Income − (Cash Payment + Maintenance cost), we have the following profits:
A1 = 850 − (300 + 80) = 470,
A2 = 800 − (250 + 50) = 500, and
A3 = 700 − (200 + 80) = 420.

The choice for best Net Profit is real estate A_2

There is no well-defined border between the models. Many problems have characteristics of more than one model.

The Rational Model

This type of model, based on the principle of bounded rationality, defines structured decision making in situations with various possible decision alternatives. The alternatives are expressed through quantitative or qualitative variables, mathematical formulas, or transactional processes that do not involve the occurrence of uncertainty or risk. Often they are simplified representations of real problems and provide us with the first trial of the decision-making process (see Example 8.1).

The Descriptive Model

In this type of model, a decision is made according to a descriptive process similar to the procedure adopted in practice. The decision making process is aided by having the person or organization assign values to risk and uncertainty in an attempt to minimize the effect of uncertainty in the choice of alternatives. The resulting decision depends on the administrative behavior or structure adopted by the organization.

Example 8.2. Decision under risk

The following table shows returns (average profits or losses for a fixed value of investment) associated with the following strategies:
A1: Invest in Savings with fixed earnings of $300 per period
A2: *Invest in Funds*
A3: Invest in the Stock Market.

The average returns vary according to the economic situation and were obtained taking into account the possible states of the economy (Recession, Stability, or Expansion).

		Strategy A1	A2	A3
Possible States of the Economy	Probabilities	Invest in Savings	Invest in Funds	Invest in Stock Market
S$_1$:Recession	0.40	$300	$400	-$100
S$_2$:Stability	0.40	$300	$300	$200
S$_3$:Expansion	0.20	$300	$200	$700

The decision is based on the value of the Expected Monetary Value (EMV):
$EMV_1 = 0.40 \times 300 + 0.40 \times 300 + 0.20 \times 300 = \$ 300$
$EMV_2 = 0.40 \times 400 + 0.40 \times 300 + 0.20 \times 200 = \$ 320$
$EMV_3 = 0.40 \times (-100) + 0.40 \times 200 + 0.20 \times 700 = \$ 180$.

Using the criterion of maximum EMV, the best decision is strategy two.

Example 8.3. Decision on a strategy for developing a project with multiple objectives and distinct scenarios

---

A company must choose one of the following strategies to develop a certain large project:

Scenario One-

Strategy A1: Develop a project entirely inside the company itself with:
- a 20% chance of finishing the project for a Cost of $130 million and two month Delay, or
- a 30% chance of finishing the project with a Cost of $130 million and three month Delay, or
- a 50% chance of finishing the project with a Cost of $90 million and five month Delay.

Scenario Two

Strategy A2: Outsource the project taking charge of supervision with
- a 60% chance of finishing the project for a Cost of $150 million on time or
- a 40% chance of finishing the project at a Cost of $80 million with a five month Delay;

Scenario Three

Strategy A3: Develop the project in partnership with a multinational company with
- a 20% chance of finishing the project at a Cost of $150 million with no Delay, or
- a 40% chance of finishing the project at a cost of $130 million with a one month Delay, or
- a 40% chance of finishing the project at a Cost of $120 million with a three month Delay

---

The Political Model

In this case, while the decision can be based on a rational model or a descriptive model, the increase in size and complexity of the problem does not allow an individual or small group of persons to choose the best alternative, since it could depend on a more extended analysis of the problem or, on negotiation or consensus among the parties involved (Example 8.3).

Ambiguous Model

Depending on the nature of the problem and type of persons involved, problems whose description is difficult or incomplete can occur. The problem may be described in an insufficient or imprecise way. On the other hand, the problem can be well formulated, but the decision making process can be difficult or fuzzy. As a result, decisions alternatives may be "ambiguous", as frequently happens with qualitative judgment or judgments involving the merits of people or organizations.

Example: Selection of Used Cars

The evaluation of used car usually involves a number of subjective criteria such as status of interior and exterior aspects of the car other than price, mileage, and year of fabrication. Each used car available in the inventory of a used car dealer, receives a preference or utility value (graded from 0 to 1) for each item to be evaluated. The dealer keeps the computerized record of evaluation of the items, and a number of photos of the car showing its actual status is available. Thus a client can examine any car available for sale even those stored in different shops.

In the example presented by Terano et al. (1984), the selection of a car is made using three criteria defined by Shafer (1978):

- *additive evaluation* (E_{add}) corresponding to the arithmetic mean of the utility values,
- *substitutive evaluation* using the Belief function or Lower Expected Value (E_{lower}) of fuzzy theory, and
- *complementary evaluation* based on the *Plausibility function* or Upper Expected Value (E_{upper}) of fuzzy theory.

Substitutive evaluation indicates the lower limit for the existence of negative values of an evaluated car, and complementary evaluation indicates the upper limit for the existence of positive aspects.

The following five criteria, placed in ascending order of importance, can be fixed (by the dealer):

OI = { s1 = year of fabrication, s2 = exterior aspects, s3 = interior aspects, s4 = mileage , s5 = price }.

According to this order of importance, criterion "s5 = price" is the most important criterion, while "s1 = year of fabrication" is the less important criterion.

A list of subjective preferences or weights for each criterion, indicated by m(si) or mi, defined by a certain client is:

Table 8.1. Utility values for six used cars (adapted from Terano et al., 1984)

Car code	s1=year	s2=exterior	S3=interior	s4=mileage	s5=price
M718	0.4	0.3	0.4	0.6	0.8
B738	0.9	0.0	0.5	0.2	0.8
X768	0.0	0.0	0.4	0.4	0.0
Z780	0.0	0.7	0.9	0.9	0.0
A783	0.8	0.0	0.8	0.6	1.0
X785	0.5	0.3	0.8	0.9	0.5

Table 8.2. Results of evaluation of six cars according to three expected values (adapted from Terano et al., 1984)

Number	E_{lower}	rank	E_{add}	rank	E_{upper}	rank
M718	0.589	1st	0.632	3rd	0.800	3rd
B738	0.333	4th	0.505	4th	0.807	2nd
X768	0.0		0.169		0.282	
Z780	0.0		0.447	5th	0.635	5th
A783	0.588	2nd	0.749	1st	1.000	1st
X785	0.457	3rd	0.639	2nd	0.782	4th

$$PI = \{\ m1 = 0.075, m2 = 0.139, m3 = 0.026, m4 = 0.460, m5 = 0.294\ \}.$$

In this case, we can see that there is strong preference for the criterion "mileage" followed by "price" and "exterior aspects."

As we can see, there is a difference between the "importance" and "preference" of a criterion. Criterion s5 is the "most important," while the criterion s4 is the "most preferred" by the client. Mathematical reasons (Shafer, 1978) for this difference will be presented in Chapter X.

The utility values u (rl, sj), for each used car rl, l = 1, 2, ..., 6 and each criterion sj, j = 1,2,...,5 , are shown in Table 8.1.

We can note that, with the exception of car number X768, every car presents at least one positive aspect (i.e., preference value is equal to or greater than 0.7), showing that we have not the occurrence of dominance factor to eliminate some of these cars.

The values of the three expected values (E_{lower}, E_{add} and E_{upperr}) and the respective ranking number for each car are listed in Table 8.2. Details for the calculation of these results will be shown in Chapter X.

Comments

Car A783 seems to be the best choice, showing two first places and one second place, although it has a score of zero for the "exterior aspects". However, as this criterion s2 is one of the least important criteria, it could not affect this customer's selection.

Car M718 presents a more balanced situation and it is the best car with respect to the limit of negative aspects (E_{lower}). It is in a slightly lower position with respect to the limit of positive aspects ($E_{upper} = 0.800$) and the arithmetic mean, when compared with car A783.

As it would be expected, car X768 presents the worst performance in every aspect of the evaluation.

How Decision-Making Process is Analyzed in the Literature

Usually *decision-making models* fall into one of the following categories:

a.   **Normative Models** – discuss and present the mathematical or algorithmic aspects of the decision making process, taking into consideration the formal aspects (theoretical or "ideal") about *"what should be done"* in a decision making situation. Because they usually consider quantitative values, decision-making problems at the operational and tactical levels are mostly analyzed. The books of Keeney and Raiffa (1976), Luce and Raiffa (1957), Gregory (1990), and Bunn (1984) are worthy of note in this category.

b.   **Descriptive Models** – show discussions and cases involving practical aspects of *"what is usually done"* in decision making without distinguishing among the operational, tactical, or strategic decision levels. The books of Clemen and Reilly (2001), Saaty (1980, 1994, 2001) and Goodwin and Wright (1996), are examples of this category of books.

c.   **Prescriptive Models** – seeks to answer the question *"what can be done most realistically"* to improve the decision-making process, including analysis and resolution of problems with multiple criteria, conflicting objectives, and fuzzy variables. Books of Saaty (1980), Poulton (1994), Kickert (1978), and Negoita (1985) belong to this category. The books in categories a) and b) also make a prescriptive analysis of the decision-making process in their final sections.

d.   **Decision Support Systems (DSS) and Business Intelligence (BI) using Data Mining techniques** – present a general analysis of the models, structure of data and mathematical algorithms utilized to form a guide to orient the use of Decision Support Systems and Data Mining techniques. The books of Mallach (2001), Turban and Aronson (1998) and, Witten and Frank (2000) are examples in this category.

Conclusions

Starting with the model of the **administrative man** suggested by Herbert Simon, we present different ways to classify a decision-making process in order to see the characteristics of decision models mostly used for strategic decisions. We know that for the decision-making process to be viable, we need to adopt concepts based on **bounded rationality** such as "near resolution of problems" or "minimizing uncertainties."

We can list some of the factors that can contribute to successful decisions:

a.   **Responsibility and Transparency** – there are laws and penalties that should be obeyed by people or organizations making decisions.

b.   **Expertise** – each decision should be based on the deep knowledge of an expert.

c.   **Coordination** – the best decision alternatives are not sufficient if there is no coordination to transmit the orders that should be obeyed and to manage the decision-making process. We can recall that in the Battle of Waterloo, lack of coordination was one of the main factors in Napoleon's defeat by Wellington of England and Blücher of Prussia.

d.   **Economy Factor** – a decision can have a negative result or a single battle can be lost, but at the end of the war the force of economic power allied to good sense in decision making can help to make up for the loss of some battles.

e.   **Time** – an abundance of time acts with a force similar to the economy factor, allowing one to wait for favorable opportunities. On the other hand, lack of time can minimize uncertainly, but it can increase the risk of making a hasty decision. Long-term planning always involves a greater level of uncertainty.

f.   **Consensus or negotiation** – when there is an increase in the number of factors or in the complexity level of a problem, a more extended analysis of the problem and negotiation or consensus among the parties involved should be sought.

The final conclusion of this chapter is: based on Table 8.1, decision problems can be classified into structured, semi-structured and nonstructured problems. Structured decision problems have low levels of complexity while nonstructured problems present medium to high levels of complexity. To start with the structuring process and the analysis of strategic decision problems we can use these two criteria. Then, it is possible to say that, *strategic decision problems* are semi-structured or nonstructured decision problems with medium to high level of complexity.

Case Studies: Strategy and Decisions in Perspective

Case – LTCM

The near bankruptcy of the giant hedge fund shows the lack of transparency, poor investor preparation and many other problems.

(Condensed from: O Estado de S. Paulo, October 25, 1998, p. B9, written by Timothy L. O'Brien & Laura M. Holson, *The New York Times*).

Stanford Weil, one of the senior executives of the Citigroup, is an experienced risk evaluator. ...However, with regard to the gigantic hedge fund, the Long Term Capital Management (LTCM), Weil admitted that he didn't know enough about the dangerous bets that the fund was making.

LTCM...almost went bankrupt — and only survived thanks to an injection of capital...made by large real estate brokers and investment banks, under the guidance of the North American regulatory authorities, concerned with the possibility that the fund's collapse might seriously harm the global economy.

...Among the fund administrators were acclaimed economists and operators well known for making enormous profits.

"...When you have a team comprised by renamed economists and a cast of stars as operators and they have managed to obtain extraordinary profits for several years, it reinforces the Fund's image."

Large banks in the United States, Europe, Asia, and Latin America invested between US$10 million and US$100 million each, in the fund for this privilege (to receive research data and private information about the market).

Nevertheless, when the Long Term partners visited a bank abroad, this bank never sent their lower level employees — only the highest level executives met with the Long Term partners.

Fund participants agreed to provide only vague information about their methods and not to give information to some investors, loan recipients or commercial partners.

Usually, banks loan money to hedge funds for one day operations and request daily information to re-evaluate the quality of the extra guarantees. However, some institutions loaned to LTCM for months without examining the accounting ledgers. Although some institutions requested daily information, Long Term did not meet these requests. Long Term feared that if its positions were disseminated, competitors would take advantage of them, and the fund financiers deliberately did not share information among themselves.

Questions for Reflection and Discussion

1. Considering the case in the section titled LTCM, List the main causes of *"near bankruptcy"* of the fund broker LTCM.

2. What is the decision-making model of the Economic man, according to Simon?

3. What is the decision-making model of the Administrative man, according to Simon?

4. What are the basic rational concepts adopted to define a modern business model?

5.   What is understood by a structured problem? Give examples.

6.   What is understood by a semi-structured problem? Give examples.

7.   What is understood by a nonstructured problem? Give examples.

8.   Describe a rational model for the decision-making process. Give examples.

9.   Describe a descriptive model of decision. Give examples.

10. Describe a political model of decision. Give examples.

11. When does an ambiguous model of decision occur?

12. What are the basic requirements for success in the decision-making process?

Exercises

1.   Decide into which category (structured, semi or nonstructured) and at what level of decision (operational, tactical or strategic) each of the following decision-making problems falls:

   (a)   inventory management;

   (b)   sales;

   (c)   CAD/CAM system buyer;

   (d)   adoption of ISO 9000 and ISO 14000 standards by your company;

   (e)   machine replacement.

2.   Decide when and how changes in the category of problems or in the level of decision occur for each situation of the last question. For example, when does a semi-structured problem become a structured problem? When does a strategic level decision become a tactical and operational level decision?

References

Bass, B. M. (1983). *Organization decision making*. Homewood, IL: Richard D. Irwin.

Bunn, D. W. (1984). *Applied decision analysis*. New York: McGraw-Hill.

Choo, C. W. (1998). *Knowing organizations*. Oxford, UK: Oxford University Press.

Clemen, R. T., & Reilly, T. (2001). *Making hard decisions with decisions tools*. New York: Duxbury Press.

Cohen, M., et al. (1972). A garbage can model of organizational choice, *Administrative Science Quarterly, 17*(1), 1-25.

Cook, T.M., & Russel, R.A.(1993). *Introduction to management science*. NJ: Prentice-Hall.

Cyert, R. H., & March, J. G. (1963). *A behavioral theory of the firm*. NJ: Prentice-Hall.

Dyson, R.G. (Ed.) (1990). *Strategic planning: Models and analytical techniques*. New York: Wiley.

Goodwin, P., & Wright, G. (1996). *Decision analysis for management judgment*. New York: John Wiley & Sons.

Gregory, G. (1980). *Decision analysis*. New York: Pitman Books.

Hillier, F., & Libermann, G. J. (1980). *Introduction to operations research* (3rd ed.). New York: Holden Day.

Keeney, R., & Raiffa, H. (1976). *Decisions with multiple objectives: preferences and value tradeoff*. New York: Wiley & Sons.

Kickert, W. J. M. (1978). *Fuzzy theories and decision making: A critical review*. Boston; London: Martinus Nijhoff Social Science Division, Leiden.

Kinoshita, E. (1996). *Introduction to management science* (in Japanese). Tokyo: Sakurai Publishers.

Luce, R. D., & Raiffa, H. (1957). *Games and decisions*. New York: John Wiley & Sons.

Luftman, J.N., et al. (1993). Transforming the enterprise: The alignment of business and information technology strategies. *IBM Systems Journal, 32*(1), 198-221.

Mallach, E. G. (2000). *Decision support and data warehouse systems.* Singapore: McGraw-Hill International Editions.

Monks, J. G. (1985). *Operations management.* Schaun's Outline Series, New York: McGraw-Hill.

Negoita, C.V. (1985). *Expert systems and fuzzy systems.* CA: The Benjamim/Cummings Publishing.

Porter, M. E. (1980). *Competitive strategy.* New York: The Free Press.

Poulton, E. C. (1994). *Behavioral decision theory: A new approach.* Cambridge, UK: Cambridge University Press.

Saaty, T.L. (1980). *The analytic hierarchy process: Planning, priority, resource allocation.* New York: McGraw-Hill.

Shafer, G. (1976). *A mathematical theory of evidence.* NJ: Princeton University Press.

Simon, H. (1958 and 1997). *Administrative behavior* (2nd and 4th eds.). New York: The Free Press.

Terano, T., et al. (1984). *Fuzzy systems: Theory and its applications* (in Japanese). Tokyo: Ohm Publishing.

Turban, E., & Aronson, J.E. (1998). *Decision support systems and intelligent systems* (5th ed.). New York: Prentice-Hall.

Chapter IX

The Structuring Of The Strategic-Decision-Making Process

Introduction: A Systematic Procedure for Structuring the Decision-Making Process

The basic types of decision models presented in the previous chapter (rational, descriptive, political, and ambiguous models) relies on quantitative values (money, time, or probabilities) that are most suitable for structured and semi-structured decision problems. These basic models can be used as starting models to guide the structuring process of strategic decision problems. First, a systematic procedure for structuring the strategic decision making process is presented, using decision matrix and decision trees. The need for the sensitivity analysis is introduced, and will be illustrated with more detail in the next chapter. Some problems that must be considered in this structuring process are illustrated in form of *hidden traps* and *paradoxes*.

The first step in the decision-making process is to formulate the problem. It is possible that an inadequate formulation of the problem leads to a result that reduces efficiency and efficacy, since an incorrect formulation can define a wrong problem.

The person responsible for structuring the decision making model in a business is in charge of "*asking the right questions, discovering the relevant elements; identifying the significant parameters; determining the significant relationships among the selected elements and parameters; speculating about the "right size" and "correct formulation" of the problem; and evaluating the temporal characteristics (life cycles, duration, stability and discontinuity)*" (Luftman et al., 1993).

Structuring a decision-making process depends on:

a.   the *purpose* of the decision;
b.   *time* and *cost* limitations; and
c.   the *complexity* of the problem.

The solution to any decision making problem can be visualized in five stages:

1.   perception: visualizing the need and opportunity for the decision;
2.   formulation of the action alternatives: evaluate the alternatives in terms of their contributions;
3.   choosing one or more alternatives to be executed;
4.   implementation; and 50 feedback.

These stages are based on procedures known in Management Science as PDCA (Plan, Do, Check, and Action). A more specific systematic procedure for structuring a decision-making process is (Monks, 1985; Simon, 1997; Clemen & Reilly, 2001):

1.   *Define* the problem and the relevant variables (*parameters*);
2.   Establish the *criteria, factors, goals,* or *objectives* of the decision (*);
3.   Relate the parameters to the objectives, i.e., *model* the problem;
4.   Generate the decision *alternatives and the possible alternative scenarios,* for different values and parameters;

5.   Evaluate the alternatives and choose that which best satisfies the objectives;

6.   Implement the decision chosen and monitor the results through:

   (a)   *Sensitivity analysis* of the results to be able to answer "what if?"-type questions.

   (b)   *Learning,* using feedback from the results to be able to change or improve the method.

   (*)   In decision analysis, *criteria, factors, goals, and objectives* are terms used without a clear distinction. In *mathematical programming,* a *goal or an objective* is expressed by a mathematical function to be optimized.

Building the Model

A model describes, represents, and imitates the procedures that happen in the real world, establishing the relationship of the variables with the objectives in the best way possible, observing the time and cost limitations. The models can be of various types (Gordon, 1978; Monks, 1985):

a.   **Verbal** – when described and represented by phrases and sentences (examples: questionnaires, expert systems, etc.);

b.   **Physical** – when represented by some kind of material or hardware, changing their dimensions, size, or format (examples: miniature models, prototypes);

c.   **Schematic** – when represented by graphics, tables, diagrams, or decision tree;

d.   **Mathematical** – when represented by mathematical equations, numerical values, or symbolic logic values [examples: Linear programming, (Hillier & Lieberman, 1980); Neural Networks, (Takefuji, 1996), etc.]

Examples of Decision Problems

a.   **Marketing Manager:**

To launch a new product or not:

Possible decision alternatives:

  A1: Launch a new product in the market, or

  A2: Do not launch a new product in the market.

Possible states of the market:

  S1: Market in recession,

  S2: Market stable, and

  S3: Market in expansion.

b.   **Inventory Manager:**

Buying decisions:

  A1: Purchase 100 units of a product.

  A2: Purchase 300 units of a product.

  A3: Don't buy.

Possible states:

  S1: High demand,

  S2: Low demand, and

  S3: Unknown demand.

c.   **Production Manager:**

Mix of products to be assembled: $x1$ = automobiles, $x2$ = utility vehicles, $x3$ = trucks and $x4$ = buses.

Decisions:

  A1: Produce 100 units of $x1$, 50 of $x2$, 45 of $x3$ and 20 of $x4$,

  A2: Produce only automobiles,

  A3: Produce 100 units of $x1$, 100 units of $x3$ and 35 of $x4$, or

  A4: Produce 1 utility vehicle for each 5 automobiles produced.

States:

  S1: only for internal market,

  S2: only for export, and

  S3: for both internal and export market.

d.   **Service:**

Decisions:

A1: Contract two vehicles for service,

A2: Contract one larger vehicle, and

A3: Acquire a utility vehicle for one's own use.

States:

S1: Forecast of up to 50 services per month,

S2: Between 50 and 100 services per month, and

S3: Over 100 services per month.

A mathematical model can be seen as a *black box* that receives the *inputs* (parameters, exogenous variables, and decisions), and processes this information to produce *outputs* (*endogenous variables* or decision results).

Decision Problem in Matrix Form

A mathematical decision model can be organized in a matrix form where:

a.   **The columns of the matrix represent the alternatives of decision.** Each column of the matrix represents one of the possible alternatives. A_i is presented to the decider or the person who makes the decision. All the possible alternatives for the decision should be formulated. We then can say that the set of possible alternatives is exhaustive and covers all the fields of definition of the problem. The alternatives should also be mutually exclusive, i.e., one decision alternative excludes the others. The unknown alternatives should be grouped into just one set to form the alternative, "other alternatives".

b.   **Possible states assumed by the problem are set out along the line of the matrix.** All the possible states of the problem should be placed along the lines of the matrix, i.e., the alternative states that the problem can assume. The states represent the possible results of the problem (market, economy, population, etc.), or the results of actions taken by an adversary when there is a situation of conflict. The possible states S_j should form an exhaustive and mutually exclusive set. Unknown states should appear grouped along one of the lines of the matrix marked as "others." A probability value estimating the possibility of occurrence $P(S_j)$ is attributed to each S_j state.

Each element g_{ji} of the decision matrix represents the gain (profit, loss, or cost) of alternative A_j (column j of the matrix) when state S_i occurs. The values of these results should be predefined for all the possible alternatives and states. In general, these values are approximated or estimated values based on past experience and problems of the same type.

The occurrence of each state is not always certain as to what happens with no-risk-rational-decision problems. In the case of uncertainty or risk, each Sj state is associated with a probability $P(Sj)$. Since the possible states should form an exhaustive set and should be mutually exclusive, the sum of probability of all the states is equal to one. The value of each probability also should be estimated by an expert or by the group of person of the decision-making process.

A decision matrix has the following format:

States	Probabilities	Decision A_1	Decision A_2		Decision A_n
S_1	$P(S_1)$	g_{11}	g_{21}	...	g_{n1}
S_2	$P(S_2)$	g_{12}	g_{22}	...	g_{n2}
...					
S_m	$P(S_m)$	g_{1m}	g_{2m}	...	g_{nm}

Decision Tree

A decision matrix represents a decision process to be resolved in a single stage. A decision tree is used to represent a sequential decision making process through more than one stage of the decision (Figure 9.1).

A decision tree is a schematic representation useful for representing the process of decision making with multiple variables, multiple objectives, and multiple decision stages, while the decision matrix represents just one of the stages in the decision-making process.

The decision tree structures any complex decision problem in a clear way since it can identify the alternatives, the states and the possible scenarios. However, its visualization becomes difficult when the size and complexity of the problem increase, even using the resource of a computer software. This restriction is true for all other types of representations of decision problems.

Figure 9. 1. A decision tree

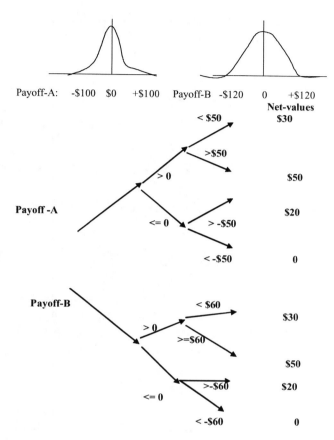

Basic Structures of Decisions Problems

We are now ready to present the basic structures of decision problems found in the literature of decision analysis. In the next chapters, these structures will be expanded in the sense to include the complex factors and nonstructured aspects that are common in strategic-decision problems (Clemen & Reilly, 2001; Keeney & Raiffa, 1976; Naylor et al., 1971).

Decision problems to select the best alternative under no-risk, uncertainty, or risk situations will be discussed. For all cases, decision problems with single or multiple criteria or goals, using utility values, will be presented. Also, a decision model updated using feedback from additional information will be presented.

Decision Problem with No Risk and One Criterion or Goal

This decision problem has:

a.   several decision alternatives (for instance, property A1, A2 and A3), and

b.   one criterion or goal: cash payment, payment in 4 or 12 installments.

Since this is a problem with no risks or uncertainties, all the relevant information (gains or losses referring to each decision alternative) is known and the decision maker chooses the alternative related to the best possible result.

Example 9.1: Select a Property According to Highest Net Income

Company XYZ analyzes 3 alternatives for buying a building for a branch office, based on the Net Income Criterion which depends on the different forms of payment used. For each property, A1, A2. or A3, there are three payment alternatives (cash, 4 or 12 installments), and the Net Incomes, in thousand of dollars, are:

Decision Matrix

Criteria \ Properties	A1	A2	A3
Cash	$ 470	$ 500	$ 420
4 installments	460	470	415
12 installments	460	450	450

This decision involves no risk or uncertainty, since the three alternatives are known and mutually exclusive and the choice of payment depends entirely on the decision maker's wish. Alternative A3 has all decision values lower or equal to those of A2 and, thus, it is *dominated* by A2 and can be discarded from the decision process. So, there are only two alternatives left, A1 and A2.

The decision can be made using the Min/Max or Max/Min principles (Hillier & Lieberman, 1980; Cook & Russel, 1993). The Min/Max principle is known as the *optimistic* decision; since it minimizes the highest income, while the Max/Min principle is know as the *pessimistic* decision, since it maximizes the lowest income.

a. **Decision using the Max/Min principle.** Using the Max/Min principle, one should *"choose the strategy offering the highest value among the lowest values of each strategy"*, that is, Max/Min = Maximum (Minimum value of A1 and A2) = Max (460, 450) =460. This value refers to alternative A1.

b. **Decision using the Min/Max principle.** According to this criteria, one should *"choose the strategy offering the lowest value among the highest values of each strategy"*, that is, Min/Max = Min (470, 500) = 470. This value also refers to alternative A1. Thus, we have Min/Max = Max/Min, in this example.

Decision with No Risk and More Than One Criterion or Goal

When a decision problem has several criteria or goals expressed in different units, (for instance, expected income, distance, etc.) it is necessary to transform each one of these values into the same *unit of measurement.* In a given decision, the value of income cannot be mixed with other objective, such as competitive edge, (expressed by the property's location), comfort (the number of rooms, visibility, etc.), or area (in square meters).

All these values should be transformed into the same unit called *satisfaction level or utility,* whose values vary from 0 (to the worst level of satisfaction) to 1 (to the best level of satisfaction) (Luce & Raiffa, 1957; Goodwin & Wright, 1996).

Another difficulty refers to the conflicting nature of these goals, as in the case of *minimization of cost and maximization of employee labor conditions,* because the best solution to minimize cost usually may not maximize labor conditions. The three goals (net income, competitive edge and available area) of Example 9.2 are to be maximized, but the best solutions for each goal correspond to different alternatives.

There is no solution fully satisfying all goals considered. A consensual solution based on the Pareto's principle is usually adopted.

> The *Pareto's Principle (Goicoechea et al., 1982; Hillier & Lieberman, 1980)*
>
> *If a solution x* of a problem with k goals f_k (x) is such that it is not possible to find any solution x with f_k (x) better than f_k (x*) for all k goals, then x* is an optimum Pareto solution.*

Example 9.2: Select a Property Considering Net Income and Two Kinds of Benefits (adapted from Goodwin & Wright, 1996)

Company XYZ studies three alternatives for buying a property for a new branch office, according to three different goals: *net income*, based on cash payment, *competitive edge*, given by the distance of the property from the commercial center, and *total available area*. We have the following values:

Criteria \ Properties	A1	A2	A3
1 – Net income (thousands of $)	$ 470	$ 500	$ 420
2 – Competitive edge (Distance from commercial center)	150 m	250 m	500 m
3 – Available area	600 m^2	400 m^2	1500 m^2

Establishing Utility Values

The worst and the best values of each goal should correspond to values 0 and 1 of the utility function, respectively. Utilities for the intermediate values are determined using different utility curves and will be explained in the next chapter.

For example, we can have the following utility values:

	Net Income	Utility	Distance	Utility	Available Area	Utility
Best Value	$ 500	1	150 m	1	1500 m2	1
	$ 470	0.7	250 m	0.6	600 m2	0.3
Worst value	$ 420	0	500 m	0	400 m2	0

Weighting the Criteria or Goals

In general, the three criteria should not be given equal weights, and the company should choose the criterion with the greatest importance. If, for the company, Net Income is the most important criterion or objective, then it gets a *relative weight* equal to 1.

Each of the other criteria should get a relative weight according to the answer given to the following question:

> *What is the importance of this criterion, in percentage terms, in relation to the Net Income?*

If the answer is "lower than 20%," possibly this criterion could be discarded, simplifying the solution of the problem.

The following table shows the relative and the normalized values of weights, the utility values for the three properties, and the weighted average:

Criteria/Property	Relative weights	Normalized Weights	Values A1	Of A2	Utilities A3
1 – Net Income	1.00	W1 = 0.43	0.7	1	0
2 – Distance from center	0.50	W1 = 0.22	1	0.6	0
3 – Available area	0.80	W3 = 0.35	0.3	0	1
Sums	2.30	1.00			
Total average			0.626	0.562	0.350

Thus, property A1 should be chosen according to the best value of weighted utility average.

Sensitivity Analysis

The value of weights may alter the decision result. If we attribute a zero weight to Net Income and the same relative weights of 0.50 and 0.80 are kept for the two other criteria, the property chosen will be the property A3.

In order to analyze the variation of the three weights it is possible to use a two-dimensional chart, placing the variation of the sum of two of the three weights (for instance, $p = W2 + W3$) on the horizontal axis, and the variation of the utility average on the vertical axis. The third weight W1 corresponds to the value 1 − p. For instance, for p ≤ 0.5, the best decision is to buy property A2, while for p between 0.5 and 0.9, the best decision is property A1. For p ≥ 0.90 and weight (Income) W1 ≤ 0.1, the best decision is property A3.

Subjective Perception of Risk

(Excerpted from: *Subjective Perception of Risk*, Mark Fenton-O'Creevy and Emma Soane, Financial Times, Mastering Risk, Part I, May 2, 2000, pp. 14-15).

Risk perception is a complex and subjective process. In finances, risk is usually considered as a combination of the values of expected loss or gain and the variability of this expected result. Human perception of risk acts in a different way. There are two important risk components affecting our perception: the *fear factor* — referring to fear of potential result — and the *control factor* — referring to the level of control over events. For instance, risk perception is very high in a nuclear accident due to the fear factor or, it is higher for a car passenger than the driver, due to control perception. In the financial market, both factors are important – fear and anticipation of losses often control our actions. One financial broker stated that "we often make decisions based more on the fear of losing, than the hope of winning."

The largest risk perception component is in how we perceive gain and loss. Persons in a winning position of a game increasingly have an aversion to risk, since they want to keep their gains, while individuals in a losing position are more willing to take risks, because they have less to lose.

However, what we perceive as gain or loss depends on the personal standpoint, which changes according to the situation and over time.

Decision Problem Under Uncertainty or Risk

Economic and financial theories often make sure that a person makes optimum use of available intuition as a basis for a rational decision, but research and verification of daily behavior shows that human behavior is significantly different from this statement.

In many decision problems, the states of nature occur with a certain level of uncertainty known as risk. It is then no longer possible to apply the Min/Max or Max/Min principle since the risk occurrence with different probabilities does not allow the choice of a greater or smaller gain value. One needs to obtain the average or expected values.

In order to establish the probability values representing the uncertainty level or risk, the decision maker must receive information by (Charan, 2001; Edwards, 1975; Li & Ye, 1999):

- consulting experts,
- gathering data,
- bibliographical research on the issue, etc.

In this chapter, the application of sensitivity analysis and the use of different types of utility function are explained with more detail, using the Example 8.1 shown in Chapter VIII as an example of the descriptive model of decision.

Example 9.3: Decision with Uncertainty (presented as Example 8.1 - Descriptive model of decision, in Chapter VIII)

The following table shows the average return (profits or losses for a certain investment value) associated to the following strategies:

A1: Investing in savings accounts with fixed earnings of $300 per period

A2: Investing in fixed earnings funds

A3: Investing in the stock market

The average return varies according to the economic situation considering the possible economy states (recession, stability, or expansion).

		Strategy A1	A2	A3
Possible states of the economy	Probabilities	Savings	Funds	*stocks market*
S_1:Recession	p1 = 0.40	\$300	\$400	-\$100
S_2:Estability	p2 = 0.40	\$300	\$300	\$200
S_3:Expansion	p3 = 0.20	\$300	\$200	\$700

Decision based on the highest average or expected monetary value.

As we already know by the example of descriptive model of decision shown in Chapter VIII, the Expected Monetary Values (EMV) of the alternatives are:

$$EMV_1 = 0.40 \times 300 + 0.40 \times 300 + 0.20 \times 300 = \$300$$
$$EMV_2 = 0.40 \times 400 + 0.40 \times 300 + 0.20 \times 200 = \$320$$
$$EMV_3 = 0.40 \times (-100) + 0.40 \times 200 + 0.20 \times 700 = \$180$$

The best decision is strategy A2, followed by A1, and finally A3.

Figure 9.2. Sensitivity Analysis Chart: Best decision alternative for several values of probabilities p1, p2, and p3 = 1 –p1 –p2, for example 10.1. (adapted from Clemen & Reilly (2001)

p2											
1.0	*A1= A2*										
0.9	*A1*	A2									
0.8	*A1 = A3*	*A1= A2*	A2								
0.7	A3	*A1*	A2	A2							
0.6	A3	A3	*A1= A2*	A2	A2						
0.5	A3	A3	*A1*	A2	A2	A2					
0.4	A3	A3	A3	*A1= A2*	A2	A2	A2				
0.3	A3	A3	A3	A3	A2	A2	A2	A2			
0.2	A3	A3	A3	A3	*A1= A2*	A2	A2	A2	A2		
0.1	A3	A3	A3	A3	A3	A2	A2	A2	A2	A2	
0.0	A3	A3	A3	A3	A3	*A1=A2=A3*	A2	A2	A2	A2	A2
	0.0	0.1	0.2	0.3	0.4	0.5	0.6	0.7	0.8	0.9	1.0 p1

Sensitivity Analysis

It is helpful to check the variation of expected values for different probability values p1, p2, and p3, thus getting a chart that allows the analysis of strategic limits of investments risks.

In order to assess value variations for p1, p2, and p3, the chart suggested by Clemen and Reilly (2001) is adopted and shown in Figure 9.2. Since there are three variables p1, p2, and p3, the values for p1 are placed on the horizontal axis and p2 on the vertical axis. Values of p3 are implicitly expressed by the property p1 + p2 + p3 = 1. For instance, if p1 = 0 and p2 = 0, then p3 = 1; if p1 = 0.2 and p2 = 0.2, then p3 = 0.6, and so on.

In case of more than three risk possibilities, the sensitivity assessment using a chart becomes impossible. In Sensitivity Analysis chart of Figure 9.2, each point (p1, p2) contains the name of the best Aj alternative for a given risk value (p1, p2, p3). For instance, in the numerical example seen, we have p1 = 0.4, p2 = 0.4 and p3 = 0.2 with the expected EMV_1 values = 300, EMV_2 = 320 and EMV_3 = 180. Thus, point (0.4, 0.4) will have A2 as the best alternative.

Once the best expected value is obtained for all different probability values, expressed by the points (p1, p2) in the chart, the strategic regions where each Aj investment alternative is the best solution are easily known.

The Role of Utility Function

A "*decision based only on expected monetary values*" may not be perfect since it does not analyze every earning possibility, such as highest profit or worst loss. Besides, expected value based on numeric values such as money, dimension, or age does not allow the inclusion of nonquantitative criteria such as "client satisfaction", "product quality", etc. The decision based on the "*level of satisfaction or utility function*," associated to each quantitative or non quantitative (or qualitative) value, best expresses the decision alternatives.

In the Example 9.3, a decision should consider other factors involving the decision maker's interests. Using the expected monetary values EMV, a player or decision maker should never get the highest earning of $700 given in alternative A3, even at the risk of losing (-$100). Utility function transforms quantitative and qualitative values in corresponding utility values, allowing better analysis of complex decision problems.

Risk Neutral Decision-Making

If the decision maker is risk neutral, he or she would use the risk neutral curve of Figure 9.3 and would probably not choose alternative A3, where $700 is the highest earning value and $100 represents a loss.

A risk neutral decision maker is usually a midsized or large organization with long experience in its activity. Thus, data placed on the decision matrix were analyzed by a consultant team, and there would be no reason to doubt the linear behavior of these values.

Risk Averter Decision-Making

Using the risk aversion curve of Figure 9.3 for the Example 9.3, one may have, for instance:

Monetary values	Utilities
$ 700	1
400	0.85
300	0.75
200	0.62
− 100	0

Figure 9.2. Utility curves for Example 9.3

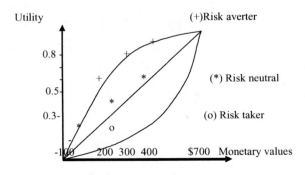

The average values using these utility values are:

$$EMV_1 = 0.4 \times 0.75 + 0.4 \times 0.75 + 0.2 \times 0.75 = 0.75;$$
$$EMV_2 = 0.4 \times 0.85 + 0.4 \times 0.75 + 0.2 \times 0.62 = 0,764; \text{ and}$$
$$EMV_3 = 0.4 \times 0 \quad + 0.4 \times 0.62 + 0.2 \times 1 = 0.448.$$

Risk averter decision makers wishing to maximize their personal satisfaction with the utility function would choose alternative A2. A risk averter person or organization is one with small amount of resources or with little experience in this kind of decision. A risk averter cannot count on counseling or assistance from other people or organizations to explain the pros and cons of the alternatives presented. However, there are different risk aversion levels, depending on whether there is greater or lesser knowledge of the problem. For instance, when buying real state, both the homemaker who wishes to buy a house and the real estate broker may be risk averters. The homemaker's risk aversion level is usually higher than the broker's.

Risk Taker Decision-Making

By using the curve expressing *"risk taker or risk preference"* in Figure 9.2, the decision maker may get, for instance, the following expected earnings: $EMV_1 = 0.18$, $EMV_2 = 0.217$ and $EMV_3 = 0.25$ and thus could choose alternative A3, where there is highest risk, but with earning possibilities of $700. A person or organization prefers to take risks when believes that the reward is worth the risk or when the time frame limit enforces a risky alternative.

Decision Model with Learning, Using Additional Information

Learning process in descriptive models of decision can be made using the adaptive or feedback model of statistics. The best known learning process is made using Bayes' Theorem, in which prior values of probabilities can be updated by additional information collected through a new sampling process (Shamblin & Stevens, 1980; Hillier & Liebermann, 1980; Takahashi, 1997). This process can be repeated many times, renewing the values of probabilities at each step of decision. The following Example 9.4 illustrates this process.

Example 9.4. Renewing Probabilities in an Opinion Survey

Senator Bill Hernandez (BH) is a candidate for the next presidential election. His supporting committee hired an opinion research company to conduct, in each month prior to the election day, a nationwide opinion survey about the preference of the electoral population, whether preferring Senator BH or the other adversary. The results of the last research, expressed in probability terms were: $P(S1)= P(BH$ wins$)= 0.3$, $P(S2)= P$ (there is a tie$)= 0.3$, and $P(S3)= P$ (Adversary wins$)= 0.4$.

After each round of the research, one of the following decisions must be taken by the supporting committee:

A1 = {Raise more funds for the campaign} or

A2 = {Invite the other candidate for a debate in nationwide TV network} or

A3 = {Continue the campaign as previously planned}.

The payoff values in terms of numbers of voters estimated to be won or lost for each probability value and decision alternative, are:

Results Sj of research	Probability	Decision A1 Raise more funds	A2 Debate in TV network	A3 Continue the campaign
S1: BH wins	0.30	100,000	100,000	50,000
S2: Tie	0.30	150,000	200,000	-50,000
S3:Other candidate wins	0.40	50,000	150,000	-200,000

Average values of win or loss of number of voters for each decision alternative are:

$$EA1 = 0.3 \times 100,000 + 0.3 \times 150,000 + 0.4 \times 50,000 = 95,000;$$
$$EA2 = 0.3 \times 100,000 + 0.3 \times 200,000 + 0.4 \times 150,000 = 150,000; \text{ and}$$
$$EA3 = 0.3 \times 50,000 + 0.3 \times (-50,000) + 0.4 \times (-200,000) = (-80,000).$$

Thus, the best decision alternative is A2.

Fifteen days after the nationwide survey, a small scale opinion survey including only the major capital cities, is conducted in the sense of updating the results of the previous survey. The result of this small scale survey, called *additional information* F, predicted that F = {BH wins in the major capital cities}.

Based on this addition information F, the opinion research company will predict whether or not candidate BH wins. The difficulty is that the result of this small scale survey, made only in major capital cities, does not always coincide with the final result of the election.

In the past, the supporting committee observed that 60% of the time, this additional research predicted that "BH wins in major capitol cities", then the election was actually won by BH. This fact can be expressed as the conditional probability P (F / S1)= 0,6.

On the other hand, 40% of time the additional research predicted that "BH wins in major capitol cities", the election ended in a tie between the two candidates, while only 20% of time, the election was actually won by the other candidate. Then, for the additional information F we have the other two conditional probabilities: P (F / S2) = 0.4 and P (F / S3)= 0.2. Using probability formula we have:

$$P (F) = P \{BH \text{ wins in major capitol cities}\}=$$
$$0.3 \times 0.6 + 0.3 \times 0.4 + 0.4 \times 0.2 = 0.38.$$

New probabilities values (known as posterior probabilities) updated by this additional information F, according to Bayes' Theorem are:

$$\text{Prob}(S1 / F)= (0.3 \times 0.6)/ 0.38 = 0.474,$$
$$\text{Prob}(S2 / F)= (0.3 \times 0.4)/ 0.38 = 0.316, \text{ and}$$
$$\text{Prob}(S3 / F)= (0.4 \times 0.2)/ 0.38 = 0.210.$$

The new payoff table using these probabilities is:

Results Sj	Probability	Decision A1 Raise more funds	A2 Debate in TV network	A3 Continue the campaign
S1: BH wins	0.474	100,000	100,000	50,000
S2: Tie	0.316	150,000	200,000	-50,000
S3:Other candidate wins	0.210	50,000	150,000	-200,000

After this additional information F, average values of win or loss of voters for each decision are:

$$EA1 = 0.474 \times 100,000 + 0.316 \times 150,000 + 0.210 \times 50,000 = 105,200,$$

$$EA2 = 0.474 \times 100,000 + 0.316 \times 200,000 + 0.210 \times 150,000 = 165,800,$$
and

$$EA3 = 0.474 \times 50,000 + 0.316 \times (-50,000) + 0.210 \times (-200,000) = -34,100.$$

Best decision is again A2, and the additional information F = {BH wins in major capital cities} reinforces this strategy.

Each month, after the results of the nationwide opinion survey, this updating process can be repeated.

Additional Problems That Must Be Considered in Structuring a Strategic-Decision-Model

It is important to remind us that in a strategic-decision-making procedure many other factors become more and more difficult and complex in a systematic way to structure the decision process. The systematic structuring methodology presented in the previous sections are valid for decision problems of tactical or operational levels and must be considered as a starting procedure for strategic-decision problems.

Many types of difficulties must be considered when a strategic-decision problem is to be structured. These difficulties are reported by researchers in the form of *paradoxes* or *hidden traps* that reflect the different aspects of human behavior under uncertainty, risk or complexity to determine a consistent list of decision alternatives.

Most of the difficulties are related to the problem of how an individual or group's risk attitude can change depending on the way the decision problem is posed. A person may have different attitudes (risk neutral, risk preference or aversion to risk) to lose a certain amount of money during the initial and final phase of a gamble or, when the total amount of money available to play the game or invest in the stock market is small or large.

A person's or group's attitude can change depending on many factors such as time, financial situation, or responsibilities according to the problem to be solved. This fact is known as *framing problem* because different persons can see different frames (of values or structures), simplifying the reality.

The effects of *hidden traps* mentioned in a Case Study, as well as *Allais or Ellsberg's paradox* can be minimized forming different decision alternatives given by different groups of persons. These alternatives are discussed and a final decision can be reached by negotiation or by the use of votes. *St. Petersburg's paradox* is concerned with the possibility of unknown value of probability expectation but the use of utility value can help to solve the problem.

The Paradoxes

St. Petersburg's paradox (Takahashi, 1997; Clemen & Reilly, 2001; Goodwin & Wright, 1996)

Let us consider the following two types of coin tossing game which must be held until the first occurrence of "head."

Game I:

If the first *head* occurs in the first trial, the player receives $2; if it occurs in the second trial, he or she receives $4, and son on, until the occurrence of head in the k-th trial, when he or she receives $$2^k$.

Game II:

Whichever trial occurs head for the first time, the player receives a fixed amount of money $W. Which one of the games must a player select?

Game II gives always the Expected Value E2 = $ W.

Expected Value of Game I is E1 = ∞, according to probability theory. Thus, the profit in Game I is, at least theoretically, greater than any value of profit in Game II. But in Game I, we assume that the profit is greater than any amount $W if the coin is tossed an infinite number of times. What is the meaning of "infinite number of times"? The answer is the number K of trials of a coin until the first occurrence of a head has a geometric distribution with expected value E(K) =

1/p, or E(K) = 2, for the case of the coin, where p=1/2. Thus Game II will be preferred when the expected monetary value $ W is greater than $2, which is a value far from infinite.

This paradox can be solved using the utility function, that shows that game II must be preferred when the monetary value $W is more than $4, which satisfies the decision based on the expected value of the geometric distribution.

b.   Allais's Paradox (Takahashi, 1997; Goodwin & Wright, 1996; Raiffa, 2002)

This paradox presents the following two games in which decision based on utility values reaches contradictory relations.

		Profit	Probability
Game 1	Option A	$ 200	1.00
	Option B	$1000	0.10
		200	0.89
		0	0.01
Game 2	Option C	$ 200	0.11
		0	0.89
	Option D	$1000	0.10
		0	0.90

Questions

Which of the two options (A or B) would you choose in Game I?

Which of the two options (C or D) would you choose in Game II?

Game 1:

Usually, due to the fixed profit of Option A, persons consider that the utility value of A is greater than the utility value of B, or:

U(A)>= U(B), or

U(200)>= 0.10 x U(1000)+ 0.89xU(200)+ 0.01x U(0) and then

0.11 x U(200)>= 0.10 x U(1000) + 0.01 x U(0).

Game 2:

The probability of profit $200 of option C is similar to the probability of profit $1000 of option D. It seems reasonable that persons prefer a greater profit ($1000 versus $200). Using utility we have:

U(C)<=U (D)or

0.11 x U(200)+ 0.89 x U(0)<= 0.10 x U(1000)+ 0.90 x U(0)and then

0.11 x U(200) <= 0.10 x U(1000)+ 0.01 x U(0).

Thus, this paradox presents two contradictory inequalities, which may be explained by the fact that utility theory does not attempt to describe the way in which people choose a utility value.

c.   A final paradox (Ellsberg's Paradox) solves Allais's paradox considering different attitudes of persons' preference with respect to uncertainty and risk: neutral to risk, aversion to risk, and preference to risk, relaxing the fundamental law of probability theory, where the sum of the probabilities of all the events must be equal to 1.

Conclusions

In this chapter, steps to structure a decision model through a systematic way, based on the PDCA (Plan, Do, Check, and Action) principle, were presented. The decision matrix and decision tree are tools used to organize a starting model of a strategic-decision problem. A decision matrix is used to represent a one-stage decision problem while a decision tree is used to represent a sequence of decision-making stages.

Examples of problems to select the best alternative under no risk, uncertainty, or risk situation were presented. For all cases, decision problems with single or multiple criteria or goals, using utility values, were presented. A decision model updated using feedback from additional information was also presented.

Difficulties to be considered in the structuring process of decision models are illustrated in the form of *paradoxes* or *hidden traps* that reflect the different aspects of human behavior under uncertainty, risk, or complexity, to determine a consistent list of decision alternatives.

In the following chapters, we will extend the structuring process described in this chapter, to more general and different kinds of strategic-decision-making problems.

Case Studies: Strategy and Decisions in Perspective

Case – The Hidden Traps in Decision-Making

(Excerpted from "The Hidden Traps in Decision Making ", by J .S. Hammond, R. L. Keeney and H. Raiffa, *Harvard Business Review*, September- October, 1998, pp. 47 to 54)

"In making decisions, your own mind may be your worst enemy."

What are the causes of a bad decision? Due to the complexity in structuring and formulating a decision-making problem and the high level of subjective judgment, bad decisions occur frequently. The "hidden traps" which accompany the decision-making process can cause errors in the formulation and structuring of a decision problem, as well as in choosing the correct alternative.

The main traps are:

1.   **"the anchoring trap"** – one of the most common types of an anchor (a weight that hangs from the ship in the same place) is a fixation on the "historical past" or "worldwide trend" or on "tradition";

2. **"the status-quo trap"** – the innovative alternatives tend to be similar to those that have been abandoned, or are just the same idea presented in a different way, i.e. there is an accommodation to remain in the same status;

3. **"the sunk-cost trap"** – many decisions try to take losses (or gains) from the past into account, even though they are irrecoverable;

4. **"the confirming-evidence trap"** – many decisions are based on evidences assumed in a polemical manner, such as "investing in television advertising is essential", "we must invest in R&D", etc.;

5. **"the framing trap"** – the same problem can be represented by a decision tree or table in a different way, depending on the point of view adopted;

6. **"the estimating and forecasting trap"** – the effects of subjective or superficial judgments should be minimized in the estimation of values or demand forecasting;

7. **"the overconfidence and prudence trap"** – excessive confidence or caution is not recommended in obtaining information or making decisions.

One way to minimize the occurrence of "bad decisions" is to use the process of Sensibility Analysis, submitting a decision to controlled variations of the values involved. This analysis can be done if there is an opportunity to ask questions such as "WHAT IF?" at any given moment.

Questions for Reflection and Discussion

1. Consider the case in the section titled *The Hidden Traps in Decision-Making* and comments on the "hidden traps" existing in the decision-problem examples in this and in the previous chapter.

2. Explain the role of a sensitivity analysis in a decision-making process.

3. What are the elements of a decision matrix?

4. What are the steps for systematically structuring the decision-making process?

5. What is a decision tree and what is it used for?

Exercises

1. Project:

   Make up several groups with five people at most in each. Use the Sunday classified ads from some national newspapers and construct the decision model (the decision matrix and the decision tree) for the following problems:

   (a) Select a residential property;

   (b) Select a piece of land to install a branch office of your company;

   (c) Choose a job;

   (d) Select a candidate for the position of manager;

   (e) Choose a new automobile;

   (f) Select a used car.

   Each problem should have at least five decision alternatives, i.e., choose five residential properties, five pieces of land, five cars, etc. The parameters and objectives or criteria for the decision should be defined by each group. Compare the decision matrixes constructed by different groups and discuss the causes for existing differences.

2. The Zeta Company has two alternatives to advertise an event in a newspaper, in its next special edition. The conditions for each ad are:

Conditions/Newspaper	A	B
Cost	$5000	$4000
Page	2nd	5th
Payment	Cash	3 installments
Circulation	High	Medium

   Find the best alternative.

3. Explain the main difficulties caused by the problems mentioned in the paradoxes.

References

Bass, B. M. (1983). *Organization decision making*. Homewood, IL: Richard D. Irwin.

Charan, R. (2001). Conquering a culture of indecision. Harvard *Business Review, 79*(4), 75-82.

Clemen, R. T., & Reilly, T. (2001). *Making hard decisions with decisions tools*. New York: Duxbury Press.

Cook, T.M., & Russel, R.A.(1993). *Introduction to management science*. NJ: Prentice-Hall.

Dyson, R.G. (Ed.). (1990). *Strategic planning: models and analytical techniques*. New York: Wiley.

Edwards, W. (1975). Cognitive process and the assessment of subjective probability distributions. *Journal of the American Statistical Association, 70*(350), 291-293.

Goicoechea, A., et al. (1982). *Multi-objective decision analysis with engineering and business applications*. New York: John Wiley & Sons.

Goodwin, P., & Wright, G. (1996). *Decision analysis for management judgment*. New York: John Wiley & Sons.

Gregory, G. (1980). *Decision analysis*. New York: Pitman Books.

Hammond, J. S., Keeney, R. L., & Raiffa, H. (1998). The hidden traps in decision making. *Harvard Business Review, 76*(5), 47-58.

Hillier, F., & Libermann, G. J. (1980). *Introduction to operations research* (3rd ed.). New York: Holden Day.

Keeney, R., & Raiffa, H. (1976). *Decisions with multiple objectives: preferences and value tradeoff*. New York: Wiley & Sons.

Kinoshita, E. (1996). *Introduction to management science* (in Japanese). Tokyo: Sakurai Publishers.

Li, M., & Ye, L.R. (1999). Information technology and firm performance: Linking with environmental, strategic and managerial contexts. *Information & Management, 35*(1), 43-51.

Luce, R. D., & Raiffa, H. (1957). *Games and decisions*. New York: John Wiley & Sons.

Monks, J. G. (1985). *Operations management*. Schaun's Outline Series, New York: McGraw-Hill.

Naylor, T., et al. (1971). *Computer simulation experiments with models of economic systems*. New York: John Wiley & Sons.

Phillips, M. E., & Brown, C. E. (1991). Need an expert? Ask a computer. *Journal of Accountancy, 5*, 91-93.

Raiffa, H. (2002). *Negotiation analysis — The science and art of collaborative decision making*. Cambridge, MA: Harvard University Press.

Shamblin, J., & Stevens, G.T. (1980). *Operations research: An algorithmic approach*. New York: McGraw-Hill.

Takahashi, N. (1997). *Decision analysis inside the organization* (in Japanese). Tokyo: Assakura Publishers.

Takefuji, Y. (1996). *Neural computing* (in Japanese). Tokyo: Corona Publishers.

Turban, E., & Aronson, J.E. (1998). *Decision support systems and intelligent systems* (5th ed.). New York: Prentice-Hall.

Chapter X

The Nature Of Strategic-Decision-Making Models

Decision with Multiple Criteria and Multiple Scenarios

We will now study more complex problems considering:

Multiple criteria or goals:

- considering earnings or costs, delays, client satisfaction, etc, and

Multiple scenarios:

- where each scenario has a different risk level.

In the multiple goal function problems, there is no optimum solution fully satisfying all goals at the same time. The individual goal's functions are, in general, conflicting and it is not possible to have an optimization method to solve the problem. There is usually a *consensus* solution satisfying minimal criteria of optimum values for each individual goal function. This consensus is based on the *Pareto's principle* presented in chapter nine. The optimal decision making in problems with multiple goals will be analyzed at the end of this chapter (Goicoechea et al., 1982; Keeney & Raiffa, 1976; Dyson, 1990; Saaty, 1980, 1994; Bonabeau, 2003; Charan, 2001; Choo, 1998; Day et al., 1997).

In considering restrictions across several scenarios, the problem solution becomes more difficult due to the high number of possible combinations of goal functions and scenarios to be considered.

Using classical mathematical programming notation, the optimization problem with k goals and w scenarios could be formulated as follows:

Maximize (or Minimize) $F(x) = (f_1(x), f_2(x),..., f_k(x))$

With restrictions:

Scenario 1: $g_{1j}(x) \leq 0$, $(j=1,2,..., m_1)$ *and* $x \in R^n$;

...

Scenario w: $g_{wj}(x) \leq 0$, $(j=1,2,..., m_w)$ *and* $x \in R^n$;

An efficient algorithm for this kind of problem has not yet been presented, unless using some kind of heuristic techniques. It should be noted that the mathematical programming problem formulated above does not consider the event of uncertainty or risk, which, in this case, would involve stochastic or probabilistic mathematical programming.

Thus, the decision-making process is one of the methodologies indicated to resolve these problems, since it does not depend on complex mathematics involving scenario restrictions and multiple goals' functions (Warfield, 1978, 1994).

Example 10.1.

A strategic decision with multiple goals and different scenarios (Presented in Chapter VIII, as Example 8.3. Illustration of a political model of decision.)

A company must choose one of the following strategies to develop a large project.

Strategy or scenario A1:
Develop the project entirely in the company, with:

- 20% chance of finishing the project at a cost of $130 (million) and delay of 2 months,
- 30% chance of finishing the project at a cost of $130 and delay of 3 months, or
- 50% chance of finishing the project at a cost of $90 delay of 5 months.

Strategy or scenario A2:
Outsource the project and supervise it with:

- 60% chance of finishing the project at a cost of $150 (million) without delay, or
- 40% chance of finishing the project at a cost of $80 with a delay of 5 months.

Strategy or scenario A3:
Develop the project in partnership with a multinational company with:

- 20% chance of finishing the project at a cost of $150 (million) without delay,
- 40% chance of finishing the project at a cost of $130 with delay of 1 month, or
- 40% chance of finishing the project at a cost of $120 with delay of 3 months.

Decision Tree

By placing the problem on a decision tree we have:

Strategy	Probabilities	Goal 1 Delay (months)	Goal 2 Cost
A1: Develop inside the company →	0.2 →	2 →	130
	0.3 →	3 →	130
	0.5 →	5 →	90
A2: Outsource →	0.6 →	0 →	150
	0.4 →	5 →	80
A3: Partnership with multinational company →	0.2 →	0 →	150
	0.4 →	1 →	130
	0.4 →	3 →	120

Utility Values

As shown before, the conversion of any kind of value (quantitative or non quantitative values) into utility values is made, first, by placing each goal value in order. Then, the value with highest preference is given the utility value of one and the value of lowest preference receives the utility value of zero. The utility values for the intermediate values are reached using the utility curve shown on Figure 10.1. The *risk neutral utility* curve shows the following results:

Delay (months) $x1$	Utilities $u(x1)$
0	1
1	0.8
2	0.6
3	0.4
5	0

Costs $x2$ ($ millions)	Utilities $u(x2)$
80	1
90	0.9
100	0.8
110	0.5
120	0.4
130	0.3
150	0

Joint Utility for the Two Goals: Delay and Cost

Since there are two goals (or attributes x1 and x2) each value of the utility must be found by combining utilities u(x1) and u(x2) of these goals, using a method known as *swing weight* (Clemen and Reilly (2001)), given by the formula u (x1, x2) = k1 . u (x1) + k2 . u (x2), where k1 and k2 are weights satisfying the equality k1 + k2 = 1.

In this method, it is presumed that the utility of the Delay u(x1) is independent from the utility of Cost u(x2) and vice-versa, and that there is no interaction between the two goals in determining the utility value. It can then be said that goals x1 and x2 are *mutually independent* in regard to utility. If we establish a preference saying that Cost is more important than Delay and that Delay has 70% of the importance of Cost, we would have k1 = 0.7 x k2. Since k1 + k2 = 1, we have k1 = 0.7 x (1- k1), and then k1 = 0.4 and k2 = 0.6.

These weights address the following conditions:

$$u(\text{worst delay, worst cost}) = u(5 \text{ months}, \$150) = 0.4 \times 0 + 0.6 \times 0 = 0$$
$$u(\text{worst delay, best cost}) = u(5 \text{ moths}, \$80) = 0.4 \times 0 + 0.6 \times 1 = 0.6$$
$$u(\text{best delay, worst cost}) = u(0 \text{ months}, \$150) = 0.4 \times 1 + 0.6 \times 0 = 0.4$$
$$u(\text{best delay, best cost}) = u(0 \text{ months}, \$80) = 0.4 \times 1 + 0.6 \times 1 = 1.0.$$

Figure 10.1. Utility curve for Example 10.1

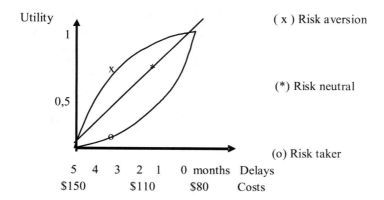

By replacing costs and delays values by their respective utility values, and reaching the joint utility values u (x1, x2), we have a new decision tree:

Strategy	Probabilities	Delay u (x 1)	Cost u (x2)	u (x1,x2) (*)
A1: Develop in the company →	0.2 →	0.6 →	0.3 →	0.42
	0.3 →	0.4 →	0.3 →	0.34
	0.5 →	0 →	0.9 →	0.54
Average of u (x1, x2)				0.456
A2: Outsource →	0.6 →	1 →	0 →	0.40
	0.4 →	0 →	1 →	0.60
Average of u (x1, x2)				0.48
A3:Partnership with multinational company →	0.2 →	1 →	0 →	0.40
	0.4 →	0.8 →	0.3 →	0.50
	0.4 →	0.4 →	0.4 →	0.40
Average of u(x1 , x2)				0.44

(*) u(x1, x2) = 0.4 u(x1) + 0.6 u(x2).

The Expected Utility Values are:

$$EUV1 = 0.2 \times 0.42 + 0.3 \times 0.34 + 0.5 \text{ x } 0.54 = 0.456,$$
$$EUV2 = 0.6 \times 0.4 + 0.4 \times 0.60 = 0.48, \text{ and}$$
$$EUV3 = 0.2 \times 0.4 + 0.4 \times 0.5 + 0.4 \times 0.4 = 0.44.$$

Thus, the company that prefers to be risk neutral will prefer strategy A2.

If the company prefers to choose the utility curve with "risk aversion" we may have the following values: EUV1 = 0.541, EUV2 = 0.48 e EUV3 = 0.608, and the best decision for the company with risk aversion is A3, where costs are not the best but there are better delivery possibilities. Using the curve expressing *risk preference or risk taker*, in Figure 10.1, the company may choose alternative A1.

Sensitivity Analysis and "What If?" Question

In example 10.1:

a.   the company, preferring to be risk neutral, should choose strategy A2;

b.   risk averting company would choose strategy A3, where costs are not the best but there are better delivery possibilities; and

c.   the risk preferring company may choose alternative A1.

In any decision problem, one should not consider a decision based only on a scenario with fixed values of the parameters involved, since several subjective assessments were used for structuring the decision problem. The decision maker tries to make a decision based on the "best information available" out of the several possible variations involved. Which are these variation alternatives?

A *decision support system* should provide the possibility of answering *"What– if"* questions, that is, the chance to answer the question

"WHAT WOULD HAPPEN to the strategy IF the earnings values, the schedule or the probabilities were different?"

Considering that strategy A1 — Developing the project inside the company — was the best decision only in the case of risk taker or preference, the company could make the following question.

"What – if?

What to do, or in which conditions is strategy A1 the best solution in a risk neutral case?"

Since the example 10.1 is a complex decision case, involving different values of delays and costs for each scenario, the analysis of the best strategy for each possible combination of the variations of values demands hard work and is not always recommended, since it involves several cases with no practical interest. The sensitivity analysis chart used in the previous example, varying probabilities $p1$ and $p2$, and leaving the third probability $p3 = 1 - p1 - p2$ implicit, is also not useful, for the same reasons.

The sensibility analysis should then be limited to the variations of parameters (probabilities, costs, or delays) of strategy A1, where the company can alter these values. The two other strategies, including the involvement of other companies and the change in the values of these scenarios, depend on negotiations with them. Even in strategy A1, only one of the three variables should be examined at a time (probability, delay, or cost), leaving the others as they are, to avoid the explosive increase in the number of possible cases.

For instance, the following cases can be examined:

Sensitivity analysis a:

Analysis of other probabilities values of strategy A1, leaving the values for Delay and Cost unchanged.

Strategy	Probabilities (new values)	Delays u (x 1)	Cost u (x2)	u (x1,x2) (*)
A1: Development in the company →	0.3 →	0.6 →	0.3 →	0.42
	0.1 →	0.4 →	0.3 →	0.34
	0.6 →	0 →	0.9 →	0.54
			Average	0.484

(*) u(x1, x2) = 0.4 x u(x1) + 0.6 x u (x2)

The best strategy is now A1 because its EUV or average value is greater than those of other scenarios.

Sensitivity analysis b:

Changing the values of Costs in Strategy A1, leaving unchanged the values of probabilities and delay.

Altering costs for $120, $120 and $90 with utilities 0.4, 0.4 and 0.9, respectively we have:

Strategy	Probabilities	Delay u (x 1)	Cost u (x2) (new values)	u (x1,x2) (*)
A1: Develop in the company →	0.2 →	0.6 →	0.4 →	0.48
	0.3 →	0.4 →	0.4 →	0.40
	0.5 →	0 →	0.9 →	0.54
			Average	0.486

(*) u(x1, x2) = 0.4 x u(x1) + 0.6 x u (x2)

Sensitivity analysis c:

Changing the values for Delay on strategy A1, leaving unchanged the values for Probabilities and Cost.

The delays now are of 1, 3 and 4 months, with new utility values.

Strategy	Probabilities	Delay u (x 1) (new values)	Cost u (x2)	u (x1,x2) (*)
A1: Develop in the company ➔	0.2 ➔	0.8 ➔	0.3 ➔	0.50
	0.3 ➔	0.4 ➔	0.3 ➔	0.34
	0.5 ➔	0.2 ➔	0.9 ➔	0.62
			Average	0.512

The best strategy again, is A1.

Optimal Decisions

In the previous chapters, it was stated that a decision problem cannot be solved just by scientific models and that, in order to define a decision-making model, it is necessary to adopt the *"satisfactory model"* based on "bounded rationality" such as the "near conflict resolution" or "minimizing uncertainty".

Further, it was stressed that the search for a solution should neither be random nor exhaustive. The search for a solution within the organization should be focused on the main problem goals and the possible alternative solutions should be looked for in the vicinity of these goals.

However, it is often interesting, or even necessary, to represent and analyze a decision problem from the standpoint of its optimum or optimized solution. In an optimization scenario, criteria or goals may be considered as objectives to be optimized or as part of restricting conditions. In the formulation of Nonlinear Mathematical Programming models, every goal or criterion except one can be described as a restriction, in order to maintain the mathematical formulation of the optimization problem with a single objective (Hillier & Liebermann, 1980; Shamblin & Stevens, 1980).

In Linear Programming (LP) both a single function goal z and the m restriction equations should be *linear,* in order to enable the applications of the method known as SIMPLEX, on a convex region of feasible solutions. If any of these equations is *nonlinear*, the optimization problem should be solved using the Nonlinear Programming or Dynamic Programming methods, whose resolution is usually very difficult.

Optimal Multiple Criteria (or Multi-Objective) Decision-Making in Industry

In problems with multiple goals it is not possible to establish an optimum solution satisfying every goal or objective. Solutions that address all criteria or goals, called "ideal solutions" usually cannot be found among the feasible solutions of the original problem. The individual goals are usually conflicting, and it is necessary to find a compromise solution based on Pareto's principle. The pre-established restrictions of the available resources may not enable the search for an "ideal solution" outside the region of feasible solutions. That means that, the ideal solution is unfeasible, as shown in Figure 10.2.

a.   In the case where existing restrictions or resources are not limited, the restrictions may be extended or "relaxed" until they encompass the ideal solution restrictions. That is what happens with the formulation called "De Novo" programming reported in Tabucanon (1988).

Figure 10.2. The "ideal" and "compromise" solutions (adapted from Tabucanon, 1988 (*) and Kinoshita, 1996 (**)

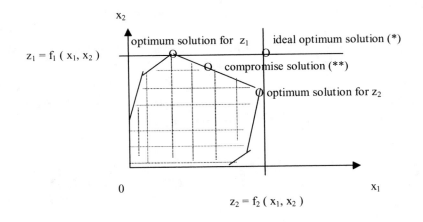

Table 10.1. Technological coefficients of products, availability and machine costs

Machine	Product 1 (hours)	Product 2 (hours)	Product 3 (hours)	Available time (hours)	Cost of the machine
Milling machine	12	17	0	1400	$75 per hour
Lathe	3	9	8	1000	60
Grinder	10	13	15	1750	35
Jig Saw	6	0	16	1325	50
Drill press	0	12	7	900	115
Band saw	9.5	9.5	4	1075	65

Note that the total cost of the production capacity of this system is:
75 x 1400 + 60 x 1000 + 35 x 1750 + 50 x 1325 + 115 x 900 + 65 x 1075 = $ 465,875.

b.   If the existing resources do not enable this relaxation, so as to include the ideal solution in the restriction area, it is necessary to find a compromise solution close to the ideal solution, respecting the original restriction area. The formulation used in this case is called "global criterion" or the weighting method used by Kinoshita (1996).

The difficulties in solving nonlinear problems occur even when the number of variables is small. If the goal function is not linear, there may be the case of optimization with several maximum and minimum points. In the case that one of restriction equations (or all of them) is nonlinear, the area of feasible solutions may be formed by nonconvex regions, and then optimization problem requires heuristic algorithms. Usually, the optimization problem of great interest to corporations is the optimization of nonlinear problems with multiple goals.

The best known methods for multiple criteria optimization problems are:

- "Global criterion" method (Kinoshita, 1996),
- "De Novo" programming (Tabucanon, 1988), and
- Goal programming (Hillier & Liberman, 1980).

The first method builds a new goal function by weighting multiple goals functions and preserving the area formed by the restrictions equations. The second method relaxes (altering the restrictions equations) the restriction area so as to hold an optimum solution called "ideal solution." Goal programming tries to reach a compromise establishing qualitative goals to address the demands of the optimization problems.

Example 10.2: Optimization Problem with Three Objective Functions (Tabucanon, 1988)

This example considers a machine shop with six machines producing three kinds of products. The time spent to produce each of the three products, the maximum time available and the cost of the use of each machine are shown in Table 10.1.

By using the data above one can formulate the following linear optimization with three goals, that is, maximization of the Profit obtained by the sale of the products, Product Quality and Worker Satisfaction.

Maximize
$$z_1 = 50\ x_1 + 100\ x_2 + 17.5\ x_3 \quad \text{(Profit)}$$
$$z_2 = 92\ x_1 + 75\ x_2 + 50\ x_3 \quad \text{(Quality)}$$
$$z_3 = 25\ x_1 + 100\ x_2 + 75\ x_3 \quad \text{(Worker satisfaction)}$$

subject to:
$$12\ x_1 + 17\ x_2 \le 1400$$
$$3\ x_1 + 9\ x_2 + 8\ x_3 \le 1000$$
$$10\ x_1 + 13\ x_2 + 15\ x_3 \le 1750$$
$$6\ x_1 + 16\ x_3 \le 1325$$
$$12\ x_2 + 7\ x_3 \le 900$$
$$9.5\ x_1 + 9.5\ x_2 + 4\ x_3 \le 1075;$$

where x_1, x_2 and x_3 are the quantities of Product 1, Product 2 and Product 3 to be produced.

By solving the linear programming problem referring to each goal function, the following solutions are given:

Profit:
$$z_1 = 8041.14 \text{ for } x_1 = 44.94,\ x_2 = 50.63 \text{ and }\ x_3 = 41.77;$$
Quality:
$$z_2 = 10950.59 \text{ for }\ x_1 = 92.27,\ x_2 = 0 \quad \text{ and }\ x_3 = 47.95; \text{ and}$$
Worker satisfaction:
$$z_3 = 9355.895 \text{ for }\ x_1 = 45.22,\ x_2 = 49.61 \text{ and }\ x_3 = 43.52.$$

None of these three solutions maximizes all three goal functions at the same time. Two ways of addressing this problem must now be examined.

"De Novo" Programming

This method reaches an "ideal solution" outside the area of feasible solutions, enabling the existing restrictions on the initial cost of the machines to be relaxed. Using the "De Novo" programming formulations, the ideal system for the total production cost of $465,875 refers to $z^* = (z^*_1 = 10\ 916.813, z^*_2 = 18\ 257.933, z^*_3 = 12\ 174.433)$. The ideal solution can be reached by solving the following system of three linear equations (see details in Tabucanon (1988)):

$$z^*_1: 50\ x_1 + 100\ x_2 + 17.5\ x_3 = 10\ 916.813$$
$$z^*_2: 92\ x_1 + 75\ x_2 + 50\ x_3 = 18\ 257.933$$
$$z^*_3: 25\ x_1 + 100\ x_2 + 75\ x_3 = 12\ 174.433$$

The solution of this system is: $x_1 = 131.341$, $x_2 = 29.683$ and $x_3 = 78.976$.

Machine availability to reach this ideal solution, which is a nonfeasible solution of the original problem, should be increased to the values presented on the following table:

Machine	Available Time	Machine Cost
Milling machine	2080.703 hrs.	$75 per hour
Lathe	1292.978	60
Grinder	1184.64	35
Jig saw	2051.662	50
Drill press	909.028	115
Band saw	1845.632	65

Note that the total production cost of the ideal system is: $75 \times 2080.703 + 60 \times 1292.978 + 35 \times 1184.64 + 50 \times 2051.662 + 115 \times 909.028 + 65 \times 1845.632 = \$602,181.20$. The new cost, when compared to the initial budget cost of $465,875, refers to an additional cost of $136,306.20.

Global Criterion Method (Kinoshita, 1996)

Let us suppose that no additional cost, besides the initial $465,875 is permitted. It is possible to distribute this value proportionally to the recommended capabilities and reach a solution that is close to the ideal. The steps of the global criterion method are:

Step One:

The optimum solution for each of the goal functions is:

$$\text{Profits: } z^*_1 = 8041.14 \text{ for } x_1 = 44.94, \ x_2 = 50.63 \text{ and } \ x_3 = 41.77;$$
$$\text{Quality: } z^*_2 = 10950.59 \text{ for } x_1 = 92.27, \ x_2 = 0 \ \text{ and } \ x_3 = 47.95 \text{ and}$$

Workers satisfaction:

$$z^*_3 = 9355.895 \text{ for } x_1 = 45.22, \ x_2 = 49.61 \text{ and } \ x_3 = 43.52.$$

Step Two:

The Global Criterion function is defined as:

$$F(X) = \{ (z_1^* - z_1(x))/z_1^* \} + \{ (z_2^* - z_2(x))/z_2^* \} + \{ (z_3^* - z_3(x))/z_3^* \}$$

or

$$F(X) = \{ (8041.14 - (50x_1 + 100 \ x_2 + 17.5x_3)) / 8041.14 \} +$$
$$+ \{ (10950.59 - (92x_1 + 75 \ x_2 + 50 \ x_3))/ 10950.59 \} +$$
$$+ \{ (9355.9 - (25x_1 + 100 \ x_2 + 75 \ x_3))/ 9355.90 \},$$

and

$$F(X) = 3 - 0.0173 \ x_1 - 0.02998 \ x_2 - 0.01476x_3$$

A new LP problem can be solved using Simplex method:

$$\text{Minimize } F(X) = 3 - 0.0173\, x_1 - 0.02998\, x_2 - 0.01476 x_3$$

$$
\begin{aligned}
\text{Subject to:} \quad & 12\, x_1 + 17\, x_2 && \leq 1400 \\
& 3\, x_1 + 9\, x_2 + 8\, x_3 && \leq 1000 \\
& 10\, x_1 + 13\, x_2 + 15\, x_3 && \leq 1750 \\
& 6\, x_1 + 16\, x_3 && \leq 1325 \\
& 12\, x_2 + 7\, x_3 && \leq 900 \\
& 9.5\, x_1 + 9.5\, x_2 + 4\, x_3 && \leq 1075
\end{aligned}
$$

Global Solution:

The optimum solution obtained by the Simplex method is:

$$x_1 = 45.22, \quad x_2 = 49.61 \text{ and } x_3 = 43.52.$$

This solution satisfies the individual goals functions as follows:

Profit:

$z_1 = 7983.90$ that corresponds to 99% of best Profit $z_1 = 8041.1444.94$;

Quality:

$z_2 = 10057.38$ that corresponds to 91% of best Quality $z_2 = 10950.59$ and

Workers satisfaction:

$z_3 = 9355.895$ which is the same value previously obtained. This compromise solution ($x_1 = 45.22$, $x_2 = 49.61$, $x_3 = 43.52$) can be considered as an acceptable solution.

Example 10.3. Selecting the best route in a supply chain problem

> *Supply chain management* is a concept with a holistic focus, requiring management to act beyond the company's borders. It is clear that there are relevant gains in trying to conduct strategically the whole chain towards end customers' satisfaction, higher productivity, etc.
>
> *Company A usually makes its delivery by highway, several times a month, to town Z. After trying several different routes for the last few months, and collecting information on them, the company decided to study and choose which route is best, considering 5 possible routes and several relevant factors [adapted from Konno (1997)].*

Multi-Criteria or Multi-Objectives Decision Analysis

 In the optimal multi-criteria (or multi-objective) decision problems presented in the last section, both the objective and restriction equations are defined by linear functions, to make possible the use of the Simplex method of Linear Programming. Today's management systems have become complex and are seldom evaluated in terms of quantitative linear components. Multi-criteria problems arise in the design, modeling, and planning of many complex systems in the areas of industrial production, urban transportation, energy production and distribution, health delivery, etc. These problems can be formulated and optimized using the quantitative approach of linear or nonlinear mathematical programming, but real-life decision problems involve many conflicting goals expressed by quantitative and/or qualitative criteria.

Possible routes R_i

R_1: Company A → Highway X1 → City C → City D → Destination Z

R_2: Company A → Highway X2 → City D → Destination Z

R_3: Company A → Highway X3 → City E → City F → Destination Z

R_4: Company A → Highway X4 → City G → City D → Destination Z

R_5: Company A → Highway X5 → City H → City F → Destination Z

Factors or Criteria Fi

F1: time spent on urban traffic between company A and the entrance to the highway;

F2: average time on the highway;

F3: cost of fuel and tolls;

F4: number of inspections stations, plus average time waiting inspection or weighing;

F5: total average time from company A to town Z;

F6: highway's comfort and safety level;

Information collected based on the average of the last six months are:

	R1	R2	R3	R4	R5
F1	190 minutes	200	210	190	140
F2	600 minutes	620	650	580	540
F3	$700	$730	$750	$650	$750
F4: number of stations	3	2	2	3	3
F4: waiting time	15 minutes	15	5	20	20
F5	700 minutes	790	750	760	770
F6	Bad	Normal	Bad	Bad	Good

We briefly describe the use of AHP (Analytic Hierarchy Process) to solve this problem. Other multi-objective decision methods, such as ELECTRE I and ELECTRE II, described by Goicoechea et al. (1982) and by Roy (1968), can solve this problem using a different approach.

The AHP Method

AHP is a method for choosing the best decision alternative considering multiple criteria and goals expressed by qualitative or quantitative values. This method created by Saaty (1980) has been used for the decision problem to establish: priority definition, cost and profits assessment, resource deployment, benchmarking, market survey, strategic decisions, conflict negotiation and resolution, social or political decisions, and forecasts.

The AHP is based on parity matrixes to express subjective assessment values attributed to variable pairs of each factor or criterion involved in the problem. AHP is a single-step decision process, which does not consider risk or uncertainty.

Since manual calculation is difficult for decision problems with a large number of factors or alternatives (usually more than five criteria and five alternatives), an AHP software known as EXPERT CHOICE should be used. The description of AHP presented in this section is based on an alternative approximation method for calculation of the eigenvector to determine the relative priority vector, described by Cook and Russel (1993).

We do not present the entire sequence of numerical procedure for this problem, because of the subjective nature involved to define each one of the pairwise preference matrixes, and also because there is the need to reevaluate these

Figure 10.3. Decision hierarchy of route selection problem

Level 1	Level 2	Level 3
Goal	Decision criteria	Decision alternatives
	➔F₁	➔(R₁,R₂,R₃,R₄,R₅)
	➔ F₂	➔(R₁,R₂,R₃,R₄,R₅)
Select the best	➔ F₃	➔(R₁,R₂,R₃,R₄,R₅)
Route	➔ F₄	➔(R₁,R₂,R₃,R₄,R₅)
	➔ F₅	➔(R₁,R₂,R₃,R₄,R₅)
	➔ F₆	➔(R₁,R₂,R₃,R₄,R₅)

Table 10.1. AHP pairwise comparison scale (Saaty, 1980)

1 – Equally Preferred	6 – Strongly to Very Strongly Preferred
2 – Equally to Moderately Preferred	7 – Very Strongly Preferred
3 – Moderately Preferred	8 – Very to Extremely Strongly Preferred
4 – Moderately to Strongly Preferred	9 – Extremely Preferred
5 – Strongly Preferred	

matrixes according to the value of an index called a *consistency ratio*. Instead, we present comments on some problems presented by the AHP method.

The AHP consists of the following four basic steps:

1. Develop the decision hierarchy of levels of decisions elements.
2. Collect preference data for each decision element by performing pairwise comparisons.
3. Determine the relative priority or weight of each decision element using the eigen-value method or alternative approximation method.
4. Aggregate the relative priorities of the final decision alternatives relative to the overall goal.

Step 1. Decision hierarchy of the route Example 10.3 is shown in Figure 10.3.

Step 2. Determining preferences by pairwise comparisons.

The AHP uses a scale from 1 to 9 to rate the decision maker's preference for each pair of criteria in the hierarchy. Table 10.1 shows the pairwise comparison scale.

The Pairwise Comparison Matrix

The matrix FF below summarizes one of the decision maker's preferences for the six criteria relative to getting the best route. For instance, criterion F2 is strongly preferred to criterion F1 and therefore creates a 5 in the F2 row relative to the F1 column. This pairwise comparison also creates a 1/5 in the F1 row relative to the F2 column. Criterion F2 is equally preferred to F3, creating 1 in the F2 row relative to F3 column and vice-versa.

FF	F_1	F_2	F_3	F_4	F_5	F_6
F_1	1	1/5	1/3	1	1/7	¼
F_2	5	1	1	5	1/3	4
F_3	3	1	1	3	1/3	2
F_4	1	1/5	1/3	1	¼	1
F_5	7	3	3	4	1	3
F_6	4	¼	½	1	¼	1
Sum	21	5.65	6.17	15	2.31	11.2

Next, a pairwise comparison matrix for the criterion F1, relative to each route Ri is defined using the same comparison scale:

Factor F_1	R_1	R_2	R_3	R_4	R_5
R_1	1	1	1	1	1/5
R_2	1	1	1	1	1/5
R_3	1	1	1	1	1/5
R_4	1	1	1	1	1/5
R_5	5	5	5	5	1
Sums	9	9	9	9	9/5

This matrix shows that, concerning criterion F1 (time spent on urban traffic), route R5 is *strongly preferred* to all others routes, creating values of 5 in the row relative to R5.

The other five pairwise comparison matrices should be defined for each one of the remaining criteria F2, F3, ..., F6.

Step 3. Using the eigen-value method of the software EXPERT CHOICE or the alternative approximation method described by Cook and Russel (1993), it is possible to determine the relative priority or weight of each decision element.

For instance, considering the pairwise matrix FF, we divide each matrix entry by its column total to normalize these values. Then we calculate the arithmetic mean of each row. These arithmetic means are estimates of the relative priorities (eigenvalues) of the six factors Fi, as shown in the following:

FF	F1	F2	F3	F4	F5	F6	Row Mean
F1	.048	.035	.054	.067	.062	.022	0.048
F2	.238	.178	.162	.333	.144	.355	0.235
F3	.143	.178	.162	.200	.144	.178	0.167
F4	.048	.035	.054	.067	.108	.089	0.067
F5	.333	.532	.487	.266	.434	.267	0.387
F6	.190	.042	.081	.067	.108	.089	0.096
Totals	1	1	1	1	1	1	1.000

These relative priorities indicate that the decision maker places most emphasis on criterion F5 (priority = 0.367) fallowed by priority F2 (priority 0.235).

We must repeat this procedure for the six pairwise comparison matrix of each criterion Fi relative to the routes Ri, to follow to step 4.

Step 4. Aggregating the relative priorities of the final decision alternatives relative to the overall goal.

For instance, the final decision priority value could be:

Route 1 = 0.193, Route 2 = 0.188, Route 3 = 0.155. Route 4 = 0.230, and Route 5 = 0.234; , which indicates that route number 5 and number 4 are the best alternatives.

The quality of the final decision is dependent upon the consistency of the judgement throughout the pairwise comparison process. A measure of consistency called *consistency ratio* is used to determine the decision-maker consistency after the development of each pairwise comparison matrix. If the consistency ratio is large, the decision maker should revise the pairwise comparison matrix. The decision maker can also revise the subjective judgment giving more preference to one of the criteria or one of the objectives.

This revisions procedure may introduce changes in the final priority. For instance, for a different pairwise comparison values, the priority could be: Route 1 = 0.182, Route 2 = 0.108, Route 3 = 0.171. Route 4 = 0.369, and Route 5 = 0.170. According to the new decision preference, route number 4 becomes the preferred alternative.

AHP is one of the most used methods for making decisions with multiple criteria involving complexity and subjectivity. One of the difficulties pointed out for the AHP is the amount of required parity comparisons, which increase rapidly with the number of criteria depending on the complexity of the decision tree. The reversal effect of the priority order, which occurs when the dominant alternatives are altered due to the inclusion or exclusion of irrelevant alternatives, is another problem pointed to by AHP critics (Harker, 1987). The order reversal effect is attributed by researchers as a "side effect" of the calculus used to normalize the priority vector. In response to this problem, Saaty (1977 & 1980) created the "ideal mode" calculation, indicated for the case when only the best alternative is desired.

The ANP — *Analytic Network Process* (Saaty, 2001) is a generalization of AHP where one of the axioms (independency of the factors) may be relaxed. While AHP hierarchic structure has a concept of dominance of one level over another, in ANP there may be closed cycles where there is a net structure that can give a new dimension and view for structuring complex problems.

Decision Based on Fuzzy Possibility Theory

In decision problems involving uncertainty or risk, classical probability theory (also known as Bayesian probability) defines probabilities pi (pi >=0 and Σ pi = 1) in such a way that, if the probability P(A) of a subset A $\subset$ S is known, the probability of the complementary sub set A^c, is defined by $P(A^c) = 1 - P(A)$, meaning that the decision maker must know the value of this probability. As in a practical problem with uncertainty or risk this fact is seldom possible, authors (Shafer, 1978; Terano et al., 1984) recommend the use of fuzzy possibility theory, in which this restriction may be relaxed.

Let $S = \{ sj \}$ be a finite set of criteria formed by subsets Ai $(i = 1,2,...)$ defined by probabilities $m(Ai)$, known as *basic probabilities* of Ai, such that $0 \leq m(Ai) \leq 1$, $m(\varphi) = 0$ and $\Sigma\, m(Ai) = 1$, (for all $Ai \subset S$ and $i = 1, 2, ...$).

Following definitions occurs:

a.   Lower Probability or Belief Function (Bel):

$P*(Ai) = \Sigma\, m(Aj)$, (for $Aj \subseteq Ai$), is the sum of all basic probabilities of subsets of Ai,   and

b.   Upper Probability or Plausibility Function (Pel):

$P*(Ai) = 1 - P_*(Ai^c) = 1 - \Sigma\, m(Aj^c)$, (for $Aj^c \subseteq Ai$), is the sum of basic probabilities of subsets Aj containing or related to set Ai, i.é, $Aj \cap Ai \neq \varphi$.

In decision problems defined by k criteria sj of S, n alternatives of decisions r_l and basic probabilities $m(Ai)$ (for all $Ai \subseteq S = \{ sj \}$), using the utility values $u(r_l, sj)$, for each alternative r_l and criterion sj, it is possible to define two expected values with respect to Bel and Pel probabilities.

If sj $(j = 1,2,...,k)$ are ordered according to the importance given by the decision maker, we can consider weights wj such that $(wo = 0) < w1 < w2 < ... < (wk = 1)$ and define subsets $A_q = \{ sj / wj^3 w_q \}$, $q = 1,2,...,k$, such that $m(s_q) = w_q - w_{q-1}$. Then,

Lower Expected Value $E*$ of alternative rl $(l = 1,2,..., n)$
   $E*[\,rl\,] = \Sigma \min (Aj)) \times m(sj)$, and
Upper Expected Value $E*$ of alternative rl $(l = 1,2,..., n)$
   $E*[\,rl\,] = \Sigma \max (Aj) \times m(sj)$

Example 10.4: Selection of Used Car

(Presented in Chapter VIII as Example 8.4 to illustrate an ambiguous model of decision).

According to the description presented in Chapter VIII, we have the following five criteria, placed in ascending order of their importance.

$OI = \{ s1 = $ year of fabrication, $s2 = $ exterior aspects, $s3 = $ interior aspects, $s4 = $ mileage , $s5 = $ price $\}$,

and a list of preference weight m(sj) or mj for each criterion

$P1 = \{ m1 = 0.075, m2 = 0.139, m3 = 0.026, m4 = 0.460, m5 = 0.294 \}$.

The criterion s5 is the "most important" because when states or criteria sj (j= 1,2,...,k) are ordered defining subsets $A_q = \{ sj / wj \geq w_q \}$, q= 1,2,...,k, the last criterion s5 appears in every subset Aq, in order to evaluate the values of lower and upper expected values. The criterion s4 is the "most preferred" because the preference decision maker has resulted in the highest value of basic probability m4 = 0.460.

The values of utility function u (rl, sj), for l = 1, 2, ..., 6 used cars and sj = 1,2,...,5 criteria are presented in Table 10.2.

We can note that, with the exception of car number X768, every car presents at least one positive aspect (i.e., preference value is equal to or greater than 0.7) showing that we have not the occurrence of dominance factor to eliminate some of these cars.

For instance, for car M718 we have, we can define the subsets:

$A_1 = \{ s_1, s_2, s_3, s_4, s_5 \} = \{ 0.4, 0.3, 0.4, 0.6, 0.8 \}$ with min (A1) = 0.3 and max (A1)= 0.8;

Table 10.2. Utility values for six used cars (adapted from Terano et al., 1984)

Car code	s1 = year	s2=exterior	S3=interior	s4=mileage	s5 = price
M718	0.4	0.3	0.4	0.6	0.8
B738	0.9	0.0	0.5	0.2	0.8
X768	0.0	0.0	0.4	0.4	0.0
Z780	0.0	0.7	0.9	0.9	0.0
A783	0.8	0.0	0.8	0.6	1.0
X785	0.5	0.3	0.8	0.9	0.5

$A_2 = \{ s_2, s_3, s_4, s_5 \} = \{ 0.3, 0.4, 0.6, 0.8 \}$ with $\min(A2) = 03$ and max $(A2) = 0.8$;

$A_3 = \{ s_3, s_4, s_5 \} = \{ 0.4, 0.6, 0.8 \}$ with $\min(A3) = 0.4$ and max $(A3) = 0.8$;

$A_4 = \{ s_4, s_5 \} = \{ 0.6, 0.8 \}$ with $\min(A4) = 0.6$ and $\max(A4) = 0.8$; and finally

$A_5 = \{ s_5 \} = \{ 0.8 \}$ with $\min(A5) = \max(A5) = 0.8$.

The weights are

$m(s_1) = w_1 - w_0 = 0.075$; $m(s_2) = w_2 - w_1 = 0.215 - 0.075 = 0.140$; $m(s_3) = w_3 - w_2 = 0.240 - 0.215 = 0.0.25$; $m(s_4) = w_4 - w_3 = 0.706 - 0.240 = 0.466$; and $m(s_5) = w_5 - w_4 = 1.00 - 0.706 = 0.294$, resulting in

$w_1 = 0.075$, $w_2 = 0.215$, $w_3 = 0.240$, $w_4 = 0.706$, $w_5 = 1.00$ } such that $m(s_q) = w_q - w_{q-1}$ for $q = 1, 2, .., 5$. Then we have

Lower Expected Value E* or Elower

$E^*[r2 = \text{car M718}] = \sum \min(Aj) \times m(sj) = 0.3 \times 0.075 + 0.3 \times 0.140 + 0.4 \times 0.025 + 0.6 \times 0.466 + 0.8 \times 0.294 = 0.589$, and

Upper Expected Value E* or Eupper

$E^*[r2 = \text{car M718}] = \sum \max(Aj)) \times m(sj) = 0.8 \times (0.075 + 0.140 + 0.025 + 0.466 + 0.294) = 0.800$.

Table 10.3. Results of evaluation of six cars according to three expected values (adapted from Terano et al., 1984)

Number	E_{lower}	rank	E_{add}	rank	E_{upper}	rank
M718	0.589	1st	0.632	3rd	0.800	3rd
B738	0.333	4th	0.505	4th	0.807	2nd
X768	0.0		0.169		0.282	
Z780	0.0		0.447	5th	0.635	5th
A783	0.588	2nd	0.749	1st	1.000	1st
X785	0.457	3rd	0.639	2nd	0.782	4th

Other values of upper, lower expected values and arithmetic mean E_{add} are obtained in a similar way (Table 10.3).

Comments

Car A783 seems to be the best choice, showing two first places and one second place, although it has a score of zero for the "exterior aspects." However, as this criterion s2 is one of the least important criteria, it could not affect this customer's selection.

Car M718 presents a balanced situation: it is the best car with respect to negative points (E_{lower} or E_*) and has slightly lower value with respect to the arithmetic mean and positive points ($E_{upper} = E^* = 0.800$), when compared with car A783. Car A783 has two first places, but it has a zero entry for the criterion s2. That, however, is one of the less important criteria.

Car X785 presents more negative points ($E_{lower} = 0.457$) and less positive points ($E_{upper} = 0.782$) than the two cars previously considered. As it would be expected, car X768 presents the worst performance in every aspect of analysis.

Case Studies: Strategy and Decisions in Perspective

Case – The Value of Scenarios

(Excerpted from: *The Official Future, Self-Delusion and the Value Of Scenarios;* Peter Schwartz, *Financial Times,* Mastering Risk, series, Part II, May 2, 2000, pp. 6-7).

> *"Intelligent people and companies still make some very bad decisions.... IBM and the retail giant Sears Roebuck lost several billion dollars betting on one on-line provider; American banks lost money and more money with the successive crises in Latin American countries during the nineteen eighties; Long Term Capital Management (LTCM) lost billions in 1996 (read more on*

LTCM in the Case Study of chapter 8), because they did not take important scenarios into account in their mathematical models."

In each of the above mentioned cases, the mistake made was not asking themselves the critical question: "what happens if we are wrong — and very wrong?" In other words, they mistakenly assessed the risks inherent to their decisions or did not make the correct scenario planning.

There are two very different kinds of scenario planning. The first is exploratory, an attempt to understand the outlines of an unknown scenario — the future — especially in a general interest context. Exploratory planning may find potential unforeseen risks, but is not always relevant to the decision maker.

The second kind of planning tries to reach an understanding of risk management. Decision-making scenarios are not created from the abstract. One must know who the decision makers are, since they also make decisions based both on perceptions and facts.

For the *scenario planning*, it is important that the team developing the range of future alternatives is sure that the "*official future*" is included in the range of alternatives. Only after analyzing this scenario, with a well-made survey, should other possibilities be considered.

How to identify and describe the *official future*? It is necessary to examine the decision makers' knowledge, their organizational environment and the market where they act. This test could be condensed into five questions:

- **First question:** If it were possible to find a fortune teller, what question would you ask concerning the future?

- **Second question:** In reference to a given decision, what would be the *scenario for the best possible result?*

- **Third question:** Which would be the *scenario for the worst possible result?*

- **Fourth question:** If you were about to retire or to leave the company, what you like your colleagues to consider your legacy?

- **Fifth question:** Are there important barriers to change in your organization?

Scenarios may be used to train decision makers in recognizing signs of change on the proper occasions. Scenarios are useful to introduce gradual changes in the decision-making models themselves. In sum, scenarios show the decision makers their own perception of the risk environment.

Conclusions

In this chapter, complexity in decision problems due to uncertainty or risk factor, multiple scenario definition and multiple criteria decision, were presented. Subjective assessment of probability values, scenario definition and multiple criteria decision with or without optimized solution, are problems that do not have definitive answers, requiring several steps of the decision-making process to reach favorable and consensual results.

In addition to the basic structure of the decision-making process of semi-structured and tactical models of decision, we are facing new factors that encompass the complex and nonstructured nature of strategic decision problems.

Complex problems and nonstructured (known also as ill-defined) problems are often considered similar problems, but it is possible to find complexity (in the sense of NP or Non-Polynomial complexity defined in Mathematics) in well-defined problems (small number of variables and functions), as in the case of optimization of nonlinear problems or matrix inversion problems.

Summarizing the results of a decision based on the models and examples shown in this chapter, one can say that the selection of the best or top best alternatives of decision is a difficult task. We may think about certain personal considerations and organizational biases a decision analysis should overcome, and the concept of "good" rather than "best" decision must be considered.

The choice of an adequate decision-making methodology will be one of personal or organizational preference, and we can not decide a priori which particular methodology is appropriate. Rather, we may analyze a problem according to different points of view to see what the outcomes for different ways of analysis are, and in this way determine which course of action is most justifiable.

Questions for Reflection and Discussion

Considering the case in the section titled The Value of Scenarios Hidden Traps, analyze the exercises with multiple scenarios presented in this chapter and give answers to the five questions for an efficient scenario planning. For instance, what would be the best and worst scenarios or the scenario for the official future? List and comment on the "hidden traps" existing in the decision problem examples in this and in the previous chapter.

1. What is a decision problem with risk?

2. What are *utility values* used for?

3. What is the importance of *the sensitivity analysis* in a decision problem?

4. What is a *decision scenario*?

5. Explain, using an example, how a Linear Programming problem with more than one goal function is formulated and solved.

6. Give examples of decisions problems with risk, multiple goals and multiple scenarios. Build a decision tree for each example.

7. What is and how is calculated the joint utility value $u(x1, x2)$ of two goals $u(x1)$ and $u(x2)$?

8. Explain each kind of utility curve: with risk aversion, risk neutral, and risk preference. Draw the utility curve graphic for $u(x1, x2)$, using the example developed in the chapter.

9. How to make a Sensitivity Analysis of a decision problem with multiple goals and multiple scenarios? Why is the sensitivity analysis for this kind of problem complex?

10. What is and what is the purpose of the "What–if" question? Give examples.

Exercises

1. Investment Model With Multiple Scenarios

   Company BYS must choose one of the following alternatives:

A1: do not invest in a new product development

A2: invest in the development of new product paying the cost in cash

A3: invest using bank loan

A4: invest in partnership with a multinational company.

Scenario One

The national market might present one of the following situations:

S1: There is no demand for the new product, with probability P(S1)=0.2 as shown by a market research,

S2: There might be a sales average of 100.000 units of the new product with probability P(S2)=0.4, and

S3: There might be a sales average of 200.000 units of the new product with probability P(S3)=0.4.

The complete decision matrix, with earnings established after exhaustive risk analysis of the possible situations, expressed in millions of dollars, is the following:

Possible States	Probability	A_1: Do not invest	A2: Invest with cash	A3: Invest with bank loan	A4: Invest with partner
S1:No sales	0.2	0	-200	-100	0
S2:Sales of 100.000 units	0.4	0	600	300	100
S3:Sales of 200.000 units	0.4	0	3500	2000	500

Scenario Two

The foreign market might present the following possibilities:

S1: There may be an average sale of 150.000 units of the new product ($P(S_1)$) = 0.6)

S2: There may be an average sale of 300.000 units of the new product ($P(S_2)$) = 0.4)

The complete decision matrix, including earnings in million dollars is the following:

Possible States	Probability	A₁: Do not invest	A2: Invest with cash	A₃: Invest with bank loan	A₄: Invest with partner
S₁:Sales of 150.000 units	0.6	0	700	500	200
S₂:Sales of 300.000 units	0.4	0	3000	3000	1000

Considering that the company cannot address both scenarios at the same time:

- Which one is the best decision based on the best average earnings?
- Which is the best decision using the best utility average value, with neutral risk, risk preference, or risk aversion utility?

References

Bonabeau, E. (2003). Don't trust your gut. *Harvard Business Review, 81*(5), 116-223.

Charan, R. (2001). Conquering a culture of indecision. *Harvard Business Review, 79*(4), 75-82.

Choo, C. W. (1998). *Knowing organizations*. Oxford, UK: Oxford University Press.

Clemen, R. T., & Reilly, T. (2001). *Making hard decisions with decisions tools*. New York: Duxbury Press.

Cook, T.M., & Russel, R.A. (1993). *Introduction to management science*. NJ: Prentice-Hall.

Day, G.S., et al. (Eds.). (1997). *Wharton on dynamic competitive strategy*. New York: John Wiley & Sons.

Goicoechea, A., et al. (1982). *Multi-objective decision analysis with engineering and business applications*. New York: John Wiley & Sons.

Goodwin, P., & Wright, G. (1996). *Decision dnalysis for management judgment*. New York: John Wiley & Sons.

Gregory, G. (1980). *Decision analysis*. New York: Pitman Books.

Harker, P.T. (1987). Incomplete pairwise comparison in the AHP. *Mathematical Modeling, 9*(11), 837-848.

Keeney, R., & Raiffa, H. (1976). *Decisions with multiple objectives: Preferences and value trade off*. New York: Wiley & Sons.

Kinoshita, E. (1996). *Introduction to management science* (in Japanese). Tokyo, Sakurai Publishers.

Konno, H. (1997). *Introduction to decision analysis* (in Japanese). Tokyo: Assakura Publishers.

Roy, B. (1968). *Classement et choix en presence de points de vue multiples (la methode ELECTRE)*. Review Française d'Informatique et de Recherche Operationnelle, 8, 57-75.

Saaty, T. L. (1977). A scaling method for priorities in hierarchical structures. *Journal of Mathematical Psychology, 15*, 234-281.

Saaty, T.L. (1980). *The analytic hierarchy process: Planning, priority, resource allocation*. New York: McGraw-Hill.

Saaty, T. L. (2001). *Decision making with dependence and feedback: The analytic network process* (2nd ed.). Pittsburgh, PA: RWS Publications.

Shafer, G. (1976). *A mathematical theory of evidence*. NJ: Princeton University Press.

Tabucanon, M. T. (1988). *Multiple criteria decision making in industry*. New York: Elsevier.

Terano, T., et al. (1984). *Fuzzy systems: Theory and its applications* (in Japanese). Tokyo: Ohm Publishing.

Warfield, J.N. (1978). *Societal systems: Planning, policy and complexity*. New York: John Wiley & Sons.

Warfield, J.N. (1994). *A science of generic design: Managing complexity through systems design* (2nd ed.). Iowa State University Press.

Chapter XI

The Role Of Simulation And Modern Business Games

Probabilistic or Stochastic Process

"Probability or stochastic process" is a name used to designate mathematical models that represent the behavior of phenomena described by probability theory, ranging from a simple game of coin tossing up to more complex phenomenon like "Brownian motion theory", "investment analysis", etc. Stochastic process uses mathematical models to represent phenomena ruled by the probabilistic variation of some variable over time.

Simulation methods, also known as Monte Carlo methods, are stochastic processes that use mathematical models that have similar behavior of real problems, feeding these models with random values generated according to some probability distribution. The term Monte Carlo is used as a synonym for simulation since in some problems the generation of probabilistic values was historically linked to the use of the roulette wheel.

In this chapter we show how simulation method can be used to evaluate complex decision problems involving uncertainty. This kind of problem involves knowledge of probability distribution (such as uniform, Poisson, or Normal distribution) used to represent the probabilistic process and the value of respective parameters (such as the average value and the standard deviation).

Simulation is the most appropriate tool for visualizing, testing, and evaluating the parameters and the dynamic behavior of a probabilistic process. Simulation uses algorithms that generate a population of probabilistic events which makes possible the estimation of the values of parameters of the problem. The results of a simulation can be proven to be valid approximations of the values of the real phenomenon which they simulate.

Using Simulation to Compare Multiple-Stage Strategic Decisions

In previous chapters, several aspects of decision problems, involving the choice of the best alternative, uncertainties, multiple scenarios, multiple goals, etc., have been studied. However those were cases of decision for only one stage. Many complex strategic-decision problems are formed by a dynamic sequence of decision problems involving multiple stages of decisions. These problems are more appropriately represented using a *decision tree*, and simulation is used to make comparisons of different strategies along the decision tree.

Let us consider the following two-stage strategies:

Strategy A

Stage one: Invest in a high-risk stock whose payoff (Payoff-A) can be negative or positive values. Past data show that the payoff value varies from -$100 (maximum loss) to +$100 (maximum profit);

Stage two:

a.   if Payoff-A is a positive value less than $50, then the investor must pay $30 as expenses, or if Payoff-A is a positive value greater than $50, then the investor must pay $50 as expenses;

b.   if Payoff-A is a negative value between $0 and (-$50), then the investor must pay $20 as expenses, or if Payoff-A is a negative value less than (-$50), then the investor pays $0 as expenses.

Strategy B

Stage one: Invest in a high-risk stock whose payoff (Payoff-B) can be negative or positive values. Past data show that the payoff value varies from -$120 (maximum loss) to +$120 (maximum profit);

Stage two:

a.   if Payoff-B is a positive value less than $60, then the investor must pay $30 as expenses, or if Payoff-B is a positive value greater than $60, then the investor must pay $50 as expenses;

b.   if Payoff-B is a negative value between $0 and (-$60), then the investor must pay $20 as expenses, or if Payoff-B is a negative value less than (-$60), then the investor pays $0 as expenses.

In this simple project, the selection of strategy A or B depends on the results of the following events:

a.   "Payoff-A" and "Payoff-B", with two possible results: positive or negative values;

b.   "positive value of Payoff A or B" results in two possible values for expenses;

c.   "negative value of Payoff A or B" also results in two possible expenses; which provide 2×2×2 = 8 possible results.

Stochastic Analysis to Compare Two Similar Strategies

The analysis of a probabilistic decision problem to a broader band of variation of the parameter values is made by a simulation study, using probability distribution attributed to each value of the estimated parameter.

The estimated value of a parameter is used as the mean or average value of the distribution. Asking an expert, it is possible to define an "upper limit" for this average, such that only 5% of the possible values of this parameter surpass this upper limit. In a similar fashion, it is possible to define a "lower limit" such that only 5% of the possible values will be lower than this limit. In probability terms, this procedure corresponds to defining a confidence interval for the average value with 90% confidence.

If the decision maker and the expert agree that the average value provided by the estimate is located in a symmetric position with relation to these two limits, the normal distribution can be used. If not, one can evaluate the possibility of using other type of distributions such as the exponential, log-normal, beta, gamma distribution, etc.

In our case, we are assuming that the value of the Payoffs (negative or positive values) has a normal distribution with the average equal to the value estimated by the expert and the standard deviation equals to 25% of the difference between this average and one of the limits found. In the case of normal distribution an interval defined by the expression $\mu \pm 4\sigma$ (the average value plus and minus four times the standard deviation) corresponds to approximately 90% of the possibilities of occurrence of the values of this distribution.

Using these distributions the first stage of strategy A and B becomes:

Strategy A

Stage one: Invest in a high-risk stock whose payoff (Payoff-A) is distributed according:

To N (μ= $0, σ = $25), a Normal distribution with average value and standard deviation equal to $0 and $25, respectively; and

Strategy B

Stage one: Invest in a high-risk stock whose payoff (Payoff-B) is distributed according:

To N (μ= $0, σ = $30), a Normal distribution with average value and standard deviation equal to $0 and $30, respectively.

We are admitting that events in stage two do not involve probability distribution. Payoff's normal distribution functions and decision trees for strategies A and B are as shown in Figure 11.1.

The simulation process to generate the Net values (Payoff minus expenses) for both strategies A and B is the following:

Figure 11.1. Payoff-A and Payoff-B probability distributions and the decision tree

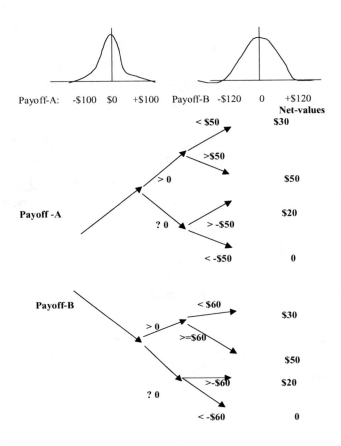

- generate a normally distributed random value (using an algorithm or appropriate software for simulation);
- using this random value make appropriate calculation of stage two to have the final net value (positive or negative) for the strategy A or B.

For example, if the Payoff-A value generated is $76, the expenditure will be $50 and then the net value is $26; if Payoff-B value is -$67, the expenditure is zero and the final net value is -$67, and so on.

Table 11.1 presents results of 30 simulated events (net values) for strategy A and 30 events for B. The first column of this table shows intervals for the net

Table 11.1. Frequency, probability, and cumulative distribution function values of net values for strategy A and B

Net values $	Frequency of A	P (A)	CDF(A)	Frequency of B	P (B)	CDF(B)
less than -70	1	0.033	0.033	2	0.067	0.067
-70 ~ -50	2	0.067	0.100	3	0.100	0.167
-50 ~ -30	3	0.100	0.200	3	0.100	0.267
-30 ~-10	5	0.167	0.367	5	0.167	0.434
-10 ~ +10	8	0.267	0.634	9	0.300	0.734
+10 ~+30	7	0.233	0.867	5	0.167	0.901
+30 ~ +50	3	0.100	0.967	2	0.066	0.967
more than +50	1	0.033	1.000	1	0.033	1.00
Totals	30	1.000		30	1.000	

values (from negative to positive values), the second and third columns show the frequency (number of occurrences) and the probability (p(A)= frequency divided by 30) of final net value in each interval. In the fourth column, the values of cumulative probability distribution function (CDF(A)) are registered. The values of CDF will be used for the comparison of the two strategies using the *stochastic dominance* technique. Table 11.1 contains also the same values for strategy B.

Placing the two strategies on the same graph of cumulative probability distribution function, we get the graph of "stochastic dominance" in which it is possible to compare the two strategies (Figure 11.2). This comparison is based on the fact that:

> *"If a cumulative probability distribution value of a strategy is to the right of the cumulative probability distribution value of another strategy for a value of an event, this means that this strategy has smaller probability of occurrence than the other strategy of the event considered."*

In Figure 11.2, we can see that "strategy B" (indicated by arrows ➜) has stochastic dominance over "strategy A" (indicated by curves), because CDF curve for B is always located to the left of CDF curve for strategy A. This means that strategy B has greater probability to have negative net values but also greater probability to have positive net values than strategy A.

We need to compare both the lengths of the ranges for which a strategy is dominant and the differences between the CDF values. This comparison can be

Figure 11.2. Graph of stochastic dominance between **strategy A** *and* **strategy B**

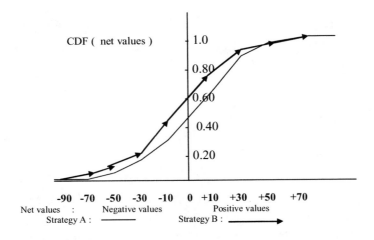

made using the sizes of the areas of the two CDF curves. For instance, the area defined by CDF curves B and A for the positive net values, looks smaller than the area defined for the negative values. This means that strategy B has more possibility to have negative net values than positive values. Further analysis of stochastic dominance requires the use of other probabilistic techniques (see, for instance Goodwin & Wright, 1996).

The probabilities of occurrence of each event need to be estimated in a subjective mode, referring to the opinion of an expert involved in the project. The expert can attribute the probability values to each node of the decision tree by examining each node from left (starting node) to the right of the decision tree. Usually strategic projects are represented by complex decision trees with many branches and nodes. The estimation of probabilities made in each node may be dependent or independent of the estimate made in previous nodes. If dependency exists, one must estimate the probability of the event conditioned to the occurrence of events in previous nodes. This fact causes difficulties in the development of the subjective reasoning of the expert, leading to unlikely estimates. The subjective estimates of conditional probabilities in each node may lead to a biased estimation of the probabilities in the final events of the decision tree.

A more natural and logical procedure is to attribute the probability values, exploring the decision tree from the end to the beginning, that is, from right to left. For example, an expert consulted about the probability of success of a project to launch a new product may estimate that, based in his or her knowledge about market demand for this type of product, the probability of success of this project is, for instance, P(Success) = 0.7 and then the probability of failure will be P (Failure) = 0.3. After fixing these values, the expert can estimate the probability of events located in the antecessor nodes to the events Success and Failure. After admitting of some "facts" (or the probability of their occurrence) it seems easier to estimate the probabilities of the events that caused these facts.

The following case study illustrates the assessment of probability values in a complex decision tree.

Business Game Simulates Competition Among Companies

Long-term conflict or competition occurs when companies or countries find themselves in prolonged confrontation such as in the market share problem. It is necessary to establish a line of action or a decision sequence to take best advantage of each stage of competition. A decision in situation of competition can be examined by simulation software known as BUSINESS GAME. Business games have been formerly created based on the experience of strategic competition found in models of war games. In business games, the concepts of victory or defeat used in war games are replaced by the analysis of the behavior of the companies involved in competition, expressed in terms of economical results over a certain period of time.

A business game can be defined as:

> *"A sequential decision making exercise structured using a business strategy model or operational model, where participants assume the role of managers."*

The term "game" always connotes competition, but business game's main purpose is to systematically train the participants in the sense to have better understanding of the business strategies and operations using virtual business competition environments simulated in a computer. Competition arises as a stimulus to create an environment of interest for understanding and testing alternatives for the simulated strategies or operations.

The "game" cannot be seen as an entertainment, as is the case of video games. The business game forms part of Game Theory, created by Von Neumann and Morgenstern, which is a mathematical model used to represent a situation of conflict in a general way.

Business game creates a complex environment with uncertainty simulating the alternatives for business decisions. Business game is a useful tool for demonstrating, testing, and training strategic decision making in companies, because it retains the effect of the diffusion of the results of a decision through future periods, taking into account the participation of rival companies.

The advantages of a business game are:

- it creates appropriate training conditions and environments for executive and manager's decision-making process which are difficult to have by other tools;
- it allows for the repetition of the conditions for analyzing a decision under different economic and financial aspects;
- it permits testing of the different alternatives for an strategy or operation using different organizational structures for individuals, groups, functional hierarchy, etc;
- it allows interactive mid or long-term projection of the results of a strategic policy.

Some disadvantages are:

- **Cost and time factors:** the cost of a software is high and the time spent to play a business game is long, since it requires several rounds of plays conducted by a team of professionals to operate the software;
- **Validity of the results and training:** even though practicing the game clarifies the company's strategic or functional mechanism, there is not a valid evidence that results of the game or the performance of game players will necessarily be repeated in real problems;
- **Danger of rashness:** the mechanism of the simulation is regulated by mathematical equations of micro and macro economy theory. Some factors can be stressed over others, such as the importance of the low

price of the product, investment in advertisement or R&D, etc. to leverage the financial results of the game, without having fully taken into account all the complex effects of these factors.

Games for Competition

Game One: Competition Between Two Companies Having Different Material Resources (adapted from Kinoshita, 1996)

Let's consider the competition between two companies BURGER-A and BURGER-B with respect to the number of sales points.

BURGER-A (designated as A) has α sales points while BURGER-B (designated as B) has β sales points.

The game consists in taking or losing the sales points through competitions simulated by tossing a coin. Thus,

- if HEADS occurs, A wins the first competition and takes possession of one of B's sales points and
- if TAILS occurs, B takes possession of one of A's sales points.

The game ends when one of the companies loses all its sales points. For instance, starting with the values $\alpha = 2$ and $\beta = 1$ we have:

a. **First competition:**

   If HEADS occurs, then A wins and stays with $\alpha = 3$ and $\beta = 0$ and we have a VICTORY FOR A, or

   If TAILS occurs, then B wins with $\alpha = 1$ and $\beta = 2$ and we will have the second competition.

b. **Second competition:**

   HEADS: A wins with $\alpha = 2$ and $\beta = 1$ and the game returns to the same situation of the first competition, or

   TAILS: B wins with $\alpha = 0$ and $\beta = 3$ and we have a VICTORY FOR B.

For every two competitions there exists a return to the first competition with probability P (return to first competition) = ¼, forming an infinite sequence of these two competitions.

General Formulas for Game One

For any value of α e β it is possible to show, using mathematical approximation of infinite series, that

$$P(\text{Victory for A}) = \alpha / (\alpha + \beta) \text{ and } P(\text{Victory for B}) = b / (\alpha + \beta).$$

Thus, the probability of victory is directly proportional to the value of its available resource (α and β) if the chance of winning a competition is equal for both companies.

Game Two: Competition Between two Companies with Different Material Resources and Different Chances of Winning a Competition

Let's consider that, in addition to establishing the value α and β for material resources, we can also fix different chances of winning each competition, with probability P(A wins one competition) = **a** and P(B wins one competition) = **1- a = b.**

What are the chances of VICTORY for each company?

For instance,

if $\alpha = 1$, $\beta = 1$, a = 2/3 and b = 1 – a = 1/3, then we could have

P(A wins) = 2/3 with $\alpha = 2$ and $\beta = 0$, and have a VICTORY FOR A or

P(B wins) = 1/3 with $\alpha = 0$ and $\beta = 1$, and have a VICTORY FOR B.

General Formulas for Game Two

Using mathematical approximations based on the Gambler's Ruin Problem of Probability Theory (Feller, W. – An Introduction to Probability Theory and its Applications – 2nd Edition, Wiley, 1957, p. 314) it is possible to show that:

$$P(\text{Victory of } A) = [\ 1 - (b/a)^{\alpha}\ ]\ /\ [\ 1 - (b/a)^{\alpha + \beta}]\ \text{and}$$
$$P(\text{Victory of } B) = 1 - P(\text{Victory of } A)$$

α and β are the material resources of A and B and a and b are the probabilities of victory for A and B in a single competition.

A Market Share Simulation Based on Game Two

The effect of resources α and β, while the probability of victory in each competition is **a < b**, can be analyzed using simulation. Simulations experiments make it possible to observe some interesting results as shown in Table 11.2. Each simulation experiment S was repeated 10 times and N is the number of competitions held in each simulation run.

Comments

It is possible to see that, in some cases, when the probability of victory in each competition is **a < b** (not favorable for A), A can win the competition, starting with greater amount of resources, $\alpha > \beta$. The difference between final resources α and β depends on the total number N of competitions.

A General Purpose Business Game

The basic form of a general purpose model of BUSINESS GAME [Naylor & others (1971)] can be described as follows:

A business game with "N" companies competing for the market share of "M" products in "K" market places.

For each period of simulation, the N companies fill out a DECISION FORM containing, for instance:

DECISION 1: Unit sale price for each one of the M products;
DECISION 2: Total value invested in marketing;

Table 11.2. Simulation results of Game Two

S	N	a	b	Initial		Final* values		Remarks
				α	β	α	β	
1	20	0.4	0.6	15	10	14.79	10.26	A keeps initial α and β
2	20	0.4	0.6	20	20	19.79	20.20	A is about to lose
3	50	0.4	0.6	30	20	25.866	24.13	B becomes close to A
4	100	0.4	0.6	20	20	12.861	27.138	B wins easily
5	100	0.4	0.6	50	50	41.56	58.435	B wins
6	100	0.4	0.6	70	50	61.564	58.435	A keeps superiority
7	200	0.4	0.6	70	50	53.712	66.287	A loses superiority
8	200	0.4	0.6	85	50	68.712	66.287	Final α and β are very clo

* Expected values

DECISION 3: Estimated cost of production in this period;

DECISION 4: Expenditure to improve the factory; and

DECISION 5: Investment in product improvement (R&D).

The decisions for the First Period of simulation (first month) are based on a FINANCIAL REPORT of a period earlier to the time of simulation, which allows the participating companies to have an exact idea (in addition to the explanations given by the coordinator of the game) of the companies' past activities in the markets they participate in. In the First Period, participants receive the same Financial Report.

After the decisions for a period are made by each participant, simulation software receives the information of the decision forms. After the simulation each company receives an updated and confidential FINANCIAL REPORT, with the results from this period together with an INDUSTRY REPORT informing market data and nonconfidential data from all the companies. Table 11.3 provides a sample of the main items of a FINANCIAL REPORT.

Evaluation of the Results of the Business Game

After practicing the game for a certain number of periods, (a semester or a year), an analysis of the economic situation and performance of each company should be done. Each company prepares its FINAL FINANCIAL REPORT and BALANCE SHEET to be discussed by the participants. The person who coordinates the game should make a comparative analysis of the performance

Table 11.3. Example of a partial Financial Report of a general purpose Business Game (adapted from Naylor et al., 1971)

```
BUSINESS GAME
FINANCIAL REPORT              COMPANY  A          FIRST  PERIOD
* SALES ANALYSIS *
    Orders                          253
    Sales                           253
    Unit Price                      $40
    Sales Revenue                   $10119
    Marketing  Expenses             $600
* PRODUCITON *       INVENTORY    PRODUCTION
    Quantity                         ....
    Unit Cost                        ....
    Total Cost                       ....
*PROFIT AND LOSS *
    Revenues
    Cost Goods Sold
    Research and Development
    Depreciation
    Total Expenses
    Profit
    Taxes
    Net Profit
* CASH STATEMENT *
* BALANCE SHEET*
    Cash
    Inventory
    Value of Plant
    Depreciation
TOTAL ASSETS
```

of the companies, taking into consideration the companies' behavior based in all the factors involved, and not just in the variation of Net Profit value.

Continuous System Simulation

A discrete-event simulation becomes complex when each equation involves several variables of the problems simultaneously. One approach to simplify the numerical calculations is to consider a set of simultaneous algebraic equations or differential equations. Periods of time are advanced in uniform steps, and a model of the system is represented in the form of difference or differential equations. The variables of the model representing the attributes of the system entities are controlled by continuous equations.

Simulation of a continuous system is largely used to control complex or nonlinear engineering problems, or econometric models. Particular interest in using simulation of continuous systems relies in the fact that behavior of a system can be controlled through the coupling between the input and output of the system. The term *feedback* is used to describe this phenomenon.

Industrial Dynamics and *Business Dynamics* are models used to simulate complex industrial and business systems. Industrial Dynamics is a term created by Professor J. W. Forrester of MIT (Forrester, 1961), aiming to study the characteristics and the performance of business corporations or one entire industry. Business Dynamics is a term used by Professor J. D Sterman of MIT (Sterman, 2000), extending the research on system dynamics for advanced models of the business system. The illustrative example of Industrial Dynamics Model of an Inventory Control System (Forrester, 1969), shown in the following section, is based on the description and results presented by Gordon (1978).

Industrial Dynamics Model of an Inventory Control System

A simple model of the inventory control system can be defined by the following system of two ordinary first-order differential equations:

$$Y' = U - V \quad \text{and} \quad X' = V - S$$

V is the equation for the rate of delivery $V = Y / T1$, and U is the order rate expressed by

$$U = S + K (I - X).$$

X is the current inventory level, Y is the outstanding level of orders placed with the supplier, U is the rate of ordering from supplier, V is the rate of delivery from supplier, and S is the rate of sales. In addition, three constants need to be defined: I is the prefixed planned inventory level, T1 is the average delivery time, and K is a constant called ordering constant.

The ordering policy introduces feedback and the value of K corresponds to the amplification in the feedback loop. The value of K, along with the value of T1, will determine if the system oscillates or not.

This problem can be solved using a continuous system modeling language like DYNAMO, or directly using a numerical method for a system of two first-order differential equations, like Runge-Kutta method. The graphics shown in the Figure 11.3 corresponds to the partial results presented in Gordon (1978) using the IBM 360/CSMP (Continuous System Modeling Program).

Assume that a time is measured in units of days, and let the system be initialized at time t = 0, with the following initial conditions:

I = X = 20 units;   Y = 12 units; S = 4 items/day and T1 = 3 days.

Suppose the demand suddenly increases at time t = 4 to S = 6 items/day. The oscillations of inventory level for some values of K (K = 1 or 0.5) are shown in Figure 11.3.

Inventory level X (initial value X = 20 for t = 0).

Figure 11.3. Industrial dynamics model of an inventory control system: effects of feedback for K = 1.0 and 0.5 (adapted from Gordon, 1978)

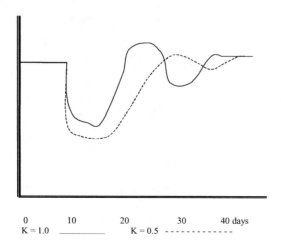

Case Study: Strategy and Decisions in Perspective

Case – The Struggle Against Uncertainty

For most of human history, people have had nothing more than instinct and superstition to guide them in the face of uncertainty. The greatest of mathematicians among the Egyptians, the Assyrians, the Greeks, the Romans and the wise persons of the Middle Ages never considered whether it was worth it to spend time measuring or managing risk, accepting uncertainty as a fatalism. Even the gambling was practiced by rules that seemed arbitrary to anyone with an elementary knowledge of probability.

Things began to change during the Renaissance and the Reformation period, when there were changes in the way of thinking about the future. In 1654, the mathematicians Blaise Pascal and Pierre de Fermat used mathematics to analyze a simple game of chance —— and thus created the basis for the theory of probability. The discoveries and developments of sampling techniques, utility, regression, and correlation, provided a solid foundation to make a rational assessment of risk management.

However, the advances of modern risk-management techniques should not lead us to think that we totally dominate risk, or that such a feat might be possible some day. It is important to remember that uncertainty is our friend, not an adversary. For example, imagine a life without uncertainties, totally ordered and predictable, that never deviates from an average pattern. Life without uncertainty would be like a movie whose end we already know.

I believe that the best way possible for us to live in this world is something close to the one what we have, a world where life is like a game of bridge or poker, and not like a game of roulette. It is worth making the effort to understand the process of evaluating and controlling risk and uncertainty because human beings learn from experience and from technology.

(Excerpted from: The enlightening struggle against uncertainty, Peter L. Berstein, *Financial Times*, Mastering Risk, Part 1, May 2, 2000, pp. 1-4).

Case – Project to Launch a New Product

The pharmaceutical company MSS is developing a project to launch a food supplement to be called PLQ in the market. This food supplement is added to sugar to inhibit the development of dental caries, especially among adolescents. Laboratory tests done up to the present have shown promising results and the company is at the point of deciding between "going ahead with the project" or simply abandoning it, absorbing the costs involved up to now. The company has earlier experience in launching products and even though this is a new product it was possible to construct a decision tree with multiple stages. This is a problem of strategic nature for the company. The project needs to be completed with the values of the parameters estimated based in past experience.

The Decision Tree

To proceed with the project for launching the product it was necessary to consider the following decision stages:

Decision 1. Proceed with other "laboratory tests" to verify the toxicity (two possible outcomes "acceptable" and "unacceptable") and efficacy of the product (three possible outcomes "good", "average", and "bad") or "abandon" the project without further laboratory tests.

Decision 2. According to the results of the laboratory tests, two possible alternatives follows: "continue the project" doing "clinical trials" with humans or "abandon" the project. The "clinical trials" can have two possible results: Positive or Neutral. The results of clinical trials will be available only after three years of testing.

Decision 3. Whatever the results of the clinical trials, it will be necessary to decide between: "launch the product" or "abandon" the project. After launching the project, there can be two alternatives depending on the economic viability: Success (S) with positive gains as a result of good acceptance of the product in the market or, Failure (F) with little or no acceptance of the product in the market. The launch of the product will occur only in the fourth year of the project, after the laboratory tests (1 year) and clinical trials (3 years).

A decision tree with 2 x 3 x 2 x 2 = 24 branches other than the three alternatives to "abandon" the project is then constructed.

The values of the costs in each node of the decision tree should also be estimated. Since the nodes of the tree are located through different future time periods during the project, each estimated value needs to be updated to the present moment so that it will be possible to compare all these values in the initial period of the project. The Net Present Value (NPV) method must be used for this purpose.

Strategy A

Taking into account that the expert estimated the probability of launching the product with success, as $P(S) = 0,7$, after exploring the decision tree from the end to the beginning, this estimate provided, for example, an Expected Monetary Value or EMV = $979 136 and the following possible events:

Events	Probabilities	Cost	(Win or Lose)
a) Abandon the project	0.416	-	$47,727
b) Launch the project with success	0.476		$2,594,578
c) Launch the product with failure	0.108	-	$2,186,516

Sensitivity Analysis

Up to this point, only one value for each cost and probability was estimated or calculated to have a strategic decision alternative. An analysis of variation of the results expressed in terms of EMV value, changing the values of the cost and/or the probabilities is called Sensitivity Analysis of the project. In decision trees of reduced size, this analysis is usually done by trying to answer the question, "*what* would happen to the project result *if* this or that values were to occur?" For example, let's suppose that another strategy has been formulated.

Strategy B

If the expert suspects that after launching the product, the chances of success or failure are equal, that is, P(Success) = P(Failure) = 0.5, redoing all the calculations and utilizing the criterion of the greatest EMV value, we have a new EMV value equals to $479,677 and the following events:

Events	Probabilities	Cost	(Win or Loss)
a) Abandon the project after lab tests	0.48	-	$47,727
b) Launch the product with success	0.30	+	$2,594,578
c) Launch the product with failure	0.10	-	$2,186,516
d) Abandon the project after clinical trials	0.12	-	$479,982

The new estimate P(Success) = 0.5 of the probability of success after launching the product reduced the final value of EMV, creating a new possibility (d) for abandoning the project.

In this case, a sensitivity analysis, based on the variation of the estimates of probabilities and costs, is extremely time-consuming. Comparison of Strategy A and B must be done using stochastic dominance technique based in Monte Carlo calculations. The results of this analysis can be found in Gregory (1980).

Source: (Adapted from Gregory, 1980).

Conclusions

Complex strategic-decision problems often require the use of multistage decision trees. For each event located at one of the tree nodes, an estimation of the probability values corresponding to the level of uncertainty of occurrence of this event is calculated. The estimations of these probability values based on historical data or subjective assessment of experts are unlikely to be efficient because of the large number of nodes and branches of the decision tree involved. The chain of conditional probability values formed along a branch of the decision tree may cause difficulty to conduct the decision based on a single value of the Expected Monetary Value.

The simulation or Monte Carlo process generates a large number of random results for the problem forming a statistically acceptable sample of the population of events of the real problem. Simulation provides the determination of the probability distribution of intermediate or final event of the decision process making it possible the comparison of different strategies using the *stochastic dominance* technique.

The decision-making process involving competition among companies can be better understood and explained through the use of appropriate *business games*. Business game is an efficient tool to create a virtual environment for strategic competitions and can be used mainly for training purpose. Cost restriction and the difficulty to find a business game tailored to the needs of a company make its use more appropriate in university courses or in a specific type of business.

Continuous system models of simulation are used to analyze the overall dynamic behavior of a system represented by a set of continuous algebraic or differential equations. Industrial Dynamics and Business Dynamics are used to represent and analyze the dynamic transformation of industrial and business activities over a period of time.

Simulation of real world problems involves many structured and nonstructured parameters requiring the use of techniques of the Expert Systems and Artificial Intelligence (Cook & Russel, 1993; Sanjay & others, 1990; Day et al., 1997).

Questions for Discussion and Reflection

1. Explain the nature and purposes of the simulation process.
2. Explain how to make the comparison of two similar strategies using *stochastic dominance*.
3. What are the objectives of a *business game*?
4. What are the advantages of a business game?
5. What are the disadvantages of a business game?
6. Considering the case in the section titled The Struggle Against Uncertainty, answer the following questions:

   • Using the exercises presented in this chapter, comment on the role of simulation and Monte Carlo Techniques to resolve the problem of uncertainty and risk.
   • What are the main roles of dynamic continuous system models of simulation?

7.   Considering the case in the section titled Project to Launch a New Product, answer the following questions:

- List the main difficulties found to resolve this project without the use of a simulation model, considering the size of decision tree.

- How is it possible to compare strategy A against strategy B? Explain the difficulties for the use of stochastic dominance technique for this case.

Exercises

1.   *The Game Using Chips*

Prepare α blue chips representing company A's material resources and β red chips representing the material resources of company B ($\alpha < 10$ and $\beta < 10$).

GAME ONE – toss a coin ($a = b = \frac{1}{2}$) to obtain the result of each competition; and

GAME TWO – use a die to draw the different probabilities of victory a and b, in each competition.

Play the game ONE and TWO several times (10 times each) for different values of a and b. Compare the results of the simulation with the result using the mathematical formula presented in this chapter.

2.   *Other Types of Business Games*

Present written reports of the characteristics, advantages and disadvantages of other Business Games you can find in the literature (or web sites), such as: *Publicity and Marketing Game, Opinion Polling Game, Game of Financial Investment*, etc.

References

Day, G.S., et al. (Eds.). (1997). *Wharton on dynamic competitive strategy*. New York: John Wiley & Sons.

Forrester, J. W. (1961). *Industrial dynamics*. Cambridge, MA: MIT Press (currently available from Pegasus Communications, Waltham, MA).

Forrester, J. W. (1969). *Principle of systems*. Cambridge, MA: Wright-Allen Press.

Goodwin, P., & Wright, G. (1996). *Decision analysis for management judgment*. New York: John Wiley & Sons.

Gordon, G. (1978). *Systems simulation* (2nd ed.). NJ: Prentice-Hall.

Gregory, G. (1980). *Decision analysis*. New York: Pitman Books.

Kinoshita, E. (1996). *Introduction to management science* (in Japanese). Tokyo: Sakurai Publishers.

Naylor, T., et al. (1971). *Computer simulation experiments with models of economic systems*. New York: John Wiley & Sons.

Sanjay, J., et al. (1990). Expert simulation for on-line scheduling. *Communications of the ACM, 33*(10), 55-60.

Sterman, J.D. (2000). *Business dynamics*. New York: Irwing/McGrow-Hill.

Chapter XII

Decision Based On Organizational Knowledge, Decision Support Systems, Expert System And Business Intelligence

Introduction

Organizations are often seeking techniques for improving the actions to structure decision models. However, with the possible exception of routine and well-structured problems, most of the decision problems found in organizations constitute a chaotic and complex family of problems. The *principle of bounded rationality* proposed by Herbert Simon suggests the use of a decision model based on a simplified model of a firm with a small number of relational concepts, such as: (a) quasi resolution of conflict,(b) uncertainty avoidance or minimization, (c) search directed around the main objective of the problem and, (d) adaptation of organizational goals based on learning.

Organizations achieve a better decision-making process by searching different levels of knowledge inside and outside the organization. According to March (1999), the pursuit of organizational knowledge (or intelligence) to structure better decision models is made particularly difficult by three problems. The first problem is the problem of *ignorance*, because not everything is known, the future is uncertain, and so on. The second problem is the problem of *conflict*, because organizations seek goals and objectives in the name of multiple, nested actors over multiple, nested time periods. The third problem is the problem of *ambiguity*, caused by ill-defined or ill-measured preferences and identities.

In order to arrive at good procedures for a decision-making process, organizations adopt some practices leading to intelligent actions. For example, the "rule-based rational action" is considered an intelligent action to estimate the future consequences of possible current actions and choose the one with the highest expected value. Procedures based on "rule-based action," used together with "organizational learning," are considered by many authors, as a way to involve assessments of the collective actions and long-term consequences rather than individual action at a particular time.

However, neither "rationality" nor "learning" always assures a reasonable final model. In Chapter IX, a list of problems considered to be the hidden traps in decision making — *the anchoring trap, the status-quo trap, the sunk-cost trap, the confirming-evidence trap, the framing trap, and estimating and forecasting traps* — is presented. According to the authors of this list, complex and important decisions problems are the most prone to distortion because they tend to involve assumptions, estimates, and the inputs from the most people (Davenport & Prusak, 1998; Matheus et al., 1993; March, 1999).

The Framework for Strategic Decision-Making

In Chapter VIII, a decision problem was presented by three levels of decision: (1) strategic decisions — which refer to the long-range goals and the policies for resource allocation; (2) tactical decisions — referring to the acquisition and efficient utilization of resources in the accomplishment of organizational goals; and (3) operational decisions — concerning the efficient and effective execution of specific tasks. In that chapter, we have noted that the main characteristics observed in strategic decision problems are: medium to long-range semi-structured or nonstructured problems with complexity.

Complexity in the decision-making process is related to one or more of the following features:

1. **Uncertainty.** In the evaluation of alternatives of action, eventual outcomes are not known for certain but only in a probabilistic level depending on subjective judgments of experts.

2. **Multiple variables or attributes.** In many real-world problems, the use of traditional mathematical algorithms such as nonlinear programming, scheduling algorithm, queuing algorithms, etc., become prohibitive when a problem with large number of variables or attributes must be considered. These problems, known as NP (Non Polynomial) complex problems, may often require the use of sophisticated meta-heuristics or Artificial Intelligence algorithms.

3. **Multiple objectives.** One of the main impacts of the decision-making process has been to provide a useful description to deal with alternatives whose outcomes have multiple, often conflicting objectives or goals.

4. **Multiple alternatives.** The development of reliable procedures to eliminate dominated alternatives — that alternative already included inside another alternative — is an important part of the decision-making process to simplify the problem. But how can we obtain powerful simplifications without the risk of missing crucial points through over-simplification?

5. **Sequence of decisions.** Many decision problems are multiple-stage problems in which a dependent or independent decision is taken at each stage and associated with the evaluation of the use of new information at particular moments in the sequence of decision-making.

6. **Imprecise or fuzzy problems.** Problems difficult to be defined precisely — due to the large dimensionality or the qualitative nature of their attributes and/or relationships — require the application of new types of algorithms such as expert systems, fuzzy algorithms, neural nets, and so on.

The environments in which management must operate today are more complex today than ever before, and the trend is toward increasing complexity. Major factors such as new technologies, global markets, competition, political stability, etc., are facing more and more the effects of increasing trends that results in more alternatives to choose, larger costs of making errors, and more uncertainty regarding the future. Decision-making today is more complicated than in the past. However, the benefits of well-structured and implemented strategic decision making are very large.

As a result of these trends and changes, it is very difficult to rely on a trial-and-error approach to management, especially in decisions involving the factors mentioned above. Managers must learn how to use new tools and techniques that are being developed in their field.

Today, an organization is not interested only in the best alternative of decision (for instance, the alternative that provides highest profit), but it is interested in knowing a set of good enough or best possible alternatives considering multiple criteria such as quality aspects, labor benefits, environmental risk, and so on. Therefore it is often necessary to analyze each alternative in light of its potential impact on several goals. In mathematical methods used to handle multiple goals (such as Utility Theory, Goal Programming, Multiple Objective Linear Programming), it is usually difficult to obtain an explicit statement of the organization's goals because the relationship between alternatives and their impact on goals may be difficult to quantify. To understand complex models and to enable flexibility and adaptation to changing conditions for different decision-making situations, the procedure of *sensitivity analysis* adopted by software of Decision Support System (DSS), Expert System (ES), and Artificial Intelligence (Nilsson, 1970; Nilsson, 1998) techniques, is recommended.

Exploiting Solutions Using Expert Systems

Seeking out and refining solutions to problems formulated by mathematical models, such as linear programming or dynamic programming, is neither efficient nor sufficient to obtain new knowledge about problems in the real world. Heuristic techniques are appropriate for obtaining near-optimal solutions in complex problems. Nevertheless, the solutions obtained by simple heuristic methods need to be improved through the procedure known as meta-heuristic techniques (Cook & Russel, 1993; Hillier & Liebermann, 1980).

Some of the better known meta-heuristic techniques are: simulated annealing, tabu search, genetic algorithm, neural network, and so on (Turban & Arsonson, 1998; Takefuji,1996).

An Artificial intelligence technique known as expert systems is recommended for solving complex problems from the real world, which takes into consideration inferences with qualitative as well as quantitative variables. In the section titled Application of an expert system, there is an example that illustrates the application of the expert system in a simple problem involving two conflicting criteria.

Application of an Expert System

The expert system is an information system (file or database managed by a computer program) which contains data or descriptive sentences about a given branch of activity such as medical diagnosis, weather forecasting, financial forecasts, machine design, consultations on geography, archeology, tourism, language, etc. The information existing in the expert system was collected and organized under the supervision of a group of experts on the subject. The system can answer questions formulated by users, as if he or she were consulting an expert person in the area.

Information is stored in the form of sentences called *production or decision rule* of the following type:

> *If* { facts are true } *then* { execute algorithm A } *else* { execute algorithm B}
>
> forming a KNOWLEDGE DATABASE. These sentences are chosen to resolve a problem, using software known as INFERENCE MECHANISM.

Example: Selecting Companies Using Two Criteria (adapted from Negoita,1985)

Information about Sales and Profit from six companies during a fiscal year was:

Company	Sales $	Profit %
A	800	17
B	750	11
C	900	18
D	1050	14
E	1150	15
F	1200	13

To classify companies according to the value of Sales and Profit, an expert system can use a decision rule based on quantitative values:

"SELECT COMPANIES WITH SALES $\geq$ \$1000 and PROFIT $\geq$ 14%"

The companies selected according to this quantitative criterion are:

Company	Sales	Profit
D	1050	14
E	1150	15

By this quantitative criterion, companies with excellent results (company C with SALES = \$900 and PROFIT = 18% and company F with SALES = \$1200 and PROFIT = 13%, were not selected.

Fuzzy Expert System

We can have a more meaningful result if we attribute fuzzy values to the variables SALES as well as PROFIT. Attributing three fuzzy values (low, medium, high) to SALES and two fuzzy values (Acceptable, Not Acceptable) to PROFIT, we have the following $3 \times 2 = 6$ rules of decision:

R1: If SALES = Low and PROFIT = Not Acceptable then DECISION = Not select.

R2: If SALES = Low and PROFIT = Acceptable then DECISION = Not select.

R3:   If SALES = Medium and PROFIT = Not Acceptable then DECISION = Not select.

R4:   If SALES= Medium and PROFIT = Acceptable then DECISION = Select.

R5:   If SALES = High and PROFIT = Not Acceptable then DECISION = Not select.

R6:   If SALES = High and PROFIT = Acceptable then DECISION = Select.

Using fuzzy inference it is possible to obtain a fuzzy classification based on a fuzzy index:

Company	Sales	Profit	Index
C	$900	18%	0.75
A	800	17	0.55
D	1050	14	0.60
E	1150	15	0.65
F	1200	13	0.40

The values of the index can vary depending on the membership function attributed to the fuzzy values. This example illustrates that the use of fuzzy values and operations allow the manipulation and ordering of data with multiple criteria.

Decision Support Systems (DSS)

Traditionally, most organizations make a decision based on successful past experiences, that is, they are refining an already known procedure. Decision alternatives are formulated and selected by quantitative methods of Operations Research, and qualitative methods employing techniques of Artificial Intelligence, formulated by expert systems and fuzzy inference. This attitude corresponds to a search for organization intelligence using a *refinement* procedure. Refinement means improving, regulating, producing, and recording existing knowledge. It involves choice, efficiency, and reliability. It normally leads to an improvement, but it can be blind to the search for new solutions.

The definitions of a DSS, according to different authors (Turban & Aronson, 1998; Cook & Russel, 1993, Li & Ye, 1990; Mallach, 2000) are:

A DDS is a set of procedures (software programs) based on a data-processing environment to analyze problems with the aim to assist managers in making decisions. The problems resolved by a DSS can be of a structured, semi-structured, or nonstructured type, according to the point of view of the people making decisions. A DSS is a flexible and expansive system, capable of giving support and providing ad hoc analysis of data and decision models, in the search to obtain efficient results in long, mid and short-term planning.

A DSS is a computer system made up of three interactive components:

a.   *a system of language (that allows communication among users and the DSS sub systems;*

b.   *a system of knowledge (that stores available data, procedures and intelligent information);*

c.   *a system for processing problems (structuring and executing appropriate models to solve problems); and*

d.   *a system that allows the sensibility analysis of the result of decision, providing a response to the "what-if?" question, such as question of the type "what would happen to this result if the data utilized were 30% greater?"*

Reasons for Using a DSS

According to Turban and Aronson (1998), in an article published in *Computer World* (September, 27, 1982), the *Firestone Tire & Rubber Co* listed the following reasons for using a DSS:

- the company was facing growing competition in the country and abroad;
- the company was having increasingly greater difficulty in monitoring its numerous business operations;
- the Information Systems department was not managing to meet the company's diversity of needs or to answer ad hoc questions raised by the managers.

According to the same source, a study done in 1983 identified main reasons that organizations began using large scale DSS:

Reasons

- DSS is seen as an organizational winner;
- Need for precise or new information;
- Managers demanded DSS;
- Reduce costs.

One important reason mentioned for the development and use of a DSS is the facility provided to end users. The end users are neither programmers nor people trained in computers and they demand friendly tools and procedures for easy use.

A DSS should have the following features, according to Turban and Aronson (1998), and Mallach (2000):

1. serve managers at different levels;
2. allow decisions by an individual or group;
3. be able to make both sequential and interdependent decisions;
4. provide a variety of decision making styles;
5. be user friendly;
6. seek efficacy and not efficiency;
7. facilitate the formulation of the problem by the end user; and
8. allow the analysis of results.

DSS is intended to improve the efficiency of the decision-making process, to provide better administrative control and to facilitate communication. It allows for the analysis of existing alternatives, the optimizing alternatives and other combinations of decision alternatives. However, it is very difficult to have a DSS available at a low cost for nontraditional and nonstructured problems. The diversity and complexity of the decision-making process makes it hard to obtain an efficient and low cost DSS.

The sensitivity analysis made by in a DSS, by asking questions of "what – if?" type, has limited capacity in exploring for new facts, because the exploration is restricted to the area around an existing solution.

A DSS is a useful and efficient tool to foresee, generate, and evaluate the alternatives for solving administrative problems.

DSS Software Tools

DSS contains standard software packages to help make decisions developed for some specific problems. These packages are made available for public use because: a) many people make these decisions, so the potential market is large; and b) the decisions factors and objectives are the same for all of them, allowing the use of standard algorithms or chart representation. The following packages of software are usually available in a DSS:

1.   Database management packages;
2.   Query and information retrieval packages;
3.   Statistical data analysis packages;
4.   Forecasting packages; and
5.   Graphing packages.

Using the Forecasting Package

In the section titled Strategy and Decisions in Perspective, an illustrative case for the use of a Forecasting package is presented. In this section a brief description of the use of forecasting method is also presented. Different methods of forecasting and their uses are described in a DSS software tool. There is no universal forecasting method for all situations and circumstances.

A simple way to classify the problems that require forecasting is in terms of functional areas to which they relate. One of the reasons for this classification is that forecasting is merely a means for improving decision making and is not an end in itself. Since decision-making problems and processes are often grouped along a functional line (marketing, finance, or production), the integrative aspect of existing forecasting methods is important in the medium and short-term planning. Although each of the functional areas of business has its own requirements for forecasts, a number of forecasts relates these functional areas and are important in the overall decision-making framework of the company.

It is possible to develop and use a single method of forecasting for a number of different situations. First, all these situations deals with the future and time is directly involved. Second, uncertainty is always present in forecasting situations. The third situation is that a forecast uses information contained in historical data.

Two types of forecasting methods can be considered: *qualitative and quantitative methods*. Qualitative methods rely on managerial judgment without the use of specific models. Qualitative methods are useful when there is a lack of data or when past data are not reliable predictors of the future. Individual or group decision makers can utilize the best available data and a qualitative approach to arrive at a forecast. Examples of qualitative forecasting method are: Delphi technique and market surveys. In chapter 13, a case study working with qualitative methods (Delphi or NGT — Nominal Group Technique) in a GDSS (Group Decision Support System) environment will be presented.

There are two types of quantitative forecasting methods: time-series and causal forecasting. Quantitative methods has gained wide acceptance for at least three reasons: a) manager's confidence on the record of past historical data; b) the adoption of computers (the forecasting package is one of the useful software tools in a DSS); and c) quantitative forecasts are much cheaper to obtain than any of the available alternatives.

Quantitative forecasting methods are used in a line of functions areas serving as an input for decisions on process design, capacity planning and inventory. Time Series forecasting methods, such as moving averages, exponential smoothing, or Box-Jenkins methods, are used for short to medium-range planning, but the integrative use in a line of functional areas makes quantitative forecasting methods useful also for long-germ strategic decision planning. For instance, information from a single forecast may be used simultaneously by marketing, production, finance, and accounting, and even by the personnel department helping in the decision of planning for the number of workers in each category to be hired and trained.

Time-series forecasting methods, considered as having a high level of accuracy and used mostly for short and medium-range planning, may assume strategic importance, for instance, when the marketing and operations departments discuss the upcoming budgeting cycle. Time-series forecasting methods offer a fast response in forecasting software available in most DSS systems.

Causal forecasting methods are used for medium to long-term range planning of aggregate production inventory, sales by product classes, or countrywide sales by industrial sectors. Causal forecasting methods using econometric models or simulation models are recommended for long-term forecasting, because of the cost involved and difficulty of working with them.

Two areas that are particularly related to forecasting are those of budgeting and planning. It is important how forecasting procedures can be integrated with at least these two existing functions to be aware of the tactical and strategic importance of forecasting procedures.

Some Cautions About the Use of Time-Series Forecasting Methods

To illustrate the basic caution to be observed in the use of a time-series forecasting package, let us consider past data of the demand for two products. Product A presented an increasing and almost linear past demand, while past demand for product B presented an irregular shape, as shown by following tables and figures.

Three different forecasting methods will be used:

a. Exponential smoothing method

$F_{t+1} = \alpha\, D_t + (1 - \alpha)\, Ft;$

where: F_{t+1} is the forecast demand for period t+1, α is a constant value used as the smoothing coefficient, and D_t is the demand during period t.

b. Trend adjusted exponential smoothing method:

$A_t = \alpha\, D_t + (1 - \alpha)(A_{t-1} + F_{t-1}),$

$T_t = \beta\, (A_t + A_{t-1}) + (1 - \beta)\, T_{t-1},$ and

$F_{t+1} = A_t + T_t;$

Table 12.1. Past demand data for product A and product B (adapted from Schroeder, 1985)

	Product A	Product B
t	D_t	D_t
1	85	66
2	105	106
3	112	78
4	132	135
5	145	

c)   Trend and seasonal component adjusted exponential smoothing (also known as Winter's method):

$$A_t = \alpha (D_t / R_{t-1}) + (1 - \alpha)(A_{t-1} + F_{t-1}),$$
$$T_t = \beta (A_t + A_{t-1}) + (1 - \beta) T_{t-1},$$
$$R_t = \gamma (D_t / A_t) + (1 - \gamma) R_{t-L}, \text{ and}$$
$$F_{t+1} = (A_t + T_t) R_{t-L+1}$$

where:

F_{t+1} is the forecast demand for period t+1, T_t is the trend component of period t, At is the average value computed through period t, L is the number of periods of the seasonal cycle (for example, if the seasonal cycles repeats on an annual basis or 12 months, then L = 12), R_t is the seasonal ratio for period t and, a, b, and g are smoothing coefficients assuming values between 0 and 1. Forecast error in period t is $E_t = / D_t - F_t /$

Table 12.2.A. Forecast for product A using: method a and method b

t	D_t	a) F_t	E_t	b) A_t	T_t	F_t	E_t
1	85	85	0	85	15	85	0
2	105	97	8	100.5	15.05	100	5
3	112	106	6	115.2	15.05	115.55	3.55
4	132	109.6	22.4	130.4	15.03	130.21	1.79
5	145	123.04	21.96	145.4	15.03	145.43	0.43
Total error			58.39				10.77

Assume: a) $D_1 = F_1 = 85$ e $\alpha = 0.6$; b) $A_o = 70$, $T_o = 15$ and $\alpha = \beta = 0.1$. (Adapted from Schroeder (1985))

Table 12.2.B. Forecast for product B using: methods a, b and c

t	D_t	a) F_t	E_t	b) F_t	E_t	c) A_t	T_t	R_t	F_t	E_t
1	66	64	4	68.66	2.66	80.5	10.1	0.804	64	2
2	106	65.2	0.8	64.87	41.13	90.1	10.0	1.195	108.7	2.7
3	78	89.68	11.68	73.30	4.71	99.5	9.9	0.799	80.4	2.4
4	135	82.67	52.33	87.20	47.80	110.1	10.0	1.201	130.7	4.3
Total error			68.81		90.98					11.4

Assume: method a) $F_1 = 64$ and $\alpha = 0.6$; method b) $A_o = 70$, $T_o = 10$ and $\alpha = \beta = 0.1$; and method c) $A_o = 70$, $T_o = 10$, $L = 2$, $R_o = 1.2$, $R_{-1} = 0.8$ and $\alpha = \beta = \gamma = 0.2$. (adapted from Schroeder, 1985)

Figure 12.1. Exponential smoothing method used to forecast demand for product A

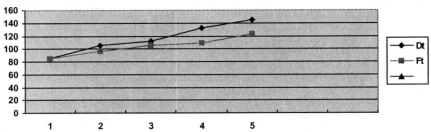

Figure 12.2. Exponential smoothing method used to forecast demand for product B

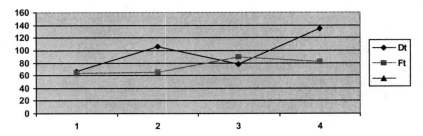

Figure 12.3. Trend adjusted exponential smoothing method to forecast demand for product A

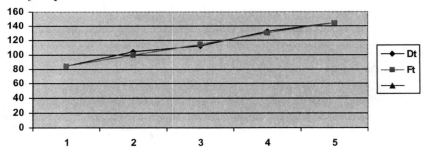

Figure 12.4. Trend adjusted exponential smoothing method used to forecast demand for product B

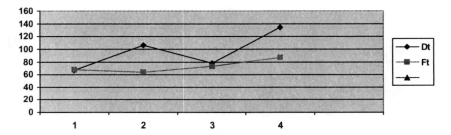

Figure 12.5. Winter's method used to forecast demand for product B

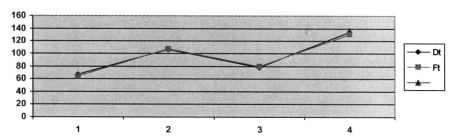

Forecast data for Product A and B, using these methods are shown in Table 12.2 A and Table 12.2B, and illustrated by Figures 12.1 to 12.5.

Comments

Forecast for product A: method b) trend adjusted exponential smoothing method fits well to the past demand (Figure 12.3).

Forecast for product B: Winter's method fits well to time-series forecasting with trend and seasonal components (Figure 12.5).

Exploring New Organizational Knowledge Using Business Intelligence (BI) and Data Mining Techniques

Another attitude known as *exploration* seeks to discover new occurrences or innovative actions for the organization, searching the organization's past database. This process involves experiments in the search for new or hidden information inside the database. It can lead to inconsistent results, but occasionally leads to new courses and important discoveries. Statistical techniques such as regression and correlation analysis have been traditionally used to explore new facts or trends.

Business Intelligence (BI), also known as KDD (Knowledge Data Discovery), technology is applied to suitably related information from different databases to discover new facts, new relationships, or previously unknown trends. Data mining techniques are used to seek out and discover new relationships and tendencies (Fayyad et al., 1996; Mena, 1999).

While a DSS is a mean to refine the existing information and data searching for refined or optimized results, a BI or KDD is a technology used to explore the data files searching for new knowledge (new information or new relationships hidden inside the database).

This new type of tool to support decision making is developed due to two main reasons: the pressure to increase the company's competitiveness and the desire to take advantage of the investments already made in information technology. The search for these objectives is made by organizing data warehouses, which are new data deposits, suitably joined with the existing database to explore the benefits offered by Data Mining technology.

The procedures for transforming existing data into new information which makes it possible to form a new step of decision making are illustrated in Figures 12.6.

Some terms and definitions used in a BI environment according to IBM (1999), Witten and Frank (2000), and Mena (1999) are:

Business Intelligence

provides a route to obtain new knowledge needed to make important decision in the organization.

Datawarehouse

is a collection of integrated, dynamic, nonvolatile subject-oriented data to support managerial decision making; or a warehouse of

Figure 12.6. Data, information and decision (adapted from IBM, 1999)

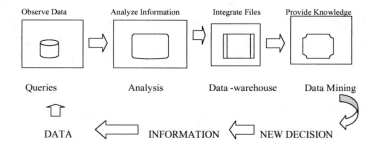

data, collected from several sources, inside and outside the organization, which is available to end users to be used in the context of the organization.

Data Mart

is a smaller version of a data-warehouse, containing data related to a certain functional area of the company.

Data Mining

is the process of extracting valid, unknown and wide ranging data from a data-warehouse, making it possible to organize new decision-making processes.

Some typical questions that can be answered through data mining are:

a.   "Who are my most important clients and what are their buying habits or behaviors?"
b.   "How should I optimize my store layout to increase profit?"
c.   "What is the composition of products in the market basket or market cart preferred by a certain type of client?"
d.   "Who commits fraud and how can I recognize it?"

Main business drivers for the application of date mining are:

a.   Saturated markets where it is difficult to find the right clients for the company's product or the right product for its clients;
b.   Imprecise borders of industrial activities, since we can find the industry from branch A (automotive, aviation, etc.) acting in branch B (services, tourism) or C (foods, soft drinks) due to the occurrence of acquisitions or mergers of companies;
c.   Lack of a clear definition to detect the type of client that the company or the competing company would like to serve;
d.   Rapid expansion of alternative marketing channels, such as e-business; and

e.   Competitive market which requires a variety of products with a shorter life cycle.

Advantages of using data mining are:

- with the aid of adequate software and a sufficient number of parameters to guide the investigation, the computer does all the work;
- the computer is not influenced by preconceived user notions about possible relationships existing in the examined database. The computer can discover unexpected relationships, some of which can be of great utility.

Some disadvantages of data mining are:

- the exploratory search through many gigabytes or terabytes of data can be a heavy load for even the most powerful (and most expensive) computers. Thus, an attempt to apply data mining is not recommended for small computers, except in very specific cases;
- in general an enormous number of irrelevant relationships are found, compared to the modest amount of "useful" information;
- it is not easy to identify a useful relationship among the mass of irrelevant relationships, since it is not easy to gauge the utility of data or relationships.

The main areas of application for data mining are listed in Table 12.3.

Table 12.3. Data mining application areas (adapted from IBM, 1999)

Marketing	Risk Analysis	Production Management
Target Marking	Customer Retention	Inventory Analysis
Market Basket Analysis	Churn Attrition Analysis (*)	Lay-out design
Cross Selling	Service Fraud	Demand Forecasting
Web Usage analysis		Business Scorecard (**)
(*) Churn model predicts which customers are likely to leave in the near future		
(**) Balanced Score Card (Kaplan & Norton, 1992) or Six Sigma		

Market Basket Analysis:
Mining Association Rules

The term "market basket analysis," used to designate the algorithm to find new association rules, has its origin in the problem classifying customers according to the contents of their market basket or cart.

A Medical Exam Data Set

Let's analyze a set of data of Table 12.4, corresponding to the results of 14 medical exams reporting the occurrence or nonoccurrence of a certain disease. The data are fictitious and serve only to illustrate the application of the data-

Table 12.4. A medical examination dataset (adapted from Witten & Frank, 2000)

Number	Sex	Age	ATTRIBUTES Weight	Fat	Cholesterol	Disease
1	male	25 or less	110 ~170	normal	normal	no
2	male	25 or less	110 ~170	normal	high	no
3	male	25 or less	110 ~170	high	normal	yes
4	male	25 or less	170 or more	high	normal	no
5	male	25 ~45	110 or less	high	high	yes
6	male	25 ~45	110 ~170	normal	normal	no
7	male	45 or more	110 or less	high	high	yes
8	male	45 or more	170 or more	normal	normal	yes
9	female	25 or less	110 or less	high	normal	no
10	female	25 or less	170 or more	normal	high	yes
11	female	25 ~45	110 or less	high	normal	no
12	female	25 ~45	170 or more	normal	high	yes
13	female	45 or more	110 ~170	high	high	yes
14	female	45 or more	170 or more	normal	normal	no

Age: in years; Weight: in pounds

mining technique. The calculation of the numerical results is based on THE WEATHER PROBLEM application presented by Witten and Frank (2000).

Item Sets

The two-items set (sex = male, age = 25 or less) appears inside rules 1, 2, 3 and 4, and then its number of occurrences is 4. Other two-item sets are:

(male, 25 ~45) occurring twice, (female , weight = 170 or more) occurring 3 times, and so on.

Other examples of item sets are:

Three- items sets

(male, 25 or less, 110 ~170 pounds) occurs 3 times, while
(female, 25 or less, 110 pounds or less) occurs only once.

Four-items sets

(sex = male, age = 25 or less, weight = 110 ~170, cholesterol = normal) occurs twice, and
(sex = female, fat = high, cholesterol = normal, disease = no) occurs twice.

Five-items sets

(male, 25 years or less, 110 ~170 pounds, fat = normal, disease = no);
(male, 110 pounds or less, fat = high, cholesterol = high, disease = yes);
(female, 170 pounds or more, fat = normal, cholesterol = high, disease = yes); and

(45 years or more, 110 ~170 pounds, fat = high, cholesterol = high, disease = yes) occur twice each.

Generating Association Rules and their Accuracy

The second step of the data-mining technique asks us to generate association rules and calculate the corresponding accuracy index. For example, the four-items set

(male, 25 years or less, 110 ~170 pounds, fat = normal, disease = no) occurs twice and leads to the following potential rules:

The one-term antecedent rule:

"if (sex = male) then (age = 25 years or less and weight=110 ~ 170 pounds and fat = normal and disease = no),

has the antecedent (sex = male) observed in 8 rules of the dataset , then accuracy of this rule is 2/8 or 25%;

The two-terms antecedent rule:

"if (sex = male *and* age = 25 years or less) then (weight = 110 ~170 pounds and fat = normal and disease = no),

has the antecedent (sex = male and age = 25 years or less) observed in 4 rules of the data set, then the accuracy will increase to 2/4 or 50%, and in the rule

The three-terms antecedent rule:

"if (sex = male *and* age = 25 years or less *and* weight = 110 ~170 pounds) then (fat = normal and disease = no)

has the antecedent (sex = male and age = 25 years or less and weight = 110 ~170 pounds) observed in 3 rules of the data set, then the accuracy is 2/3 or 66.7%.

Table 12.5. Characteristics of MIS, DSS, ES and KDD (adapted from Turban & Aronson, 1998; IBM, 1999; Mallach, 2000)

Features	MIS	DSS	ES	KDD
Type of problem	Structured	Semi Structured Integrated	Non Structured	Non Structured
Finality	Efficiency	Efficacy Refinement	Specific	Exploration
Time Horizon	Past and Present	Present and Future	Present	Future
Objective	Information	Decision	Inference	Knowledge acquisition
Cost	Medium	High	Medium or High	High
Applications	Inventory Accounting Forecast	Integrated Decision	Diagnosis Training	Market Basket Analysis

A computer program must be used to generate all the potential rules and obtain their levels of accuracy. It seems clear that only decision rules with 100% accuracy should be used to form new decision rules, but lower level accuracy of potential rules is a challenge to proceed with the data-mining process. In this example, due to the small size of the dataset, it is difficult to generate a new decision rule with 100% accuracy. However in the Weather Problem data set presented by Witten and Frank (2000), it is possible to find 58 association rules with 100% accuracy.

Comparing MIS, DSS, ES, and KDD

The main features that distinguish a MIS (Management Information System), a DSS (Decision Support System), an ES (Expert System), and a KDD (Knowledge Data Discovery system) are presented in Table 12.5 (Turban & Aronson, 1998; Mallach, 2000; Maggiolini, 1981; Li & Ye, 1999; Berry & Linoff, 2000).

Case Study: Strategy and Decisions in Perspective

Case – Using the DSS Forecasting Software Package

Sam Fordson, president of AAA Corporation was meeting with George Springfield, vice president of operations, to discuss the upcoming budgeting cycle. George said, "Sam, I'm tired of operations being forced to change forecast every month. Every fall just before budgeting time, the marketing people make their annual sales forecast, which, as you know, is updated monthly. I can tell you that this forecast is merely a composite of all the 'wish list' submitted by the marketing people. After the marketing vice president receives these forecasts, he simply adds them and adjusts the results to the situation. I think these procedures for forecasting are too crude, and something must be done about them."

Sam replied, "Well George, as you know, the market is very dynamic in our business and the marketing vice president tries to stay in close touch with the market. But if you have a better approach to forecasting our monthly demand, we'll be happy to give it try."

George reminded him that the Information Technology people recommend strongly the use software packages of the corporation's DSS. The use of the packages can be made at no additional cost and providing immediate response to standard questions formulated through the SQL (Structured Query Language) available in the DSS. Forecasting Package and Statistical Analysis Package are the two most common packages used in business decisions. George continued, "Perhaps we should test these packages to assist us in planning the short-term and annual budgets."

At this point, Peter Song, the marketing vice-president, walked into the office, and Sam and George explained the entire situation to him. Peter said, "I'm very skeptical that a computer can be used to replace the marketing judgment that we've spent years developing. How can computer methods do efficient demand forecasting when so many factors are involved?"

George reminded him that the IT people had warned that the forecasting package is formed by different quantitative and qualitative methods, and the selection of the most appropriate method or combination of methods, besides the technical or mathematical problems involved, requires decisions involving the interest of more than one manager.

George and Peter agreed to develop a forecasting model using all available historical data except those for the past year. This model would then be used to forecast demand for the past year, and the results would be compared to actual demand. All three managers agreed to meet again when the model was complete to review the results of the test and only then decide to use the results of the forecast for the short-term and annual budget planning.

Source: Based on Schroeder (1985).

Conclusions

The search for new knowledge, inside and outside the organization, exploring databases, reports, organizational history, patents, professional experience, etc., is part of the search for organization knowledge. The search for organizational knowledge depends on the availability of an efficient computer system.

An organization's strategic planning is traditionally based mostly on market analysis and financial planning. Factors such as indirect costs, customer satisfaction or preference, usually are not considered in the organization's decision strategy due to the difficulty to determine the appropriate information indicator and range. New software technologies such as the **Decision Support Systems** (DSS) and **Knowledge Data Discovery** (KDD) have been developed as an effort to obtain new knowledge to support decisions in the organization.

The DSS is an important support for strategic decision making, through sensibility analysis, known as "what – if?" questions, which allow the examination of new decision alternatives.

Data-mining techniques used inside the KDD environment utilize traditional statistical and operations research techniques to extract new knowledge, and new techniques such as Market Basket Analysis to discover new decision rules. The use of advanced software technologies such as DSS or KDD should provide important advances in the strategic decision making in the organization.

Questions for Discussion and Reflection

1.   What is a DSS? and a KDD?
2.   What is a DSS (or KDD) used for?
3.   What are the main features of a DSS (or a KDD)?
4.   What are the main differences of a DSS or a KDD in relation to MIS and ES systems?
5.   What is the role of "what-if?" questions? Give examples.
6.   What are the roles of data mining techniques? Give examples.

Considering the case in the section titled Using the DSS Forecasting Software Package, answer the following questions:

- What are the main types of forecasting methods? What are the differences between quantitative and qualitative forecasting methods?
- What are the reasons to use a time-series forecasting method? What are the problems involving time-series forecasting methods?
- Are forecasting data used by the operations department the same ones used by the marketing department or by the budget planning department? Comment on the difference of data types.

Exercises

1.   Explain the differences between *refinement* and *exploration* of knowledge. Give examples.
2.   Generate association rules and calculate accuracy indexes using the five-items sets extracted from the Medical Examination data set.

References

Berry, M. J. A., & Linoff, G. S. (2000). *Mastering data mining.* New York: John Wiley & Sons.

Clemen, R. T., & Reilly, T. (2001). *Making hard decisions with decisions tools.* New York: Duxbury Press.

Cook, T.M., & Russel, R.A.(1993). *Introduction to management science.* NJ: Prentice-Hall.

Davenport, T. H., & Prusak, L. (1998). *Working knowledge — How organizations manage what they know.* Boston: Harvard Business School Press.

Fayyad, U., et al. (1996, November). The KDD process for extracting useful knowledge from volumes of data. *Communications of the ACM, 39*(11).

IBM (1999). *Intelligent miner for data: Enhance your business intelligence.* San Jose, CA, IBM International Business Machine Corporation — SG 24-5422-00.

Kaplan, R.S., & Norton, D. P. (1992). Balanced scorecard: measures that drive performance. *Harvard Business Review, 70*(1), 71-79.

Li, M., & Ye, L.R. (1999). Information technology and firm performance: Linking with environmental, strategic and managerial contexts. *Information & Management, 35*(1), 43-51.

Maggiolini, P. (1981). *Costi Benefici di um Sistema Informativo.* Italy, Etas Libri.

Mallach, E. G. (2000). *Decision support and data warehouse systems.* Singapore: McGraw-Hill International Editions.

March, J. C. (1999). *The pursuit of organizational intelligence.* USA; UK: Blackwell Publisher.

Matheus, C.J., et al. (1993). Systems for knowledge discovery in databases. *IEEE Transactions on Knowledge and Data Engineering, 5*(6).

Mena, J. (1999). *Data mining your website.* Digital Press.

Nilsson, N. J. (1970). *Problem solving methods in artificial intelligence.* New York: McGraw-Hill.

Nilsson, N. J. (1998). *Artificial intelligence: A new synthesis.* San Francisco: Morgan Kaufmann Publishers.

Turban, E., & Aronson, J.E. (1998). *Decision support systems and intelligent systems* (5th ed.). New York: Prentice-Hall.

Witten, I. H., & Frank, E. (2000). *Data mining.* San Francisco: Morgan Kaufmann Publishers.

Chapter XIII

Group Decision And Negotiation In Strategic-Decision-Making

Introduction

In the previous chapters, decisions models have been modeled based on the economic point of view of the problem expressed mainly through quantitative values and, in some cases by qualitative representation. The economic perspective draws unique coherence from economic assumptions of rational behavior and it draws predictive power from strongly valid rules of influence that employ mathematical or logical operators. Because the decision must be expressed in a way that is compatible with the rules of inference, great simplicity, and structure are required. In strategic decision making problems great effort has been directed toward relaxing the mathematical constraints, while retaining the economic — logic inference.

Another important aspect to be considered is that in both theoretical and practical decision-making models, fixed numbers of decision alternatives or prefixed value of parameters have been considered. The major inputs to the analysis of an econometric model of decision-making process are subjective probabilities, utility values, and decision tree structures. Individuals may differ in their subjective value of probabilities, their utilities of outcomes or in their perceptions of the subsequent actions available. Strategic decision problems involve not only one person's opinion but involve a group of individuals belonging to different classes and levels of interests inside and outside the organization. No longer is the problem concerned with the selection of the preferred alternative of one person. The analysis must be extended for a group of decision-makers, each one exhibiting a certain preference structure, perceiving different consequences, and corresponding to a diverse set of interest and responsibility. In some cases, depending on the number of persons involved as well as on the nature of the decision problem (for instance, promoting or hiring persons or, electing the president) it will be necessary to adopt a voting system.

How can different groups of individual affect a decision-making process? In this chapter, we consider some behavioral aspects of individuals and group of individuals that may affect a decision-making process.

Behavioral perspectives of competitive decision-making are neither as well articulated nor as complete as those of economic view. In behavioral views cognitive limitations and the use of mental effort are emphasized. In contrast to the rational approach of the economic frame, the behavioral views acknowledge that players may adopt different kind of rationality.

Individual and Group Behavioral Models

Behavioral theory, adopted by the social sciences, reminds us that competition which occurs in practice does not take into account just systematic and logical decisions about wins and losses. The behavioral perspective examines which attitude an administrator or a business assumes when faced with a given situation. It is a way of explaining how the decision alternatives were selected to formulate the strategy. It also works to minimize the influence of the subjective determination of the qualitative and quantitative values of the parameters involved.

In general, strategic decision-making is a procedure for making decisions working against some competitor or against the state of nature. The states of nature or the scenarios that can occur involve risk or uncertainties with regard to market behavior, climatic influences, available capital, etc. A company should have knowledge about the possible scenarios and the risks built into these scenarios and choose a decision alternative.

A *competitive situation, or one of conflict,* occurs when the result of a decision is influenced by decisions made by other participants. Game theory, formulated by Von Neumann and Morgenstern (1944), analyzes decisions made where conflict exists. Game theory examines actions and reactions to the existing alternatives in order to analyze and plan a competitive strategy. It allows the administrator to analyze the systematic mode of wins and losses resulting from a given action, as well as the possible wins and losses of the competitor.

Administrators' behavior often does not rigorously obey the principles of game theory. This stance could bring about beneficial results in some cases. Experimental studies reporting on situations, where a player, with no knowledge of game theory or behavioral theory, plays against an adversary, are related by Day and others (1997). To illustrate the complexity of the behavioral perspective we show an extension of the Prisoner's Dilemma game, called the Social Dilemma game by Raiffa (2002).

The Prisoner's Dilemma Game

In a two persons non-zero sum game between two people, gain $f_1(i,j) = a_{ij}$ of player 1 and gain $f_2(i,j) = b_{ij}$ of player 2 are different when player 1 chooses strategy i and player 2 chooses strategy j. In this case, the sum of the gains $a_{ij} + b_{ij}$ is different from de zero.

The value of the game is defined by the equilibrium point or *saddle point,* which is the point (i^*, j^*) which satisfies the equalities:

$$f_1(i^*, j^*) = Max_i \, f_1(i, j^*) \text{ and}$$
$$f_2(i^*, j^*) = Max_j \, f_2(i^*, j).$$

The point of equilibrium is the point (i^*, j^*) which provides the greatest gain for player 1 as well as player 2, and is the most convenient point of gain for both players. Note that, if one of the players moves away from this point, while the adversary remains at this point, this player's gain is diminished. However, this does not always occur as we can see in the problem known as the Prisoner's Dilemma.

The Game

Two prisoners who are accused of the same crime are kept in separate cells and are being interrogated separately by the police.

If _both prisoners confess_ to the crime, both will be sentenced to 10 years in prison.

If _neither of the two prisoners confesses,_ the police, using circumstantial evidence can only sentence them to 2 years.

If just _one of the prisoners confesses_, this prisoner will receive, as a reward, a light sentence of one year in prison and the other, who did not confess, will be sentenced to 12 years in prison.

Since the years in prison are penalties (and not gains), they are represented by negative values and we can determine the equilibrium point of the game.

Prisoner A /Prisoner B	Not confess	Confess	Max i of A
Not confess	(-2, -2)	(-12, -1)	-2
Confess	(-1, -12)	(-10, -10)	-1 *
Max j for Player 2	-2	-1 *	

This example is a game between two persons with different gains (two person nonzero sum game). The following observations can be made. The equilibrium point, which theoretically would be the best decision for both prisoners, corresponds to the decision (Confess, Confess) with a penalty of (-10,-10) marked with asterisks (*).

Nevertheless, the best decision (lighter penalties) for both prisoners would be (not confess, not confess) with penalties (-2,-2), that is, 2 years in prison for each.

This example shows that the best solution is not always obtained through a mathematical principle of the equilibrium point type and that it is preferable to choose a decision where there is A SATISFACTORY AGREEMENT BE-TWEEN THE TWO PARTIES.

The Social Dilemma Game

This game, adapted from Raiffa (2002), is a generalization for N-persons, of the Prisoners' Dilemma game, where each participant can take one of two actions: Cooperate (C) or Not Cooperate (NC). The rules of the game are:

- the game is played only once;
- no type of communication is permitted among the players;
- the action (C or NC) taken by each participant is known only to the game instructor. The instructor communicates to the participants only the total number of actions C and NC;
- the gains (in dollars) are: each NC players wins $(X = a value that depends on the number of Cs) and each C players wins $ (Y = number of Cs less 0.3x N).

For example, in the case of N = 100 persons, suppose that the number of Cs is 20. Each of the 20 C players loses $ (20 – 0.3x 100) or $ (-10), paying a total amount of $200 which will be distributed among the 80 NC players. The parameter 0.30 can be adjusted by the instructor. The C players generate the capital to be divided among all.

Now let's allow reserved communication among the competitors (private choice) before the game. The number of C or NC will depend on the private communications. Nevertheless, if the communication is done in an open mode (public choice), and each player knows who is C or NC, then the number of C's should increase.

This game can be illustrated like a problem of birth control among the population. Each family decides how many children it will put in the world. What is the perspective for these children to have good quality of life? Should one family have many children? How about the others families? What is the size of population that planet Earth can adequately sustain? The game indicates the need for negotiation among the participants, and that many questions remain unanswered.

Methodologies Used in
Group-Decision-Making

Organizations make decisions in a group, due mainly to two reasons (Mallach, 2000):

- task related reasons: have to do with functional demands and techniques which make it impossible for a single person to make a decision; and
- organizational reasons: which demand that certain individuals participate in the decision making process due to the functional, structural and legal organization of the company.

Involving lots of people in the decision making process provides a greater basis of experience, knowledge, and creative insights. It is intuitively reasonable that the chances of overlooking possible events and possible courses of actions are diminished in group-decision-making. The synergy of individuals may make the overall quality of the group decisions greater than the sum of parts. The creations of juries, panels and cabinets as ways of reaching decisions can be seen to be based on this promise.

However, if the opinion and values of individuals differ, how should the differences be resolved? Difference of opinion may inhibit the expression of critical ideas, resulting in an incomplete survey of alternative courses of action or choices. Techniques to enhance group's creative potential and interaction such as Delphi, SODA (Strategic Options Development and Analysis), and even the brainstorming process are widely used.

The main difference of a group activity from an individual activity is the opportunity for interaction among the group members, which enriches the discussion and the analysis of the problem and provides a more objective choice of alternatives to resolve the problem. Today, the richness deriving from interaction can be obtained in various ways, since we have gotten beyond the phase of meeting around a table or telephone consultations and conventional mail, and we have the technology of e-mail, audio, and video conferencing. Consultations, information surveys, mergers, and big business deals can take place by means of group decisions with no need for the parties to be physically present at the same place.

Some of the well-known group-decision methods are: (Warfield, 1976; Poulton, 1994):

- brainstorming,
- Q-sort method,
- Delphi method,
- NGT – Nominal Group Technique,
- SODA – Strategic Options Development and Analysis, and
- GDSS – electronic meetings via video conferencing and e-mail using Work Flow system.

Brainstorming

Brainstorming is a meeting held to extend the discussion of a given problem stimulating the creativity and the discovery of new solutions or new directions to the problem. The informal type of discussion helps greater participation of the members of the group but a good control of the discussion as well as the documentation of important facts and results are essential.

Q-SORT

Q-SORT is a group decision process where each participant structures the decision problem, sorting a set of declarations according to his or her preference. Each participant receives a set of cards containing the declarations about the problem. A scaling measure is used to guide the sorting process of the declarations. The main advantage of this procedure is that it can be repeated many times using different sorting criteria for the problem.

Delphi

Delphi is known as a methodology useful to generate, clarify, structure, and organize a set of ideas. The methodology collects and evaluates information or expert's opinion with respect to a main subject. It is not allowed for persons of the group to maintain communication among them. A supervisory team selects a group of 30 to 100 experts giving to each expert a questionnaire based on the most significant answers received, the supervisory team prepares a new questionnaire to be distributed among the same or a new group of experts. The process continues until the supervisory team evaluates that a significant and structured set of answers has been received to solve the problem.

Main characteristics of this method, based on description presented by Goicoechea et al. (1982), are:

- the method can be applied to small or large groups;
- face-to-face contact is not necessary, and in many cases not recommended;
- relies on written responses;
- respondents can be at different locations;
- may take more than 6 weeks to complete the decision process;
- group decision is made through aggregation of individual judgments, usually after three or more rounds of distribution and analysis of questionnaires.

The execution of Delphi is made through the following sequential steps:

1. Develop the Delphi question that must be clearly and comprehensively formulated, reflecting the objective of the problem to be solved.

2. Select and contact participants that will be interested in the problem being examined, and with minimum level of expertise necessary to deal with the problem.

3. Select a group of respondents among the participants contacted in step 2. Suggested number of the sample group is 30 persons, but it can be more or less than 30 persons, depending on the problem to be analyzed.

4. Develop questionnaire number 1 and test. The purpose of this questionnaire is to identify issues. This questionnaire should be tested on a small sample of persons that are not part of the respondents. After the test, the questionnaire is sent to the respondents.

5. Analysis of the questionnaire number 1. A decision-making staff prepares a concise list of items identified in the answers of questionnaire 1, and a summary of comments made by the respondents.

6.   Develop questionnaire number 2 and test. This questionnaire asks for comments expressing agreement, disagreement or new questions about the summary list prepared in Step 5 and sent to the respondents. Respondents are asked to rank the issues of the list according to the level of importance.

7.   Analysis of questionnaire number 2. The staff prepares a summary of the comments and counts the number of votes according to the rank attributed to each item of the questionnaire number 2.

8./9. Develop questionnaire number 3 asking to do comments about the votes received by each item, and give a final vote for the items presented.

10. The staff prepares a final report that must contain: the purpose of the decision, all the intermediate results, and the final decision based on the aggregation of individual votes collected in step 9.

The final report should be discussed and approved by a representative committee formed by members of respondent groups. For purposes of feedback and closure, participants should be given a copy of the final report.

NGT

NGT-*Nominal Group Technique* is a technique similar to Delphi, used for more complex problems to be solved by a small group of persons through face-to-face contact. NGT usually can be done in 1 to 2 hours, whereas Delphi may take 6 or more weeks to complete.

Steps to conduct this technique are:

1.   Leader gives each participant (5 to 9 persons) a written copy of the question or problem being considered.

2.   Participants write their own idea or answer to the question or problem presented.

3.   The results of group thinking are presented, recording each idea on a flip chart to avoid duplication. The leader may merge similar ideas forming a new idea, with the agreement of the group. Discussions are not permitted during this step.

4.   Each idea written on the flip chart is sequentially presented and discussed.

5.   Preliminary vote of item importance is requested. Individual judgments of each idea are expressed by a numerical ranking system and an average value of the group preference for each idea will be defined. This average value serves to express the mathematical evidence of the increase or decrease of a group's preference.

6.   New discussions and new voting are permitted.

7.   Final vote.

During the step 3 and 4, the leader passes out 5 to 9 cards to each individual. Each individual is then asked to make a priority list containing a list of 5 to 9 most important items. Evidence indicates that individuals can accurately rank items of lists of this size.

Strategic Options Development and Analysis (SODA)

SODA is a methodology oriented to structure a complex problem with the support of a reduced number of persons. The basic tools used are: the *cognitive map* that helps to identify the objectives of the problem, the *key-ideas* that directs the decision process, and the *actions* to be taken to solve the problem. An interactive software called COPE-*Cognitive Policy Evaluation* is used to give support to the decision process.

GDSS

Group Decision Support System or GDSS is a system whose design, structure, and utilization reflect the manner in which members of a group interact to choose an alternative of decision. The system should have technological support for communication, file sharing, modeling activities in group, aggregating individual perspectives to form a group perspective, and other facilities that permit interaction within the group. The GDSS can encompass all the sectors of an organization or only certain activity sectors, with the possibility of expanding the participation of individuals according to the functional level of the sectors involved. The GDSS is programmed to accept appropriate input data, to analyze the objectives (such as productivity, profitability, etc.) and to provide solutions to the selected problems, generating the appropriate reports.

GDSS may be concerned with the problem of communication media richness. Media richness is defined as the potential information-carrying capacity of a data-transmission medium. Different types of media, differing in their richness, may be appropriate for different types of tasks. For instance, according to Mallach (2000), face-to-face contact is the highest ranked medium in richness, followed by video conference, audio conference, real-time electronic chat, and finally, electronic mail. Electronic mail is ranked as the medium with lowest richness. In the face-to-face contact, GDSS must consider that participants should be *in the same place* and they should work *at the same time*. In the case of a video, audio conference as well as real-time electronic chat, participants may be in different places but they should work at the same time. Using electronic mail, participants may be in different places doing work at different times.

Authors (Mallach, 2000; and Turban & Aronson, 1998) report the following three general types of GDSS:

- **Communication Management System:** provides communication flows by means of facilities to store and exchange messages. Common examples of this type of system are the electronic mail packages.
- **Content Management Systems:** provides automatic routing of messages according to the contents in a standardized way.
- **Process Management Systems:** provides important aid in both individual and group decision making process controlling: the pattern, contents, timing, and flow of the information exchange. Control of pattern and contents of the message can be made by *forms* represented by different types of documents. Control of timing and flow can be made by a *script* that defines the routing of the form. A Work Flow system, considered as an "intelligent electronic mail" is an example of this type of GDSS.

These different types of GDSS can be used to manage differences of opinion, focus on the goal of the strategic decision, control the time factor, lead to objective analysis and judgments. The following Case Study One serves to illustrate the application of group-decision-making methods.

Decisions that Depend on the Behavior of Persons

Decision models suppose that the decision maker resolves a problem by choosing the best alternative in terms of gain or profit. In Decision Analysis Theory and Game Theory this aspect is rigorously obeyed, even though in the majority of cases the formulated alternatives are simplified or condensed versions of the possible states of nature. In real-life problems, we also need to take into consideration the behavior of the individuals or organizations involved in the decision. Several authors (Cohen et al., 1972; Takahashi, 1997) present their research results involving the problem of behavior in decisions. We can classify decision problems according to the behavior of persons or organization as:

a. **Decision for the Complete Resolution of the Problem.** A decision is made to choose one of the possible alternatives, which proposes to resolve the problem completely. All decision models from Game Theory and Decision Analysis pertain to this category.

b. **Decision by Oversight.** In this case, the decision is made in a superficial or negligent way without any criteria for analyzing the problem. As an example, we cite the case of hiring someone without examining their resume, or without having them tested or submitted to any training.

c. **Decision by Flight.** Encompasses problems approved (or abandoned) due to difficulty in appropriately appreciating and resolving them, since they involve conflicts of interest, lack of objectives, lack of interest, lack of time, etc. The adoption of changes suggested by an anonymous letter could serve as an example for this type of decision.

These three types of situations can be represented by the garbage can model shown in the section titled Garbage Can Model.

Garbage Can Model

The garbage can model proposed by Cohen et al. (1972) pictures the problem of decision-making as enormous garbage can where problems to be resolved are put. Well-structured problems or those with a higher priority are resolved and taken out of the can. The other problems are taken out after a superficial examination or are taken out of the can because they are taking up space. Many neglected problems remain on the bottom of the garbage can, which requires the periodic emptying.

The garbage can model is made up of the following elements:

1. **Decision Mechanism:** is a structure or instance for deciding a problem, spending a certain amount of ENERGY, according to the difficulty or interest in resolving this problem. Examples: decision making meetings, hiring committees, committees for firing or promoting employees, parliament, congresses, etc.;

2. **Participants:** are people or organizations that are part of the decision-making mechanism and spend a certain amount of ENERGY (time, knowledge, money) to try to resolve a problem;

3. **Problems:** are proposals presented to the decision mechanism;

4. **Solution to the Problem:** decision alternatives chosen for each problem.

The occurrence of oversight or flight-type decisions can be linked to the greater or lesser importance or priority attributed to a problem. These decisions may occur due to the existence of the phenomenon called *organizational anarchy*.

According to Cohen et al., *organizational anarchy* may be the result of the existence of many problems which are difficult to describe in a precise way. Some reasons for the existence of organizational anarchy are:

1. decision participants lack clarity in defining and selecting problems;

2. difficulty in describing and applying a technology or former experience to the solution of the similar problem;

3. existence of multiple restrictions or conditions imposed on the problem which disperse decision maker's attention;

4. irregular, sporadic, or inadequate participation of persons or group of persons so that the level of energy available to resolve problems is uneven.

Organizational anarchy can be found, for instance, in some university (or some public agency) where:

Table 13.1. Some rate of occurrence of decisions of the oversight or flight type, in different positions and age groups (% and total number of persons) (adapted from Takahashi, 1997)

POSITION/ AGE	Head of division	Head of department	Supervisor/ manager	Regular employees
20~24 years				47.3% (55)
25~29			73.7 %(19)	65.5% (142)
30~34		87.0 (23)	75.8 (66)	65.3 (75)
35~39		82.5 (57)	60.7 (61)	69.6 (23)
40~44	72.4 (29)	68.6 (51)	58.8 (51)	73.9 (23)
45~49	81.8 (22)	50.0 (26)	50.0 (42)	
50~54	64.3 (14)	75.0 (16)	37.0 (27)	
55~			50.0 (10)	

1. Several decision-making organisms (schools, departments, committees, projects, etc.) are created and their problems are thrown in the garbage can represented by the university.

2. The methods employed (such as teaching, research, evaluation methods, etc.) provide uncertain results for the development of the university.

3. Professors, students, employees or community representatives participate in an irregular fashion in the decision making organisms of the university.

Table 13.1 presents the partial result of a research to evaluate the number of persons (according to position and age group) that have had experience in adopting a decision of this type (flight or oversight).

According to this research, high rates of decision by oversight or flight are observed in the first age intervals for heads of division, department, and supervisor/managers groups. Inside regular employees, the rate of decision by flight or oversight increases according to the age interval. Answers from groups with less than 10 persons were discarded.

The Impact of Psychological Types

In the behavioral model of decision making, it is important to consider the behavior of each person or group of persons regarding the psychological preference of each person. The Swiss psychologist Carl Gustav Jung (1975-1961) created and developed a theory of psychological types in an attempt to explain the apparent differences existing in people's behavior. Jung stated that he began to construct his theory when he perceived the differences of conception and behavior between him and his colleagues in analyzing the same problem, and also observing the behavior of patients and other people. Jung's theory is based on the supposition that differences among individuals are caused by the different ways that people use their minds. In using the mind, a person becomes involved with the following mental activities:

- **PERCEPTION:** contact with events or collecting information without concerning oneself with its organization or purpose, and
- **JUDGMENT:** information is "received" via a process of organizing, planning, and analysis to draw a conclusion.

For Jung, these two activities constitute the innate preferences of individuals who prefer one of the two activities.

The process of PERCEPTION can be affected in two distinct and opposite ways:

- **SENSING:** when attention is directed to what can be observed or what is real, and
- **INTUITING:** when perceiving the relationships among events, persons, or ideas, observing what is behind them.

The process of JUDGING can take place in two distinct ways:

- **THINKING:** takes the pros and cons into consideration to try to come to a conclusion in a logical manner, but can neglect some existing relationships among persons, or
- **FEELING:** takes sentimental values into consideration and can neglect logical thinking.

Jung believed that these four processes of using the mind can be applied to events from the outside as well as the interior world, and thus added the following types:

- **EXTROVERTS:** individuals who direct their thinking and energy to events from the world outside, acting and reacting with it, or
- **INTROVERTS:** those who receive information from the outside, as well as the interior world, through contemplation and reflection, keeping this information inside themselves.

Each of these psychological types affects a person's behavior in many areas, including decision-making.

The MBTI method (Myers-Briggs Type Inventory, ® trademark of Consulting Psychologists Press Inc.), developed by Briggs and Briggs-Myers determines the personality type based on combination of these eight basic personality types.

Table 13.2 is a summary of the decision techniques preferred by each of these basic personality types (adapted from Mallach, 2000).

Table 13.2. Basic personality types and some preferred decision-making techniques (adapted from Mallach, 2000)

Type	Preferred Techniques
Extrovert	Brainstorming in group Evaluating scenarios or actions
Introvert	Brainstorming privately
Sensing	Share values and ideas Many factors are considered
Intuitive	Deductive reasoning Use of images
Thinking	Classify and categorize Task analysis using graphs, trees or networks
Feeling	Listen to other's values
Judging	Evaluation using comparisons Select a solution
Perceiving	Use different or contradictory statements

Negotiation Model

The combination of the economic perspective of game theory with the behavioral perspective of group-decision-making seems to lead to a complex decision. Examining the strengths and weaknesses of the two decision perspectives, one sees that problems related to interaction among competitors did not merit due attention.

Groups of persons have to recognize that they are in a dispute to choose a decision alternative based on allocating finite resources and that this dispute needs to be resolved by negotiation. Negotiation can be about just one specific item (such as the sale price of a product) or, it can involve several items (such as positions, salaries, the number of hires, etc.) Factors such as the place of the negotiations, number of participants, time available, etc., can vary and influence the results of every negotiation.

A third perspective, represented by the perspective of co-evolution by Day et al. (1997), and by negotiation model of Raiffa (2002) (see the Social dilemma game presented in this chapter), allows one to predict the interactions among participants, which leads to a more balanced adaptation of the competition.

This third perspective permits the creation of a model where the player does not compete necessarily against a hypothetical or logically declared adversary. Participants in this game act as members of an organism where mutual rationality co-exists and all manage to survive and evolve within a limited and adverse environment. The perspective of co-evolution and the negotiation model are concepts formulated, in an independent way, by Day & others and by Raiffa.

Co-evolution is a concept based in evolutionary biology which is used in connected systems, such as the effect of a virus on living beings, the genetic system, etc. The co-evolution or negotiation model can be considered a perspective to view business as a type of system in evolution, where the result of one action can affect other results and all the results can co-evolve.

The economic perspective of win or loss of game theory, as well as the behavioral perspective shows us that by considering just one of these perspectives, certain basic knowledge can remain hidden. The third perspective can remove or clarify these obscure components. Table 13.3 lists the characteristics and relationship of these three perspectives.

Case Study Two illustrates the needs for negotiation among different departments concerning enterprise's planning and budgeting.

Table 13.3. Some features and relationships of three perspectives considered in strategic-decision-making (adapted from Day et al., 1997)

Economic Perspective	Behavioral Perspective	Co-evolution Perspective
Rationality of participants	Participants act with limited knowledge	Actions are interdependent
Use of mathematical models	Requires mental effort	Adaptation to new conditions
Decision with full and sufficient information	Considers social goals and benefits	Considers interactions
Has predictive capacity	Has predictive capacity	Negotiated results
Uses strong logical inference	Uses weak rules of inference	Uses negotiation
Learning by adaptive models	Learning occurs over time	Learning occurs through negotiation

The General Multi-Objective and Multiple-Decision Problem

A general, multi-objective, and multiple-decision-making problem introduces a great deal of complexity in comparison with a single decision maker in which the problem is concerned with the selection of a most preferred alternative by this decision maker. There exists a growing interest in group-decision-making, but the set of several factors and situations contributes to illustrate the difficulties to develop a model suitable for most significant real-world applications.

A formal model of the general multi-objective and multi-decision problem presented by Goicoechea & others (1982), is useful to visualize some of these difficulties.

Let $A = \{ a_1, a_2, ..., a_p \}$ represent a set of feasible alternatives available to a group of N persons represented by i, (i = 1, 2, ..., N). Let $x = \{ x_1, x_2, ..., x_p \}$ be the set of consequences associated with the set of alternatives.

Let us assume that, also there exists uncertainty associated to the occurrence of each alternative. Let $f_{ij}(x)$ represent the subjective probability density function attributed by each person i for the consequence of the alternative j.

Let $u_i(x)$ be the vector of utility function of the person i, $W(x)$ is the utility function associated for the group of N persons and F_j is the joint probability density function of the group for the alternative j.

In the group decision model, the group should select the alternative a_j that maximizes the group's expected utility, i.e.:

Max $E_j(W(x))$, $j \varepsilon A$

where:

$E_j(W(x)) = \Sigma W(x) F_j(x)$, for all x;
$W(x) = G(u_1(x), u_2(x), \ldots, u_N(x))$ and $F_j(x) = f((f_{ij}(x), f_{2j}(x), \ldots, f_{Nj}(x))$.

The group-decision-making problem consists of finding an aggregation rule G for the group utility function W and an aggregation "f" for the joint probability density function Fj.

An important point to be considered is whether or not it is possible to determine a function W that is satisfactory to the group of individuals. This issue is related with the problem of the satisfaction of each person of the group regarding the efficiency of the voting process used to express his or her individual preference, and was examined by Arrow's Impossibility Theorem for a specific type of aggregation rules called *social welfare functions*. Analysis of problems found in some models of voting systems leading to the Arrow's impossibility theorem is presented in following section.

Group's Preference and Arrow's Impossibility Theorem

Today, people are more and more often requested to participate in some type of electoral process, independently of age or occupation, since elections take place in schools, departments, communities, and in some cases even in the family environment. There are also elections to choose representatives for the city, state, and nation.

However, the choice of a satisfactory voting process is a controversial matter due to the conflicting interests that come into play and due to the difficulty of effecting an analysis and comparative evaluation of the existing voting systems.

We present some models of voting system that underlie the existing electoral processes, which will also permit a more structured analysis of their strengths and weaknesses. The voting systems presented here were adapted from the work presented in Konno (1997), with theoretical bases from Fishburn and Geherlein (1976), and Arrow (1976).

A. Multiple Choice Voting System

Let's consider that there are m candidates (or alternatives of choice) C_1, C_2,...,C_m and n voters E_1.,E_2,...,E_n. Each voter classifies all the candidates or alternatives of choice in a certain order of preference. For example, a certain voter establishes that the preference is $C_3 > C_1 > C_m > ... > C_5$.

In the preference of each voter, for each pair of candidates (C_i, C_j) one of the preferences $C_i > C_j$ or $C_j > C_i$ occurs. Candidate C_k will be considered the *winning candidate by simple majority* if C_k is the candidate most preferred in relation to all the remaining candidates. It is irrefutable that this process chose the best candidate. However it is not always possible to find this winner due to the occurrence of ties in voter's preference. The occurrence of ties among the candidates is due to the problem of cyclical ordering.

This phenomenon (ties among the candidates) is known as the *Condocert's paradox*. Condocert, a French mathematician, discovered that the number of ties among the candidates due to cyclical ordering increases according to the number of candidates. For instance, simulation studies showed that, for 5 candidates the probability of occurrence of ties is 0.25, while for 10, 20 and 30 candidates this probability increases to 0.49, 0.68 and 0.76, respectively (Konno, 1997).

B. Two-Stage Election With Multiple Candidate List

A two-stage election with the elaboration of a list of multiple candidates appears to be a lot better than the previous system.

This kind of election is held as follows:

STAGE ONE – The voter votes in **q** preferred candidates from among the **m** existing candidates and

STAGE TWO – The **s** most voted candidates in stage one are submitted to new voting and this time **t** among the **s** candidates are chosen. The candidate with the highest number of votes at this stage wins.

Simulation results testing various combinations of values (m,q,s,t) reported that the greatest percentage of winning votes occurs when: $q \cong m/2$; $s = 2$ e $t = 1$ (Konno (1997)). Thus in STAGE ONE, half of the candidates should be voted, and at STAGE TWO the two most voted candidates are separated and voted.

C.   Election by Approval or Rejection of Candidates

Knowing that there is no perfect election system, according to Arrow's Theorem, the following system was proposed by Brams and Fishburn (1982):

EACH VOTER VOTES FOR AS MANY CANDIDATES AS SHE OR HE WISHES AND THE CANDIDATE WHO OBTAINS THE GREAT- EST NUMBER OF VOTES WINS.

This system has the advantage of including all the features of the other voting systems.

D.   There is No Perfect Voting System

The mathematician, economist and social scientist Kenneth Arrow, made a deep analysis of the principles that should guide a perfect democratic society. He studied the existing electoral processes and managed to formulate the Arrow's Impossibility Theorem.

Arrow's Impossibility Theorem – The Impossiblity of Generalizing a Social Decision Process By Vote

---

"In a social decision process, where society and each individual or voter can fully prioritize candidates according to his or her preference, there is no perfect decision process which satisfies the principle of equality and independence of votes."

This principle, formulated and demonstrated in 1951, had a great impact on those who believed that democracy is the perfect form of government and that a social-decision-making process which obeyed the principles of democracy would be perfect. Due to this principle, Arrow was the third winner of the Noble Prize for Economics.

Case Study: Strategy and Decisions in Perspective

Case – Group Decision to Organize a New MBA Course

ABC University is reviewing and reorganizing the structure and the contents of its MBA courses for the next academic year. Particularly, the University's MBA courses committee is interested in a new course embodying important environmental problems according to the interest of state and local government agencies and local enterprises.

Considering the multidisciplinary nature of this type of course and the innovative aspects expected for this new course, the committee decided that the purpose and the structure of the course, as well as the organization of curriculum and the contents of disciplines should be organized based on the suggestions received from a wide range of persons interested in this new course.

A task force indicated by the committee to conduct this consulting work decided to organize a group-decision-making process using the advantages and flexibility of the existing GDSS to meet a fast, efficient, and transparent group-decision procedure. The committee decided to apply group-decision techniques, NGT and/or Delphi techniques, supported by an electronic meeting system available in the University's GDSS.

According to the University's regulation for a MBA course, a new course will be approved when a proposal with the following topics are presented:

a.   purpose and description of the course;

b.   types and qualification of the students to be enrolled;

c.   a curriculum composed by 10 to 15 disciplines;

d.   each discipline must be described by a short syllabus of up to ten lines, and 5 bibliographical references; and

e.   desired academic and professional background of at least two instructors for each discipline.

Case – Negotiated Decisions in the Operations Department

The president of a manufacturing company noticed that, reviewing the earnings reports of the current quarter, the profits were down once again. This was the third successive quarter in which profits were dropped. During a meeting with the vice president of operations, the president observed that the primary cause of poor profits could be found in the operations department. Product inventories were up, and the unit production cost had increased over the past year. The quality of the service had not deteriorated over time but union relations had been getting worse during the past months. The vice president of operations replied that production costs could be cut and product inventories reduced, but not without adverse effects on customer service, quality, and union relations. He suggested that the problem could be solved by more aggressive marketing, since sales had dropped along with profits.

The president and the vice president of operations realized that the problem went deeper than simply cutting back present operations costs and improve profits. They decided that, to prevent this situation from occurring again in the future, the company must do a better job of planning, decision-making, and managing within the operations function. The company must develop a system of decision making in operations to ensure that the operations department would consistently meet its cost, quality, and customer-service objectives.

This decision-making system must include better forecasting methods, more effective control over product inventories, better process design decisions, and improving quality control systems. The vice president of operations argued that he needs more decisions from the top, about how much the cost, quality, delivery, or flexibility objectives would be emphasized.

The president replied, "We've recently completed a five-year corporate plan. Doesn't it help answer your questions?"

The vice president observed that the corporate plan focuses almost entirely on market analysis and financial planning. It's presumed that operations will meet the marketing and financial goals which have been set. The market strategy and the financial plan are not always consistent with operations strategy and are not formulated at the same time. Revision of the corporate plan or the operations goals is essential to keep a dynamic operations strategy, which is an integral part of the corporate plan.

At this point the marketing vice president walked into the office and said: "I've just returned from our national sales meeting and, based on more recent market research and government decisions, it appears that sales will be up even beyond our previous forecast. Last year we lost sales because of stock-outs of certain key product models, and this hurt us more than we expected. As a result, I'm raising the forecast for next fiscal year from 100,000 units to 110,000 units.

The president interrupted, "Just two months ago, we sat here in this office and agreed on the forecast of 100,000 units. We simply do not have the plant capacity to produce 110,000 units. And what are we going to do with all of the inventory if we add the capacity and the forecast does not materialize?"

The marketing vice president replied: "Suppose for a moment the new forecast is correct, what are our options for more plant capacity? Do we have time to build a new plant?"

The operations vice president observed that: "I think our methods of forecasting are too crude, and something must be done about them. As we all know, the market is very dynamic in our business. I'm not sure how well the new computerized quantitative methods available for forecasting will work for us, but perhaps we should investigate them."

Operations management seeks to produce goods and services at low cost, but with good quality, and acceptable, flexible, delivery deadlines. It is believed that these goals are reached by employing modern equipment, a good information system, satisfied workers, and a team of competent administrators. However, these objectives conflict among themselves and it is not possible to optimize these four dimensions (cost, quality, delivery, and flexibility) at the same time. A negotiated decision is always necessary.

To take precautions against this type of situation (consecutive drops in profits), the vice president of operations must have an efficient system to review and improve the planning, programming, and control procedures of production. It is necessary to identify the critical production points, utilizing the company's best available information. How much should one sacrifice the other three objectives to reduce production costs? It is necessary to adopt a strategic corporate decision to focus on the critical production points and better adjust the four objectives.

Source: Adapted from Schroeder (1985).

Conclusion: What Constitutes a Good Strategic Decision?

Three decision-making models were analyzed in this chapter: the first model was based on the economic win/lose perspective of game theory; the second was based on the behavioral view illustrated by the garbage can model; and finally, the third model was based on a perspective of negotiation and co-evolution. An attempt to understand the characteristics and feasibility of the use of group-decision methods (NGT, Delphi and GDSS) has been made.

In any of these three perspectives, group decisions may lead to the need for a decision using a voting system. Some voting systems used by groups of persons in the choice of individual preference were analyzed. Despite the problems existing in each voting system, and the objection raised by Arrow's Impossibility Theorem, election is an important process for selecting strategic preferences. For example, according to Konno (1997), the election system by approval and rejection of candidates is being adopted more often in elections for boards of directors and councils of class associations and scientific societies in various countries. This system is particularly recommended for electing directors of universities and associations because it avoids the need for a second round.

Finally, what constitutes a good strategic decision?

Summarizing the results of a decision based on the models and examples shown in this and in the previous chapters, we may think about certain personal preferences and organizational biases a decision analysis should overcome.

The following features of a good decision, based on Bunn (1984), might be appropriate in an executive's evaluation of strategic-decision-making process. A good strategic decision is the decision that:

1.   has a favorable response from superiors and colleagues;
2.   achieves a quick committee consensus;
3.   provides the ideal outcome for the possible understanding of the problem.

According to these features, the decision-making process will not solve a problem for us. It can provide us with the means for explicitly structuring and restructuring, analyzing and reanalyzing the problem under different assumptions and criteria.

We should have gained a greater understanding of the problem situation and sharper intuition in the sense to eliminate obvious incoherence in our reasoning. We have to analyze a problem according to different points of view to see what the outcomes are for different ways of analysis.

Starting from basic and moving to more advanced models, we will have sufficient information and good sense to sit in a negotiation table, and in this way determine which course of action is most justifiable.

Questions for Discussion and Reflection

1.   What is *Game Theory*?
2.   What is a game's Equilibrium Point?
3.   Explain what is *a two-person-nonzero sum game*? Give examples.
4.   Explain the importance of the *Prisoner's Dilemma game*.
5.   Comment on the importance of the multiparty social dilemma game.
6.   What are the advantages and disadvantages of a decision made by a group of persons?
7.   What do you understand by "organizational anarchy?" Give examples.
8.   Describe the garbage can model.
9.   What are the characteristics of a negotiated decision model?
10.   What are the advantages and existing restrictions of the voting systems mentioned in this chapter?
11.   Considering the case in the section titled Group Decision to Organize a New MBA Course, answer the following questions about Group-Decision-Making:

    I.   Based on your own interest and background to take this new MBA course on environmental problems, describe the steps necessary to conduct this group-decision-making process using NGT and/or Delphi technique, supported by an electronic meeting system provided by the GDSS;

    II.   List the key issues to be asked in the first questionnaire that will to the respondents;

    III. List some categories of participants to be selected and contacted;

    IV. Describe the type of communication media and electronic meeting systems recommended in each step of the group-decision process of question 11.I.

12. Considering the case in the section titled Group Decision to Organize a New MBA Course and based on the answers given to question 11 above, select the preferred techniques (listed in Table 13.2 – Preferred techniques according to basic psychological types) to be used in each question:

- question I (steps of the group-decision-making process),
- question II (list of key issues to be asked in the first questionnaire),
- question III (list of category of participants) and
- question IV (type of communication media recommended in each step),

    Give a brief description of the reasons for the selection of the techniques.

13. Considering the case in the section Group Decision to Organize a New MBA Course, repeat the procedure (selection of preferred techniques and a brief description of the reasons for the selection of techniques) made for question 12 above, considering that the persons conducting the group-decision process have strong *judgment, thinking, and extrovert* psychological type.

14. Compare the answers for questions 12 and 13 and give comments.

15. Considering the case in the section titled Negotiated Decisions in the Operations Department, answer the following questions:

the objectives of an Operations Department's

ie role of a corporate plan?

ons to be negotiated between the marketing vice
perations vice president?

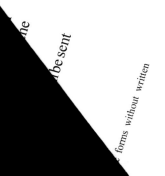

Exercises

1.   Voting to choose a restaurant for a dinner party

   The following list of choices was presented for voting on a place to have the meal:

   (A) Barbecue; (B) Chinese food; (C) Italian food; (D) Japanese food; or (E) Arabian food.

   (a)   Hold an election among friends and colleagues using the three election systems presented in this chapter.

   (b)   Compare the work involved (preparation and counting the votes) and the time spent with each of the election systems. Comment on the results.

2.   Simulating the next presidential election

   Using a group of 10 to 20 persons (friends and colleagues), simulate the election process for choosing the next president (candidates A, B, C, and D for the president of your company, university, city mayor, etc.) utilizing:

   (a)   Vote in a single candidate and a single round;

   (b)   Vote in a multiple list in two stages;

   (c)   Vote for approval or rejection of the candidates.

References

Arrow, K.J (1976). *Social choice and individual values*. New York: Wiley.

Berry, M. J. A., & Linoff, G. S. (2000). *Mastering data mining*. New York: John Wiley & Sons.

Brams, S., & Fishburn, P. (1982). *Approval voting*. New York: Birkhauser.

Bunn, D. W. (1984). *Applied decision analysis*. New York: McGraw Hill.

Clemen, R. T., & Reilly, T. (2001). *Making hard decisions with decisions tools*. New York: Duxbury Press.

Cohen, M., et al. (1972). A garbage can model of organizational choice, *Administrative Science Quarterly, 17*(1), 1-25.

Davenport, T. H., & Prusak, L. (1998). *Working knowledge — How organizations manage what they know*. Boston: Harvard Business School Press.

Day, G.S., et al. (Eds.). (n.d.). *Wharton on dynamic competitive strategy*. New York: John Wiley & Sons.

Fishburn, P., & Gehrlein, W. (1976). An analysis of simple two-stage voting systems. *Behavioral Science, 21*, 1-12.

Goicoechea, A., et al. (1982). *Multi-objective decision analysis with engineering and business applications*. New York: John Wiley & Sons.

Karlin, S. (1992). *Mathematical methods and theory in game programming and economics* (Vol.I, II). New York: Dover.

Keeney, R. & Raiffa, H. (1976). *Decisions with multiple objectives: preferences and value trade off*. New York: Wiley & Sons.

Konno, H. (1997). *Introduction to decision analysis* (in Japanese). Tokyo: Assakura Publishers.

Mallach, E. G. (2000). *Decision support and data warehouse systems*. Singapore: McGraw-Hill International Editions.

March, J.C. (1999). *The pursuit of organizational intelligence*. USA; UK: Blackwell Publisher.

Matheus, C.J., et al. (1993). Systems for knowledge discovery in databases. *IEEE Transactions on Knowledge and Data Engineering, 5*(6).

Mena, J. (1999). *Data mining your Website*. Digital Press.

Raiffa, H. (2002). *Negotiation analysis — The science and art of collaborative decision making*. Cambridge. MA: Harvard University Press.

Schoreder, R. G. (1985, 1993). *Operations management: Decision making in the operations functions* (2nd ed., 4th ed.). New York: Mc Graw Hill Book.

Takahashi, N. (1997). *Decision analysis inside the organization* (in Japanese). Tokyo: Assakura Publishers.

Turban, E., & Aronson, J.E. (1998). *Decision support systems and intelligent systems* (5th ed.). New York: Prentice-Hall.

Von Neumann, J., & Morgerstern, O. (1944). *Theory of games and economic behavior.* Princeton: Princeton University Press.

Witten, I. H., & Frank, E. (2000). *Data mining.* San Francisco: Morgan Kaufmann Publishers.

About The Authors

Tamio Shimizu earned his BS in mathematics from the University of São Paulo. He holds an MSc from the Aeronautical Institute of Technology, São José dos Campos, and a PhD in production engineering from the Polytechnic School, University of São Paulo. His research interests are information technology, intelligent manufacturing systems, and decision support systems. During the past several years, he was a professor in the Aeronautical Institute of Technology, São José dos Campos, and a professor and head of the Department of Production Engineering, Polytechnic School - University of São Paulo, until 2003. He belonged to the board of executive directors of Fundação Carlos Alberto Vanzolini. He was an IBM fellow at Rensselaer Polytechnic Institute and Union College, USA. He participated in a research exchange program between Brazilian and German governments. He was a visiting fellow of the University of Tokyo sponsored by Japan International Cooperation Agency. Currently, he is a full professor in the Department of Production Engineering, Polytechnic School, University of São Paulo.

Marly Monteiro de Carvalho has been a PhD professor at the Polytechnic School, University of São Paulo, since 1992. She holds a production engineering degree (São Carlos Engineering School, University of São Paulo), an MSc, and a PhD in the same area (University of Santa Catarina). She is research coordinator of QEP Quality and Product Engineering Group of CNPq (a federal research agency). She was a visiting fellow at Polytechnic of Milan sponsored by a State Government Research Agency (FAPESP). She participated in a program titled "International top management on quality leadership," sponsored by SIDA- Swedish International Development Cooperation Agency. She was a researcher in a project of Quality Control on Textile Industry, sponsored by the Organization of American States-OAS Paris in France. She belongs to the board of technical directors of ABEPRO- Production Engineering Brazilian Association and is editor of the Brazilian Journal called "Revista Produção." For several years she was also a researcher at the Technological Research Institute of São Paulo State (1992-2000).

Fernando Jose Barbin Laurindo has been a professor at the Polytechnic School, University of São Paulo, since 1997. He holds a production engineering degree (Polytechnic School, University of São Paulo). He holds an MSc and PhD in production engineering from Polytechnic School of University of São Paulo. He also graduated in law (University of São Paulo) and made an extension course in business administration from Fundação Getúlio Vargas. He was a visiting fellow at Polytechnic of Milan sponsored by a State Government Research Agency (FAPESP). He belongs to the Information Technology Management Group (GTI) of the Production Engineering Department. He is the research vice-coordinator of GTI group (listed in CNPq - a Federal Research Agency Research Group). Currently, he belongs to the board of executive directors of Fundação Carlos Alberto Vanzolini. For more than 10 years, he worked in IT and project and product management in companies of the industrial, financial, and service sectors.

Index

Creating Business Value with Information Technology:

Challenges and Solutions

Namchul Shin, PhD
Pace University, USA

Questions on the business value of information technology (IT), which have been raised by managers and researchers for the last decade, are not settled yet. Firms invest in IT to improve their business performance. However, some firms fail to improve their business performance while others succeed. The overall value of IT varies enormously from firm to firm. Computerization does not automatically create business value, but it is one essential component that should be coupled with organizational changes such as new strategies, new business processes, and new organizational structure. *Creating Business Value with Information Technology: Challenges and Solutions* aims to solicit the studies that yield significant insights into the business value of IT.

ISBN 1-59140-038-4(h/c); ISBN 1-931777-91-8; eISBN 1-59140-088-0
US$79.95 • 332 pages • © 2003

"...research on IT business value is valuable not only for academics but also for practitioners, since knowledge obtained through this kind of research can provide managers with a more precise rationale for making IT investments."
–Namchul Shin, PhD, Pace University, USA

Idea Group Publishing

Hershey • London • Melbourne • Singapore

An excellent addition to your library